The Body in Coaching and Training

An introduction to embodied facilitation

Mark Walsh
with contributions from Alexandra Vilvovskaya,
Maud Raber, Adrian Harris and Rachel Blackman

Open University Press

Open University Press
McGraw Hill
8th Floor, 338 Euston Road
London
England
NW1 3BH

email: enquiries@openup.co.uk
world wide web: www.openup.co.uk

First edition published 2021

Copyright © Open International Publishing Limited, 2021

All rights reserved. Except for the quotation of short passages for the purposes of criticism and review, no part of this publication may be reproduced, stored in a retrieval system, or transmitted, in any form or by any means, electronic, mechanical, photocopying, recording or otherwise, without the prior written permission of the publisher or a licence from the Copyright Licensing Agency Limited. Details of such licences (for reprographic reproduction) may be obtained from the Copyright Licensing Agency Ltd of Saffron House, 6–10 Kirby Street, London EC1N 8TS.

A catalogue record of this book is available from the British Library

ISBN-13: 9780335250110
ISBN-10: 0335250114
eISBN: 9780335250127

Library of Congress Cataloging-in-Publication Data
CIP data applied for

Typeset by Transforma Pvt. Ltd., Chennai, India

Fictitious names of companies, products, people, characters and/or data that may be used herein (in case studies or in examples) are not intended to represent any real individual, company, product or event.

The Body in Coaching and Training

Praise page

"Mark Walsh has filled this book with a treasure of information. He shares lessons learned, prioritized, collated, and delivered in a personal way to help us and our clients experience and change.

He invites us to learn from the many perspectives of emotion, dance, creativity, discipline and meditation while sharing in his personal lessons as well.

The richness of this material deserves that you take your time to read and absorb. You may want to read it all the way through first or perhaps read a bit at a time. This could allow you the opportunity to create a 'focused presence' for living with that concept for the day.

Have fun, this book will definitely change your perspective in at least one if not many ways!"
— ***Judith Aston, Founder of Aston® Kinetics***

"Whilst intended for coaches and trainers, I would say that if you work with people in any way at all: get this book! Mark has a wealth of experience and shares it with such in-depth yet easy to read generosity and intelligence that you immediately get the sense that this is someone who walks his talk. You'll be getting copies for friends and colleagues before you're half-way through."
— ***Adam Barley, Founder of ZeroOne movement practice***

"This book respects and recognises the body's rightful place in the counselling and coaching professions. It clearly recognises the importance of the interplay between body and psyche as well as energy and emotion. The author explores the idea of body consciousness not just as the physical corpus of flesh and bones but as a living organism participating in all aspects of our human experience. This book provides easy access to the depth of our experience as living, pulsating organisms that cannot be overlooked in the professions dedicated to helping others. It guides the reader through the consciousness of the psych-emotional-physical balance of being human."
— ***David Berceli, Founder and Developer,***
Tension & Trauma Releasing Exercises (TRE)

"Walsh has already made an important contribution to the field of embodiment and to humanity in general through his international conferences and determined efforts to make available world-wide the work of hundreds of embodiment teachers and healers. In this lively, wide-ranging book, he draws on his own expertise as an embodiment facilitator, and that of many of his colleagues, to help people live more self-attuned, centred and relaxed lives."
— ***Judith Blackstone, Founder of the Realization Process***

"As evidenced by this brilliant book, Mark is passionately committed to empowering and inspiring you to empower and inspire others. This book is a PhD program for embodiment facilitators to expand the depth and breadth of their work and their clients' lives. A gateway to embodied peace and flow for the citizens of the world."

—*Kathleen Booker, The Jedi of Calm*

"The purpose of coaching is to achieve positive change, through clarity of understanding that leads to conscious movement. The fact that we use the physical metaphor of movement for changes in mental state is no coincidence — they are inextricably intertwined. This book digs deep into the connectedness between coach and client and how this supports clients in the complex process of becoming."

—*David Clutterbuck, Coach, Co-founder of the EMCC and Visiting Professor at Henley Business School, Sheffield Hallam, Oxford Brookes and York St John Universities*

"Mark Walsh's book, like the man himself, is sharp, witty, and to the point. He takes us through the landscape of embodiment, cutting a path through the fluff and nonsense and revealing the common sense, genuine inspiration and cutting-edge wisdom that is at the core of embodiment practice. The book itself is full of useful information for all leaders in the modern world who want to match their passion for their subject with the information and skills that will ensure that what they teach lands on fertile ground and is useful."

—*Ya'Acov Darling Khan, Co-founder of Movement Medicine*

"In today's intense and demanding world it is so easy to value our mind over our body. In this book Mark not only brings his immense passion and experience to the field, but also reminds us that often the solution to our problems is far simpler than we realise, we need to come home to our body."

—*Alex Howard, Creator of Therapeutic Coaching and Founder of The Optimum Health Clinic*

"Walsh leads the reader on a journey of embodiment. Through personal reflections and structured exercises, readers are provided with a compassionate and integrated manual."

—*Stephen W. Porges, Professor of Psychiatry, University of North Carolina*

"In this book Mark Walsh richly demonstrates how fundamental embodied awareness is for anyone who coaches or trains. He fleshes out that demonstration with a range of perspectives from history, science, case studies and personal experience. Ultimately, though, The Body in Coaching and Training is

an eminently practical book. By equipping readers with guidelines, exercises, frameworks and prompts for personal reflection, it nourishes, provokes and guides them to lead from a place of grounded awareness."
—**Philip Shepherd, Author and Creator of The Embodied Presence Process**

"Mark's writing is perfectly aligned with who he is and how he teaches: forthright and honest, clear and helpful, fearless and with plenty of heart."
—**Martin Aylward, Meditation Teacher and Author**

"Mark Walsh is much more than a writer, he 'walks the talk' of embodiment with courage and humility."
—**John Cremer, Speaker of the Decade – The Academy of Chief Executives**

"Mark has a special ability to make embodiment work relevant and accessible."
—**Arawana Hayashi, Co-founder of Social Presencing Theater, Presencing Institute**

"Mark Walsh brings an informed, passionate perspective out into the world. His down to earth musings, and targeted checklists, especially for facilitators, generate easily digestible food for thought and a call to action."
—**Jamie McHugh, Somatic Movement Specialist and Artist**

"Mark Walsh brings embodiment to life with passion, irreverence, and grit. It makes a body want to celebrate!"
—**Ginny Whitelaw Roshi, CEO, Institute for Zen Leadership**

*To everyone in the EFC, EYP and Embodiment Unlimited communities –
'The Sangha is the Buddha'*

Contents

About the book xiii

1	INTRODUCTION: WHAT YOUR BODY REALLY IS	1
2	SCIENCE, PHILOSOPHY AND CULTURE	32
3	EMBODIED SELF-AWARENESS	62
4	EMBODIED SELF-LEADERSHIP	98
5	SOCIAL AWARENESS	134
6	SOCIAL LEADERSHIP	152
7	APPLICATIONS	170
8	PRINCIPLES OF EXCELLENCE	180
9	CONCLUSION	194

Appendices 206
Index 215

About the book

Who this book is for – and not for

This book is for trainers, coaches and facilitators of all kinds who would like to deepen their understanding of how to use the body in their work, and to gain both important personal insights and practical professional tools. It will serve all kinds of coaches wanting a complete introduction to the work, and those looking to deepen and clarify what they already do.

It is important to have a focus in any book, and not try to please all people, so it's also worth saying who this book is *not* for. Do not read this book if:

- You are brand new to training or coaching. This book presumes some familiarity with the field and common approaches like emotional intelligence and mindfulness
- You've never done any kind of awareness-based movement practice (e.g. yoga or dance) in your life. While we don't expect readers to have expertise, passing experience is helpful and a *complete* newbie to mindful movement would be better just getting out there and doing a yoga class than reading a book on awareness!
- You are not willing to do any personal work and just want quick client tools. The foundation for the pragmatic client tools in this book is self-enquiry and self-development
- You are in need primarily of healing and support, not challenging education. This book contains work that is not easy – if your life is too hard right now, it's not kind or wise to attempt what is within
- You are looking for intellectual or spiritual masturbation, and not a pragmatic framework. This book isn't a clever word game

All that said – and very likely some people scared off! – this book is *perfect* for, say, a fairly new or experienced facilitator, who knows that the body matters, has started to think about the topic, and now wants to bring their experience and knowledge together in a clear useful way, and gain some really practical tools, to help clients and develop themselves. Equally, if you're on a coach training programme and some legend put this on your readings list, then well, lucky you, it's a great place to start!

What you will get from this book

This book is a guide to working more effectively with the body in coaching, training and facilitation.

This book will provide readers with the theoretical and pragmatic essentials of the embodied approach to facilitation. It will guide you through building your own embodied presence, offer a framework for understanding the field, and give practical techniques you can use with clients immediately. Interactive exercises are offered and video demonstrations accessible for illustration. Although this book is aimed primarily at trainers, coaches and facilitators of all kinds – whom I will refer to simply as 'facilitators' throughout for ease – it is a wonderful resource for any teacher, change-maker, or any human willing to work with others skilfully in and through the body. Welcome . . . and enjoy!

Why now? The mess we're in and the hope I have

Despite the modern world's considerable technological achievements, the disembodied mess we're in is literally killing us. We are very likely the most addicted, suicidal, medicated and unhappy culture of humans who has ever lived. Disconnection to ourselves leads to physical and mental health issues, misery and an existential vacuum. When we can't feel what we truly value, nihilism, consumerism and narcissism fill the void. Through disembodiment we are also increasingly isolated from each other emotionally, despite being so linked technologically – the relational bonds so critical for human flourishing have broken down without the foundation of embodied empathy. In addition, we have lost our connection to the natural world, through losing connection to our own bodily nature, and so destroy both. We are threatening both our own lives and all life on earth with our perceived separation from it. . .

More mundanely, because the body is the most direct way to impact a human being (try punching yourself spiritually, for example), it is also the way that gets the quickest results for many clients. Most clients of mine are clever people, but they are not smart in an embodied way, as nobody taught them to be. Actually they were 'taught' the opposite. This means that while I value and use many other approaches when facilitating, the usually ignored body is often where the most 'bang for your buck' is! The most leverage can be found in what has not been tried already.

Disconnection is killing us on all three of these related levels of disconnection (self, other and planet), and we can no longer afford to treat embodiment as the luxury for a few, or as a balm for a pseudo-yogic middle class. Trickle-down spirituality has failed and time is running out. COVID created further fear and isolation has made this disconnection worse. Against this bleakness we also have new hope: emotions now matter even in business, embodiment is taking-off like never before,[1] and despite their sometimes shallow nature, there is a yoga studio (or at least Zoom room) on every corner and a mindfulness app on many a smartphone. We could yet come back to our senses and pull this one back from the edge. Gently, kindly and inclusively. We could yet romance ourselves back to sanity before we dig our children's graves numbly. So . . . this is the bigger 'why' of working with the body.

I will return to this theme at the end of the book, but I want to say upfront that you are reading it with a gun to your head, written with a sense of urgency which will become clearer as the bigger picture of this work comes to light. Enjoy the ride!

How to read this book

You could read this whole book in a few hours. Don't. Take weeks to try what's within and reflect on it. Take months even – a year would be no disaster. It took me many years to come up with it, and to take it on *fully* may take as long. Practise and *live* what's inside. Digest it and apply it. Take . . . Your . . . Time.[2]

'Facilitator'

I use the term 'facilitator' throughout the book both for ease – it conveys that I am referring to coaches, trainers, teachers and whatever the latest pretentious term doing the rounds is. I also use it as it conveys a humanistic sense that your job is to set up *experiences* and people will make their own learning, rather than you being the expert who has to get cognitive knowledge. This is aligned with what I see as embodiment's empowering ethical core. Often, of course, I combine teaching, coaching, mentoring, facilitation, etc., and it really just comes down to definitions, which it's not worth getting bogged down in here.

Who the hell am I to write about this?

– My embodied story

Mark Walsh – bio

Mark Walsh is the world's best and least modest trainer of embodied facilitators. He founded the Embodied Facilitator Course, the online Foundations of Embodiment Certification, and Embodied Yoga Principles system (taught in 20+ countries). He hosts The Embodiment Podcast (a million downloads[3]) and related YouTube channel (17 million hits+), runs The Embodiment Conference (which holds the world record for largest online event with 510,000 attendees) and leads business training company Integration Training (past clients include Unilever, Ikea, L'Oréal, the House of Lords, the NHS, Oxfam and many more). He has worked in 50+ countries including in a number of areas of conflict such as Sierra Leone, Ukraine and Afghanistan. He holds a black belt in aikido, has 25 years' yoga experience, 15 years' conscious dance experience, has an honours degree in psychology, and a 50-metre swimming badge!

Mark Walsh – a bio beyond the BS

My story is really one of failure. I was cognitively very smart as a child having an IQ measured in the top 0.01 per cent, and being from a family of teachers there was never a shortage of books at home. School was easy for me. But by 17 I found myself a criminal, broken-hearted from a first love relationship breakdown, drug – and alcohol – addicted, and suicidal. I held a razor blade to my wrists before I was even shaving and thought, 'If I'm so clever, why am I so messed up?' I had read literally every book in my sixth-form[4] library and it hadn't helped. By the time I got to university my hunch was that the real path to understanding people and life was not to be found in books, and I knew I couldn't think my way out of the mess that I was in. The hyper-cognitive approach had failed me as it's failed Western civilisation. I was learning the hard way there's more than one way to be smart!

Because I was involved with various illicit activities at the time and had just moved to the big city for university, I'd decided to study a martial art to protect my business interests. When I walked into an aikido 'dojo', however, I saw something that on a deep bodily level I knew that I needed. It resonated and said, 'You need this!' It spoke to me of grace and maturity, wisdom and philosophy of the flesh. I was profoundly touched by the integration of power and love that I saw, and dedicated myself to training.

I was not a natural as a heady 'mind-led' person (take heart, readers), but persevered and eventually made it my full-time activity. I lived in aikido schools for some years travelling around and doing odd jobs and working with kids in outdoor education seasonally to support myself. Eventually I got involved with peace and youth projects internationally that used aikido, after an especially impactful seminar with the UN in Cyprus that brought together people from warring countries.[5] Helping people through the psychological side of aikido seemed more meaningful than just throwing them around. I saw that aikido could be healing and clarified how it was character education. I'd been starting to reinvent the embodiment wheel, but what I learnt from a new thing called the internet was that somatic psychology/embodied learning existed as a field already. I was young and had no ties, so travelled the world learning from the best I could find, often living with them like an old-school apprentice. I painted walls like the Karate Kid. I took cheap flights at 6 a.m. to places I'd never heard of. I hitchhiked and got the overnight bus. I slept on couches and in basements. I charmed and begged my way into schools. I got beaten up and loved hard by mentors. I made myself useful to better men. I ate bad food and washed in a bucket of cold water. I met like-minded lunatics. I loved it.

Eventually I discovered that emotions matter more than Japanese Sensei might suggest, that dance held treasures not obvious in martial arts, that creativity was as vital as the discipline that has gotten me sober, that the West also held treasures like body therapy and trauma work, and that meditation could take it all much deeper. I spent some years applying the work in areas of conflict, working in the slums of Brazil, started a 'Peace Dojo' in a circus in Ethiopia, and had many adventures in the Middle East that can't be detailed. Eventually, somewhat burnt-out from seven years on the road, I came home to the UK and started a business training company, taking the work into leadership and stress management. I settled down and learnt to make some money! In time the business took off and I started getting requests from other facilitators to show them my speciality. Eventually this became the Embodied Facilitator Course community

About the book xvii

> which has been a source of great satisfaction and the learning in this book. It's a home now as is my body.
>
> I've learnt a lot from teaching cross-culturally and seen the world with this work. I have made it my life's mission to spread embodied knowledge and have found some innovative modern ways to do that online too, and the company now reaches numbers I never dreamed of as a small-town boy! I've made some great friends along the way, met my wife teaching about trauma to therapists working in the war in Ukraine, and am very glad embodiment has become my life. This book is a condensation of all that I've learnt the hard way about this subject. Enjoy the feast.

Safety

Reader well-being check

Embodied work can be demanding and perturbing emotionally. On my bigger courses such as EFC, FEC and the Embodied Yoga Principles teacher training, we filter quite hard to remove students who would be better served by one-to-one therapy than by challenging education, but obviously this is not possible with a book. While healing is central to embodiment as it means coming back to wholeness, the focus of this book is education not well-being. I'd suggest avoiding exercises, especially those labelled 'potentially triggering', if you are in a vulnerable place right now. If you have any of the following you may want to be especially careful:

- You're under particular work stress
- You're recently bereaved
- You have active mental health issues (or have had within the last year)
- You're in a physically unsafe environment such as an abusive home or war-zone
- You have untreated trauma history (even if you feel fine)

That being said, I believe in treating people as robust adults able to choose, so it's best perhaps to just say, consider these things and take full responsibility for yourself.

The ethical core of embodiment – consent and non-violence

Embodiment has ethics built into it. Or to put it another way – ethics are visceral.

Let's start by asking a question I often ask in workshops: *How are you different from a rock or a chair?* This difference is fundamental to how we all live, but usually not examined explicitly! Usually when I ask this, people point to awareness and responsiveness as key differences. People feel and move – two things at the heart of embodiment. I may then poke a chair and then have people do this to each other. Or perhaps I will pick up the chair and make a joking show of trying to physically pick up a stooge without their consent. By the time I talk about smashing a rock or the chair, normally people realise the ethical core of embodiment.[6] While one could get obtusely philosophical about this, or overly theoretical defining embodiment, none of us treat chairs like people, or like being treated as an object ourselves. Equally I sometimes point out that the ethical consequence of not being embodied is abuse. Inevitably. When we are not consciously embodied, we are *psychopathic*. This may seem a strong word but simply consider if under stress you treat people (hopefully temporarily) as subjects or objects. Consider the example of being on the Underground/Metro or in traffic, you're hot and stressed, you're late and people are in your way. Do they become objects not people – at least a bit?[7] We are not saints.

When we do not feel ourselves we do not feel others. Disembodiment makes us lose empathy. This is why when stressed or numb for any reason we say and do things we later regret – we are not acting according to our values and compassion, as these are embodied. Numb people hurt people (including themselves).

This ethical core of embodiment is central to this work, and other ethical norms and rules that we teach students come from it. The embodied subjectified world is a very different place from the one where we objectify each other as things for sex, work, war, consumerism, etc.

> *Kitten exercise: Warning, potentially triggering*
>
> An exercise from Paul Linden[8] that shows the visceral bodily nature of ethics is this. Imagine a small fluffy kitten (or other suitably cute baby animal if you don't like cats) sitting sweetly in the palm of your hand purring while it looks up at you with its big dark eyes. Notice how you feel and what you do unconsciously in your body. Likely you will soften and open. Now imagine strangling it brutally to death. Notice your body again. Likely you will be contracting and closing. Why? Because ethics is built into the body. Something that, despite being somewhat common sense, I've found, despite studying moral philosophy to university level, is not in the academic literature.

How not to hurt anyone with embodied facilitation – embodied ethics, precautions and safety principles

> *Warning*: It is vital that you read this before attempting any of the exercises in this book with others.

Beyond understanding the ethical core of embodiment, here are my strong recommendations for doing this work safely:

- Take on **service** as the orientation principle to clients. Aside from paying you and basic decency, students have *no* obligations to meet your other needs such as sexual needs, esteem needs, reassurance needs, or whatever, and should not be treated as even potential providers of these in any way
- Make sure you're **embodied yourself** by doing the work long-term personally, and making sure your state is sufficient to work with others in the moment (e.g. through centring – see Chapter 4). Remember this is the ethical core of embodiment and a disembodied embodied facilitator (sadly I've met some who have learnt the tools but not done the personal work) is not only ironic and lacking integrity, but also almost certainly abusive
- Appreciate that the heart of ethical embodied training is about **empowerment** and make this central to your work. This is why I ask students what *they* are doing in their bodies, rather than tell them as the expert or frame them as bodily victims; this is why we stress building range and choice; this is why we use the frame of facilitation and education, more than teaching and pathology, etc. Not telling people their experience or how to live their life is about safety as well as respect. Embodied training is 'teaching people to fish not giving them fish'
- Respect **consent**. All ethical embodied work is consensual. Specifically, this means not working with people who have 'been sent' without contracting with them (e.g. in corporate environments or with kids). It also means getting opt-in permission for exercises with groups and giving easy no-pressure opt-outs and be supportive of those who do opt out as this is when you really show if you're making requests or demands (e.g. 'If you want to do it step in, if you don't that's fine, just take a rest'; 'It's great to see two people are resting'). I suggest explicit verbal permission for any touch as a training, as most of us are conditioned not to do this
- Note that to give consent, people have to have **capacity**. This means that they are in a state where they can really agree. I often ask clients, 'Who's in charge?' and make sure they know it's themselves when doing a centring exercise with them, and get them to practise saying 'stop' or holding a hand up, should they at any point feel uncomfortable so we know they still have capacity and haven't dissociated or lost their locus of control (see above). Someone in an intense fight-flight-freeze response due to lack of calibration cannot give true consent, or someone 'high' from dancing or breathwork
- **Calibration**: when working with a partner using challenging stimuli – to work, say, with centring – we progressively elevate the intensity of the stimuli, again asking for consent each time. We have a no-questions-asked, immediate 'safety clause' if they want to stop or go to a less intense stimulus at any time. See the self-leadership Chapter 4 for more on this
- Understand **power dynamics** and how they impact consent. If you are the facilitator, many people, especially in some cultures, may feel coerced into going along with what they *think* you want, meaning you get compliance

rather than actual consent. At EFC we teach looking for the 'body no' – meaning a fight-flight-freeze response, maybe alongside a verbal 'yes'. We'd suggest only taking a body and a verbal yes as consent; and even then appreciate some people like trauma survivors may be very good at hiding their real no! A maybe = no, and if in doubt, don't
- Power dynamics also mean that entering into **dual relations** (e.g. business or romantic) with students is especially important to consider (usually to avoid). We have found that people coming from more transactional coaching or athletic backgrounds, may not fully appreciate this: tennis coaching, say, and transformational embodied coaching are fundamentally different ethically, and the latter requires a much greater degree of ethical care. Put bluntly, if transformational work goes wrong it's not, 'oops, I ruined your serve', it could be 'oops, I ruined your life'
- Read the **trauma** section in Chapter 4 and the relevant piece at the end of every chapter. Do not skip this part under any circumstances before trying things out
- Get **accountable**. Do not just trust in your own sense of ethics. By all means listen to your own body on ethical issues and the 'voice of disquiet' that accompanies some decisions, but also:
  ○ Sign up for a code of ethics like the one of the International Coach Federation
  ○ Be in a community of accountability (EFC is one, for example)
  ○ Have a trusted mentor you can go to with ethical issues
  ○ Share power where you can. On most courses I teach on, for example, there are always two trainers and both have to agree any major decision, often with the course manager too (e.g. an exam fail). I am regularly outvoted on issues even within companies that I own
  ○ Be aware you may have blind spots and cover these the best you can. I often teach with my colleague Vilya (who wrote Chapter 2) to create, for example, gender, cultural and age diversity in our courses
  ○ Know the **limits of your expertise** and refer when needed or in doubt. Being a coach who works with the body does not suddenly make you a therapist or a physiotherapist/doctor, or any other professional. I regularly refer students to good trauma therapists, healthcare professionals ('I do embodied not body' I tell them if they have a bad back or whatever, although I may work with an injury's embodied component, for example), marriage counsellors, etc. This work is about education not anything else
  ○ **Filter** students to ensure they are a good match for embodied work. I interview students ahead of larger courses regarding trauma history and who may need healing or counselling rather than education, where there may be a personality clash, and their life situations. This saves trouble for all in my experience

Many of these guidelines are influenced by therapeutic traditions which have learnt to be especially careful, and while embodied facilitation is not psychotherapy, it also goes deep so the field can learn from theirs. This section is also highly influenced by Paul Linden who works with abuse survivors, so has shown me a 'gold standard' of care. My reasoning is that I don't know people's histories or what people might be dealing with outside the training, so best to be careful and do no harm.

For brevity I have not mentioned some important ethical issues like confidentiality, which relate in the same way to embodied facilitation as they do to other modalities, as my purpose here is to present the embodied aspect in particular, not to teach basic professional ethics, which I assume you have a grasp of already. I hope it's obvious that I've really considered these and have developed them over years of experience, sometimes the easy way through learning from mentors and sometimes the hard way through mistakes. Students also tell me that while some may seem excessive at first, with reflection they see the logic of them and find both that they dramatically increase trust with clients who have a felt sense of the care, and also ruin students' enjoyment of many embodiment classes that don't live up to them, so watch out for that! Yoga teachers doing personal adjustments without asking and embodiment coaches not calibrating and using rough grabs from the outset, for example, are pet hates – note, too, that none of these are set in stone and can be taken too far. I did laugh, for example, when hearing a student asking verbal permission to 'hand touch' when offering a handshake once! Like anything, they can be taken to excess and senses of both context and humour are vital in such matters, alongside serious rules.

> **Reflections: Your ethics and fears**
>
> What in this ethical list is familiar? What is new or clarifying? Are there any you disagree with? What did you do in your body as you read them?
>
> What are your guiding ethical principles and hard lines? Get these clear, write them on a piece of paper and put it on a wall. Add what your procedure is when you hit an ethical dilemma. Our version is: 'pause, breathe, call a colleague and a mentor'.
>
> Make a list of your fears of working with the body. For example, 'people will be triggered', 'business colleagues won't take me seriously', etc.

The ethics of crediting

We are all standing on the shoulders of giants, myself very much included, and I believe it is ethical to credit wherever possible. For that reason I have tried to nod to my major influences in each chapter. This is also useful to readers if they'd like to know more about a topic, as this book is an overview. I am above all an integrator, and while some of my unique contributions to this field are here, a lot of what this book does is bring together much of what already existed scattered across diverse traditions, and it's often tricky to know where something comes from because, in 25 years of learning, I forget sources, and sometimes techniques were taught to me by multiple people. Many aikido teachers I've come across, to mention just one tradition, teach various kinds of centring, for example, and I tend to forget who actually came up with a particular technique. Also I would argue that nobody owns the idea of bodily self-regulation, bodily leadership or any other aspect of embodiment, though people have unique brands and forms.

I also find this to be partially cultural, as it is more common in legalistic America to try and copyright things for business reasons, and I take a firm stand on not bowing to anyone trying to trademark human nature, whilst, in say, Russia or Israel I've found that I'd love a little more respect for intellectual property! Personally, I love it when people use my forms (e.g. ABC centring) as long as they mention where it comes from and don't try and teach other teachers in it (which leads to degrading 'copy of a copy' skill levels, and safety issues with that). My standard request, if you use the content in this book publicly, is to credit me and the teachers that I credit, and if you'd like to include it in a teacher training to give me a call – I tend to be generous and supportive rather than protectionist as I want to see this work spread! In this book I'm giving away my best stuff – something I have done online for years, much to the dismay of some in this field with vested interests in keeping the work hidden, as I wish to see embodied training become a normal part of facilitation everywhere.

Touch in coaching and facilitation

Note that while consent is a key ethical principle throughout this book, it is especially important in regards to touch. I stress consent for touch as this reinforces the idea that a person's body is their's and not to be violated. In other words, being impeccable about consent for touch teaches boundaries and consent itself. This goes right to the heart of embodied empowerment, and sadly is much needed for *most* people, as we have been conditioned from childhood that our bodies are not our own in many ways, from demanding a kid hugs his or her grandmother, to more sinister demands in enough cases to shock anyone who grew up in a loving home who hasn't looked at the statistics.

Note, too, that some cultures (often corporate cultures, and those where male-female touch is taboo) may not allow touch and it's perfectly possible to do embodied work without it. In most corporate workshops, for example, I touch almost nobody, and during online workshops it's of course impossible. I'd advise anyone used to working with it as a necessity due to the nature of their work (e.g. bodyworkers) or their culture (most South Americans and South Europeans) to train themselves out of a habitual reliance upon it to soothe or connect with people, as a way to up their other skills. This is quite hard for some and I remember a Brazilian and a Spanish EFC student especially who really struggled! Cultures tend either to be touch-phobic or boundaryless – though sometimes a combination of the two.

Reflection

How has your familial and cultural background impacted your habitual approach to touch? Will this serve you as an embodied facilitator?

And don't worry too much . . .

Finally, here I'd also like to say do follow these cautionary guidelines but also don't worry too much! Because working with the body is still sadly taboo (sometimes in business, I get grown adults sniggering when I merely say the word and HR managers wondering about lawsuits if anyone hugs anyone), and now many are paranoid about traumatising people with a misplaced word on top of this, people can be excessively concerned about what can go wrong. Mostly working with the body is very safe, especially if you follow these guidelines – I find that people just won't 'go there', for example, if they (or you) are not up to it – and over the years fortunately have seen very few real problems occur. Not being scared of the body or making it 'weird' also helps in avoiding issues of trust and buy-in. The body is essentially a home base and a resource, not dangerous or odd.

Exercise

Notice any fear in your body as you embark on learning about working deeper with it. What are you telling yourself about the dangers here?

Now notice any hope in the body. A movement forwards or sense of 'coming home' perhaps? Is there a deeper calling to the body? Can you 'let the soft voice of the body love what it loves'?[9]

Notes

1 For example, the massive size of The Embodiment Conference, which broke the Guinness world record for largest online event in human history.
2 I bloody mean it!
3 Numbers at time of publication in 2021.
4 UK equivalent of high school more or less.
5 Training Across Borders by Aiki Extensions.

6 Actually, eco-embodiment thinkers such as Charles Eisenstein, Philip Shepherd and David Abram would also point out that objectifying the natural world as simply a lifeless resource, also leads to environmental violence. While not the main focus of this book, it is worth noting that embodied practice does lead to a deeper more subjective relationship (exactly the right word) with nature. Things stop being things.
7 This can also be simulated by asking a group to move quickly in a small space.
8 See his *Embodied Peacemaking* (CCMS Publications, 2007 e-book) for more. Paul is my primary embodiment mentor.
9 From a Mary Oliver poem.

1. Introduction: what your body really is

Few of us have lost our minds, but most of us have long ago lost our bodies.
– Ken Wilber

> **Exercise**
>
> Exercises and practice are integral to this book – you can only learn embodiment that way, which is all about experience by definition. Exercise:
>
> Feel. Take a moment to pause before this book changes your life. Breathe. Feel. Or as Lynne Forest said, 'Have an in-body experience.' Your body is a part of yourself and, just like your mind, can be educated. As the founder of Clinical Somatic Education, Thomas Hanna, wrote; *"The human body is not an instrument to be used, but a realm of one's being to be experienced, explored, enriched and, thereby, educated."*

Setting the scene

Preliminary reflection/discussion questions

The chapters begin with some reflection. This can be done internally briefly, or by using paper and pen taking more time, or in the form of a long discussion over coffee with a friend. You could even dance or draw your answers if you are more creatively inclined (some schools of embodiment use art therapy in combination). The key thing is to be active and engaged from the start, as this means you will get A LOT more from this book than just reading it through passively as information-gathering.

- What is a body to you? Complete the sentence, 'My body is . . .' 20 times in quick succession and see what your associations are. You could also ask, 'My relationship with my body is . . .' and do the same.
- What challenges that the world faces do you think involve the body, or a lack of embodiment?

2 The Body in Coaching and Training

- How do you already use the body in facilitation work?
- Do you give any embodied training already (e.g. yoga or dance) and how might this bias your perspective on the body?
- Ask yourself what it means to be truly 'body smart'. Include more than the athletic/kinaesthetic.

Promise

By the end of this chapter you will have a radically expanded view of what the body actually is, and a far more useful view for facilitators than the common understanding.

What is embodiment?

Embodiment teacher Emilie Conrad said, 'Movement is what we are, not something we do', and this sums up the meaning of embodiment, but let's go a little deeper into defining what embodiment is, especially as it's becoming something of a buzzword and '#embodiment' is starting to be used for any old nonsense on Instagram these days! I've found answering this question is best done from a series of perspectives rather than using one rigid definition.

One short definition of embodiment is that it's simply about *'how we are'*. The complexity within this simple sentence opens up, however if we give an extended version of it: 'how we are' is the manner by which (how) we (it is inter-relational) create (it is generative) our (identity is key) being (are), moment by moment in relationship to all our social, cultural and environmental contexts. 'How are you?', while a simple worldwide social nicety of a question, is also a deep ontological enquiry and the essence of this book!

Next, another deceptively concise definition: *'Embodiment is the subjective aspect of the body.'* The important distinction between 'bodily' and embodied is that the word 'embodiment' pertains to subjectivity – *who* we are, as well as *how* we are. The body as 'I' not 'it', you could say. Embodiment is about the bodily aspect of ourselves, rather than just seeing the body as an inert 'brain taxi', as embodiment teacher Francis Briers says! Or to link it to the first definition – it's 'the how of our who'! It is subjective in the sense of felt but further in the sense of our being. Some confusion comes from the 'subjective aspect of the body', as some conflate mere body awareness with embodiment. While mindfulness is the foundation of embodiment practice, the word may still suggest separateness – 'I am aware OF MY body' – as if you were separate and looking at it from afar. Embodiment could therefore be described as true inhabitation rather than awareness *of*. Embodiment refers to being aware AS a body, not just of it. This leads to this simple set of distinctions, with various ways of doing yoga used to illustrate:

Bodily: physical, but no emphasis on awareness

Yoga here would just be a form of exercise to develop muscles and flexibility, like much modern Western fitness 'yoga'

Mindful: aware *of* the body

Most traditional yoga involves attention, so would include mindful movement practices, breath posture and other aspects but only as things to correct

Embodied: awareness of the body *as* an aspect of the self

Some modern schools (e.g. my own EYP) and some classical tantric yoga schools develop the whole person using the body as the entrance point

Somewhat more philosophically – or, more accurately, linguistically – we could say embodiment is not just about the body as an aspect of the first person not third person, but about the body as a verb not as a noun (object). One to contemplate perhaps!

The opposite of embodiment – objectification

Note that the objectified body is the alternative to having a subjective view of the body. Most people are aware of the problems this causes in a sexual context – if you've ever been leered at as just a piece of meat, you'll get this. Likewise, are people who work for a business really a human 'resource' like a piece of coal to be burnt? Or consider how the fitness and dieting 'industries' (note the factory feel again) asks us to shape our bodies, or how the medical industry asks us to see health mechanically and not holistically. The implications of the endemic disembodiment we see in the world are disturbing and profound, and we'll explore this further in the ethics section of this chapter and in detail when we look at the forces of disembodiment in Chapter 2.

> *Reflection*
> In what ways are you seen as an object and not fully human? In what ways do you treat yourself this way?

The HOW of being human

Our physiology (specifically our posture, movement, tension and bodily awareness patterns) is far from being a neutral 'brain taxi'.[1] It is the mechanism of our perceptions, cognitions, emotions, behaviour, relationships, and so on (see functions of the body later in this chapter), and a partial solidification of a set of habits we call ourselves. (That's a dense sentence and the heart of this book, so read it again.) The way we hold the body, move around, attend and intend with the body, is a way of managing and expressing who we are, and we literally 'lean' towards one life or another. The unconscious self, and potentially the consciously created self, are visceral. Our shaping isn't just an expression of ourselves (body language) but *creates*. It is a response to the present moment, but is equally a solidification of past conditions and a way of creating a future based on these. Coaches take note of the last part especially.

Further, to clarify confusion around definitions, it's worth highlighting a distinction between *conscious* and *unconscious* embodiment. ALL people are unconsciously embodied, meaning that they have a set of bodily habits that are the unexamined substrate for their being (thinking, feeling, relationships, etc.), but only a few have brought these to light and gotten any choice in the matter. So are we all embodied? Yes, but some more consciously embodied than others.

A way to be smart (a set of skills)

A very pragmatic definition of embodiment that I will be working with throughout this book is that of a type of intelligence. What I like about this angle on it, is that it points to specific skill-sets that can be developed through practice. By this definition, embodiment is about skills in awareness and choice, both individually and in relationship. This creates the categories of self-awareness, self-leadership, social awareness and social leadership. This is explained in more detail later in this chapter and throughout the book, as it provides a simple framework for us.

A further way to think about how the word embodiment is used is as a catch-all term for all the practices relating to bodymind holism. It's as good a word as any to lump the various awareness-based movement/bodywork arts such as tai chi, aikido, Feldenkrais, yoga and conscious dance together. The nearest other word that could do this is 'somatic', which is sometimes used as a synonym for 'embodied', and sometimes means awareness-based movement but not with an emphasis on shifting the self. It is also associated with a specific school – Hanna Somatics – in some locations, but feels 'clunky' to us because despite its high – sounding Greek origins, it is not part of most people's daily vocabulary. A common usage of 'embodiment', of course, is as an exemplar of or a tangible form of an idea, which we think points helpfully towards the more technical and specific usage here, although I appreciate others may find this dual meaning unhelpful. Other terms that have been coined include 'bodyfulness' – which Christine Caldwell and I came up with independently, and the aforementioned 'bodymind'. In any event, it appears that 'embodiment' is the word that is catching on.

Very simply after all this word play, it is worth noting that embodiment is really about just being human. Because it is both a more accurate and kinder view of what a body is, it directs us back to the essence of our humanity – to our values, our consciousness, our relationships, and, dare I say it... to love.

More poetically, as the body is the primary site of creativity, aesthetics and artistry, we could say that embodiment simply means *coming home* to the body. When awareness and the body embrace, flesh turns from a prison to freedom, from a command to a question: a question of spirit, of love and of meaning. Embodiment is our original romance and the possibility of a life-long love affair.

Lastly, many people also experience transcendence through sex, sports, connection with nature or, less enjoyably, bodily pain or illness – so I end this section by saying the body is also a gateway to that which is most meaningful to us. There are many ways this can be phrased, including 'Your body is a temple of the holy spirit' (Corinthians 6:19–20) in the Christian tradition.[2]

Guidelines for embodied practice

This book contains many exercises, as experience is the heart of embodiment by definition. Here are some basic guidelines for them:

- **Safety first:** do no harm physically or emotionally, to yourself or others through embodied techniques. If something starts to feel very unpleasant or overwhelming (as opposed to simply odd or slightly uncomfortable), stop. Definitely stop if you start to become 'flooded' with emotion, freeze up or dissociate (space out). See also the ethics, trauma and safety section.
- **Experimental and experiential:** don't believe a word I say – test everything for yourself and remember, it's 'not knowledge until it's in the muscle',[3] so you need to try things out. Theory and practice are two wheels on a cart as Buddhists say, and just reading this book without practising is a waste of time.
- **Personalised:** we're all different and techniques must be adapted to suit each of us and those we work with. Be creative and feel free to make the work bespoke.

Exercise: Your body now – drawing

Intuitively people often have a good sense of their embodiment but may not have the words for it. One way to bring this out is to draw your current embodiment (Figure 1.1).

Focus on the subjective aspects of how you experience the body and your body being rather than just physical things. As per our definition of embodiment. You can use colours, symbols, whatever works for you. Be creative and capture your relationship to the body. It's not a work of art. You could also talk it through with a friend (though be aware this is very personal), a coach or therapist.

6 The Body in Coaching and Training

Figure 1.1 Body drawing

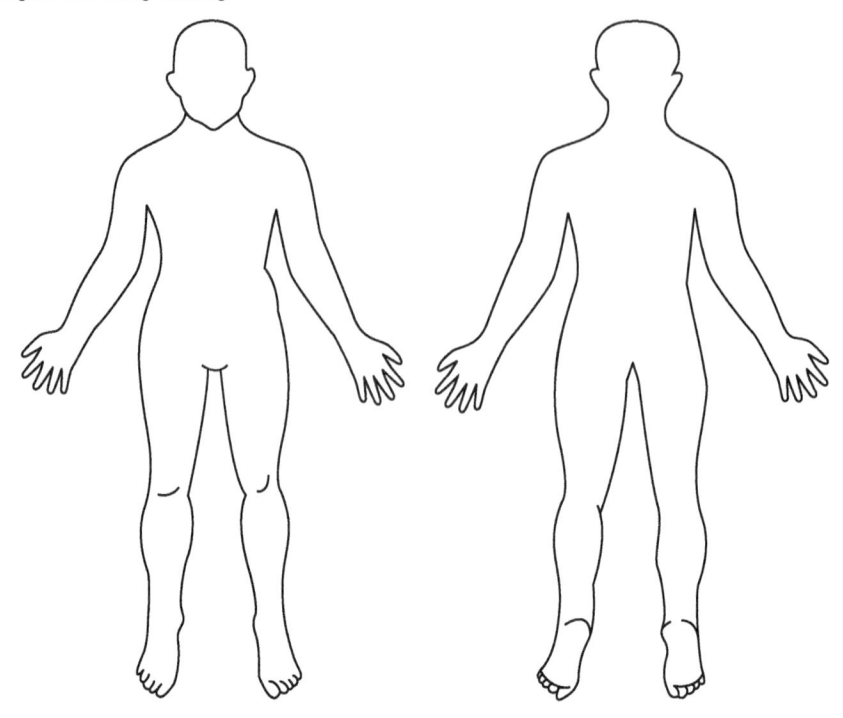

> ***Exercise: Objectifying arm exercise***
> Another exercise to bring to life experientially a definition of embodiment is to relate to your own arm first as an object and then as a part of yourself.
>
> First, look at IT as a THING, as an object. Prod it, poke it, treat it as no different from a chair. Notice how that is. Next look at your arm as part of you, feel YOURSELF through the arm, move the arm as part of you, RELATE to yourself with and through your arm. How is this different from the previous experience? You could also try this with a partner and with (consensual) touch, be warned though, they may not appreciate the objectification!

Why does the body matter in training and coaching?

Aka: Why embodiment makes or breaks facilitators.

I'm aware that readers who have not yet 'bought into' embodiment may ask, having read all the seemingly abstract definitions, 'So what?!' Fair question. Why does all this matter to facilitators?

Given that we all are embodied, it's EXTREMELY useful to know how we are shaped as people generally, and as facilitators more specifically. Why? Because our embodiment impacts others hugely, while being invisible to us, and because it dictates what we can see and do! As facilitators we need to know our strengths, weaknesses and blind spots; and also to develop flexibility. The basic embodied training model that I work with is to help people develop awareness, range and choice (rather than tell facilitators that they are wrong, and offer to fix them). People may already know their habitual coaching style, for example, but embodied training can help them easily shift that to better work with different clients, giving them state-changing skills and longer-term behavioural flexibility. When all that you have is a hammer (and maybe don't know that), then hitting nails is all you can do, and everyone looks like a nail!

Also, embodiment can help you develop yourself more deeply over time. It is not just self-awareness that makes a good facilitator but who a person is – that is, what they embody! Techniques are easy and theories plentiful, but it is the *being* of a facilitator that makes the biggest difference, not what they know about. Being underpins ALL techniques – and this is embodiment, and we cannot develop ourselves to death without using the body, and this holds all patterns in place. We could all list the many traits of a good facilitator, but HOW do we develop these without embodied practices? Clever words and good intentions don't cut it.

Hopefully this section takes the 'who' and 'how' definitions of embodiment and links them to your practical concerns as a facilitator. Yes, you'll find 'quick-wins' in this book, but more critically you'll find a map, and a practical method to developing the most important tool in your box – you.

A more client-centred answer is that if we are to get the best results, we need to work with the whole person and the body is part of a person. Embodiment is a core part of a person's being (and therefore communication, stress management, leadership, parenting – or whatever) and so needs to be considered. Furthermore, because embodied intelligence is likely to be excluded from people's education, from secondary school to MBAs, it is the area where leverage can most quickly be found. As it is the aspect most usually excluded from the helping professions too, it is often the aspect that helps when others have failed, and makes an excellent market differentiator, especially with so many coaches and trainers around these days!

The body is also the most direct and quick way to work with many issues. It may be quite laborious or take much work to talk your way around a person's world – view, for example, and all kind of 'defences' may be in place linguistically, but to just shift their posture, that's much more accessible! Because the body is the most manifest part of our being (to borrow from a tantric yoga model), it is the easiest to get a hold of!

When I'm selling embodied training to companies, we don't call it that, we just say it's interactive and therefore engaging (everyone hates PowerPoint, let's face it), goes deep quickly (people are busy) and sticks (you won't waste your money). Most of all, I demonstrate that it works, which is what my business clients really care about. I think we've all been on courses promising quick-wins and realised that air-punching emotional highs don't lead to lasting change. Embodiment is about practise and sustainably shifting over time, and while not rock and roll, this is what works. Mere information remains as useless 'shelf help', as embodiment teacher Wendy Palmer says, in reference to books that sit on shelves and don't really impact us. I like to think that if information alone was enough, then Wikipedia and Google would have solved all the world's problems, or whether you'd trust someone claiming to be a great lover because they'd read a lot of books on kissing? Likely not. Knowing *about* stuff is common these days, but embodied wisdom, that's rare . . . and what makes the real difference.

A further perspective on 'why embodiment?' is that of being VUCA-proof. In an increasingly volatile, uncertain, complex and ambiguous (VUCA) world, the view of many as to how things are heading today, it is important that we develop flexibility for ourselves and our clients, especially under the new norms of intensity and challenge. I have seen over the years of working in business that NO business client of mine has become less busy, more stable or found easier markets. The business environments that I now work in, feel more and more like war zones. Embodiment makes you anti-fragile[4] when adaptability is required for resilience and simply not being out-of-date very quickly. I see many facilitators burn out in this fast-paced . . . no . . . insanely-paced environment, and coming back to the sanity and refuge of the body is vital to avoid this.

Honestly though, these days I find that there's genuine widespread curiosity on the part of facilitators about how to work with the body, so maybe I shouldn't preach to the choir. And what I do hear is not so much, 'would it help me to work with the body?', but 'how do I work practically and safely with the body given that I'm not an athlete or yoga teacher?' People want simple tools that do the job, coming from depth but without being esoteric or too 'Californian'/'woo-woo', and this is what this book is all about. When I started this work, perhaps the world wasn't quite ready except on the leading edges, but now after the revolutions of emotional intelligence and mindfulness, the time for embodied intelligence and 'bodyfulness'[5] has come.

You already know this

While embodied facilitation may seem like an unusual subject, it is really something you already know (but may need reminding of and developing) and somewhat common sense. Often I frame it this way when introducing it to new students rather than try to sell it as exotic secret knowledge. People all feel to some degree, and we all know feeling matters – work someone hard enough and they will feel that they are tired, and nobody picks their life partner from an Excel spreadsheet after surveying data on potential mates. We can all manage our mood to some extent unless we are toddlers, we are all aware of natural rhythms to a greater or lesser degree, we all know there is a better posture for sleeping than waking (i.e. more horizontal!). A dog or a child can get a sense of someone's character by how they move, we have all felt the stress of someone next to us on a plane or a train, we all have at least a little skill in humour, 'cheering people up' or flirting (forms of embodied emotional influence), we all have 'gut instincts',[6] and there's plenty of sayings based on 'butterflies in the stomach', 'gut wrenching', etc. that show that embodied wisdom is implicit in our cultural understanding to name just one body area . . . I could go on. **The basic embodiment skill-sets are our core humanity**. Embodied training merely clarifies and refines our birth right.

A further note on language

Note that the English language – and many others besides – are FULL of embodied wisdom! Phrases like, 'stand up for what you believe', 'broken hearted' and 'gut feeling' point to the somatic. Lakoff and Johnson have suggested that the body is our most fundamental metaphor, as for example we associate a parent's literal warmth with affection, so 'warm' becomes a byword for affection.[7] I believe, however, that this is more than just linguistic or metaphorical, as the body is our basic way of making sense of the world. Those studying robotics and AI have also found this to be true.

Embodiment teacher Philip Shepherd, on the other hand, points out how disembodiment is also firmly established in language, especially in regard to leadership. We have 'heads' of companies, 'chief' executive officers and 'captains' of industry, for example.[8] What does this say about our cultural privileges?

As an exercise you could try and list how many body-based phrases you regularly use or are prevalent in your country. Spend a day, or watch a movie, making a tally of those you hear. You'll notice a lot!

Structure of the book

Overview

Let me walk you through the structure of the book. After defining terms, laying out what I mean by embodied intelligence, passing on the necessary trauma and cultural considerations to practise safely, and presenting the scientific foundation, I'll present the four main aspects of embodied intelligence, each in their own chapter. These chapters are the 'meat' of the book. Each is shorter than the last as they build on each other. After this core content, I will present chapters on other practical applications and client concerns, discuss excellence in embodied facilitation and conclude.

Format

A heap of words about embodiment is . . . somewhat ironic. To make this book closer to the essence of the content, I therefore present not just theory and descriptions of tools, but reflections and experiments. Engaging with these will deeply enhance your understanding of the book, as this work is experiential by definition. I will also guide you to your own practices as a central aspect of learning to be an embodied facilitator.

In order to keep the book to a manageable size, and because embodiment is sometimes better shown than told, video resources are mentioned throughout if you'd like to delve deeper into a subject, or to see what we're talking about. While it is not necessary to view any of these to grasp the book's central content, they will support it. These are all on the book website along with an extra chapter, a free film of a workshop that we normally sell, various supportive articles, course links and more. See: https://thebodyincoachingbook.com/

Foundation – building your own embodiment

An embodied facilitator's foundation is their own embodied intelligence. It starts at home. Critically, embodiment is a form of learning that requires experience. You certainly wouldn't board a plane with a pilot who had no practical flying experience, or get in a car with someone who'd just read a book on driving. The same need for practice applies to the field of embodied facilitation. Techniques can be learnt easily, but what makes them work well is the practitioner's own embodiment. Most of your coaching efficiency will stem from who and how you are, and what you have laid down in the flesh, not from what you know *about*.

It can be tempting and well-intentioned for a facilitator to jump straight in and start using the tools with others, but the techniques will only be safe and effective if the facilitator practises them him or herself, and embodies them with congruence. This is a matter of both integrity and efficacy, and it is sad to see coaches set themselves up as embodiment trainers after a few weekend workshops, without undertaking any long-term practise. I sure don't want this book to add to this trend! So my request of you, and prayer to the heathen gods of embodiment, is that you experience first-hand what's in this book, and develop your own embodiment through dedicated practice, and stay on this ever-deepening path. Please be humble enough not to think that other kinds of work you have done qualify you in this regard. Realistically, you can of course help others as a work in progress, and I don't expect many readers to simply develop themselves for months before working with others – the format I work with when training trainers – so we have structured the book so that each chapter has two halves, one for you and one for working with others. At least explore the first half of each chapter thoroughly and experientially before trying to take it to others.

Please also read all the essential precaution and safety information in the preliminary matter a few times before trying ANY of this work as a facilitator.

What is embodied intelligence?

The contexts of the body

Before we can understand the real function of the body, it is first necessary to understand the contexts within which we are *always* embodied. In fact, one way of understanding embodiment is *as* our primary context. The body is our constant, largely invisible and underlying context, shaping what we think, feel and do – as well as our relationships – by providing the substrate of our being. This is what 'embodiment' means.

Equally we could say that embodiment is a relational network. We are always embodied in relationship as well as in ourselves. You exist not as a permanent independent self, but are different in different interpersonal contexts, and because of those social contexts.

Lastly, we are always embodied in place, and have come to embody the places we have inhabited most frequently. Culture sits between place and people and has aspects of both to it, as will be mentioned extensively throughout this book.[9]

We can view the aspects of bodily influence happening in place and in relationship, as layers. This means that at any time a person's embodiment is influenced by the various dimensions below (Figure 1.2).

Embodiment is affected by situation (what's happening now), culture (present and past), relationships (present and past) and place (present and past) – as underpinned by universal biological aspects (e.g. the distress response), many of which we share not just with all people, but with many animals.

- **Environmental context:** we are different depending on where we are. Different cities, climates and training rooms all make a difference, for example. See the box below.
- **Situational context:** we are not embodied in the same way in all circumstances, as at work or at home, for example. Fluctuating biology (e.g. hormone cycles) could also be thought of as 'situational'.
- **Relationship context:** we are different with different people. We are also embodied in relationship to historical relationships.
- **Personal historical context:** a body is a life story, or perhaps more accurately an adaptation to a life, a way of finding love, safety and belonging. This is 'our' embodiment and if we are not aware of what it predisposes, this solidified past creates a future. Bringing this to light and creating new options is what embodied facilitation is all about.
- **Cultural context:** where we come from, and where we are now, matter.
- **Human context:** we have a universal shared physiology (e.g. the distress response).

As embodied facilitators, our job is to bring to awareness these different layers, and appreciate all of them at play. Failure to act or least acknowledge introducing the idea of embodiment to a client will lead to a 'but it depends' pushback, which is half true as it does indeed depend (on these contexts).

Figure 1.2 Contexts of embodiment

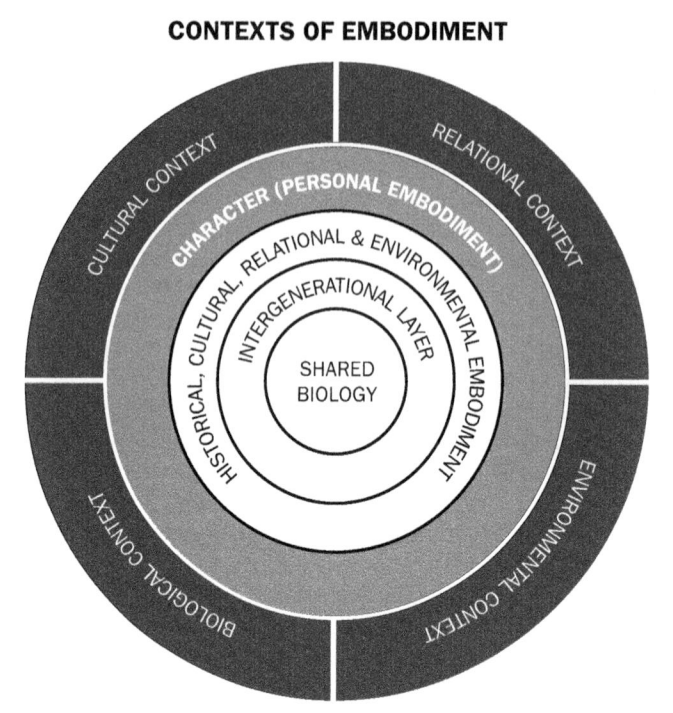

CONTEXTS OF EMBODIMENT

- CULTURAL CONTEXT
- RELATIONAL CONTEXT
- ENVIRONMENTAL CONTEXT
- BIOLOGICAL CONTEXT
- CHARACTER (PERSONAL EMBODIMENT)
- HISTORICAL, CULTURAL, RELATIONAL & ENVIRONMENTAL EMBODIMENT
- INTERGENERATIONAL LAYER
- SHARED BIOLOGY

> **The body and place**
>
> *Places have a subtle but significant impact on how we behave, so setting up your working space is important. The sensory dimension is key; research shows that people are more likely to tip the waiter or help a stranger if the sun's shining! But sensory information that's too subtle to be noticed can still have a significant impact on behaviour: A smell of burnt dust too faint to notice is enough to make people lose their appetite. What kind of sensory space are you facilitating in? The layout of spaces is also important. Think about how differently you behave in a canteen or a restaurant, a corner shop as opposed to a supermarket, or a library compared to a bar. Each space helps structure how we behave through the architecture, furnishings, layout, lighting, etc. Your coaching or training space will do the same. What's the 'mood' of the space? Is it serious and formal, calm and relaxing or quirky, upbeat and fun? How might the 4-elements model (explained later in book) apply to the mood of the space? For example, arranging the chairs in opposed lines, a circle, rows or randomly will impact on power dynamics, embodiments and how people interact. When we are in close physical proximity to someone or something, we feel closer psychologically. The opposite is also true and your layout could create 'tribes'. Different stages of coaching or training may require a different space. If you're*

using the 'four seasons' model, think about how to match the mood of your space to the task at hand.

Is 'thinking outside the box' more than just a metaphor? Researchers at Cornell University built a box big enough to sit in to find out. Those sitting outside the box were better at solving word puzzles, and those walking freely around it did best of all. There's two reasons why this happens: First, we think with metaphors all the time; second, these metaphors are embodied. The way we use the metaphor 'more is up' provides a simple example. Because in health we stand up and sickness brings us down, we tend to think metaphorically of 'more' as being 'up' ('price rises') and less as down ('stocks plummeting'). So being in a restricted space – inside the box – makes it harder to open up your thinking to bigger ideas. Some coaches and trainers work outdoors and with good reason: Walking in nature can lighten your mood, boost cognitive capacity and enhance creativity. Nature is also great for our well – being: People whose work spaces look out onto trees and flowers experience less stress, are more satisfied with their jobs and experience fewer everyday ailments like headaches.

The bottom line is that the environment we're in contributes in a significant way to our thinking, creativity and reasoning skills – we are embodied in place – so take this into account!

Further reading: www.bodymindplace.org

— Adrian Harris, MSc, PhD

Exercise: Place and embodiment

Notice the impact of places on your embodiment:

- How is it affected by the landscape and environment, climate, outdoors or indoors architecture and settings? How does your experience of self and others change with these?
- What are your key needs in terms of place (e.g. beauty)? How concretely are you taking care of them? What about where you generally do your facilitation? Are there any positive changes you could make?

What does the body actually do?

Founder of the modern conscious dance movement Gabrielle Roth said, '*Your body is the ground metaphor of your life, the expression of your existence. It is your bible, your encyclopaedia, your life story.*' The central notion of embodiment is that the purpose of the body includes much more than the standard story might suggest. Understanding this defines embodiment as a field and opens up a host of possibilities for clients. One way of thinking about the huge

14   The Body in Coaching and Training

scope of what the body encompasses is to think of embodiment in terms of *functions* that the body has.

To start with, the body relates to two aspects that are usually well known, from a 'bodily' (though not necessarily 'embodied') perspective:

- **Basics:** physical health, survival, locomotion and reproduction. This foundational aspect of the body is the standard view in mainstream culture as the body as a physical 'self-taxi'.
- **Aesthetics:** the body seeks, receives and expresses beauty. There are different levels of depth to this but the body has always been involved with beauty. The 'body positivity' movement adds new dimensions to traditional approaches.[10]

The body also relates to ten further aspects, which bring us more directly into the field of embodiment:

- **Perception:** the body is *how* we view the world. To steal a quote, 'we don't see the world as it is; we see the world as we are'[11] – we perceive the world through the lens of our embodiment (see exercise below).
- **Cognition:** the body is *how* we think. The field of embodied cognition, for instance, has established this clearly. For example, it is now established that our posture and movement patterns directly impact how creative or more structured or thinking can be. 'The body is our brain', as embodiment neuroscientist Amanda Blake[12] would say.
- **Emotion and motivation:** emotions are physiological actions we do with specific patterns of our body, and feelings are the felt sense of these actions. Emotions signal to us very clearly our underlying needs and values, which are either satisfied or unsatisfied (for more on this, see Center for Nonviolent Communication[13]). In that sense, our body guides us through our emotions to our deep motivation.
- **Identity:** the body is how we solidify and maintain *who* we are – the set of habits and dispositions that form our personality are embodied. Our sense of who we are is deeply embodied.
- **Relating:** the body is how we communicate and coordinate with others, and how we are in community. We are inter-body-beings, creatures of relationships, in and through our bodies.
- **Learning:** the body systematically records our past and predisposes our future learning around how to be and interact in the world. 'Learning' here refers in the widest sense of implicit learning to do and be, e.g. how to be safe or how to relate. Our embodied learning lies in between this solidification and the plasticity that we can create in our learning through awareness and rewiring of our habits and patterns. Our body is informed by our past, creates our future, and is our access point to the present.
- **Insight:** the body is how intuitive wisdom from experience operates. Our distributed nervous systems keep the memory of our past learnings in mostly unconscious ways. So when we access the body we can tap into

knowledge, as well as personal and perhaps transpersonal insights. While I am clear that this happens to us personally, it is worth noting that it is the only function here not scientifically well established – yet.
- **Inspiration:** the body receives creative and spiritual inspiration. I have asked many groups when they have their best ideas and participants' answers are usually: in the shower, on the toilet or walking in nature – all times when the body is both felt and relaxed. While there is little science on this one, there is a lot of wisdom and you may have relevant experience that may point to the truth of it.
- **Ethics and values:** the body tells us what we care about and what is morally right and wrong. Positive feelings and sensations give us a direct indication of ethical congruence, before and during action. Kindness and truth make us literally stronger.[14]
- **Linguistic creation:** through the body we create new possibilities in the future through language. While language is our primary and very human means of organising future actions (you never heard a dog say, 'I'll meet you next Tuesday at 4pm for a walk'), and how we plan and create different tomorrows, language is always embodied. For example, some people struggle to embody a 'no', or to make a bold declaration.[15]

Notice the word 'how' in many of these descriptions. The body is *the way in which* we perceive, think, relate, etc.!

This extended 12 functions view of the wide scope of the body's role is pretty radical, and can lead to a very different view of life. Awareness of all that the body is involved with also opens up a huge toolkit for facilitators to work directly with these areas. The fact that these areas are not widely considered 'bodily' is why this book was written. There is a wide evidence base for nearly all of these 12 functions – that is, they are proven and not just my opinion – with a couple strongly suggested by science. See Chapter 2 for more on this.

Credit: This list was influenced by the work of Richard Strozzi–Heckler,[16] The Newfield Network[17] and Paul Linden[18] among others. They are all significant influences on this book.

Exercise: Angry vs. kind bunnies – perception and cognition

Sit or stand somewhere where you can watch people unobtrusively as they walk by – outside a café, for example. First scrunch up your nose like an angry bunny rabbit, narrow your eyes and tighten your jaw and abdomen. Notice how people look at you and what you think about them.

Next try making your posture as relaxed yet expansive as possible and soften your eyes, jaw and belly. How do people look at you now and what kinds of thoughts do you have about them? The people have not changed but you have, and so might have your thoughts and perceptions.

Credit: Exercise inspired by Paul Linden's Being in Movement somatic education.

> **Exercise: Bodily identity**
>
> Can you imagine being YOU 'in' a different body. Maybe you've seen one of those goofy movies where a genie or wizard or whatever swaps two people over. Now imagine you woke up as a different biological sex, a different age, a different size and shape. Would you still be you? Imagine reacting to different stimuli with more or less triggering, having different hormones, and of course people would treat you very differently. Would you still love who and what you love? Would the world look the same? Would you have the new person's confidence or yours? Their sexuality or yours? Their politics even, or yours?
>
> What exactly is the 'you' that's floating around? Your brain? That's not really possible as neurones are all over the body, with significant clusters in the gut and the heart. Some abstract mind that doesn't depend on anything else? Makes you think, doesn't it!

Dimensions of embodied intelligence

One way to think about embodiment is as a type of intelligence, or 'a multi-dimensional way to be smart', consisting of learnable skills. In a way it is a meta-intelligence as other forms of intelligence fit within it – emotional and intuitive intelligence almost completely, for example, and even cognitive intelligence is influenced by it (see embodied cognition research in the next Chapter 2).

I created a model based on one of Daniel Goleman's models of emotional intelligence, to demystify the field and make learning embodiment practical. You can think of embodiment skills as involving awareness and choice (or leadership), for ourselves and others, across two time-frames, thus forming a simple four-quadrant matrix of embodiment capabilities, or cube if you prefer (Figure 1.3). Or to put it another way, it's about 'know' and 'grow', 'now' and 'then', with 'me' and 'them'.

Embodied intelligence (Figure 1.4) is a pragmatic perspective as it provides a map of practical skills that can be developed, so is the central model of this book; Chapters 3–6 are each devoted to one of the four quadrants. It gives a practical framework for developing oneself and supporting clients.

The basic model is self and other, awareness and choice (know and grow), over two time-frames. Note that I created this model in 2010 and started sharing it widely online soon after. Others have since come up with similar models, perhaps independently, perhaps in imitation . . . which after all is a form of flattery!

Figure 1.3 Model of embodied intelligence

EMBODIED INTELLIGENCE

EMBODIED SELF-AWARENESS	EMBODIED SOCIAL AWARENESS
- of short-term state	- of short-term state
- of long-term pattern	- of long-term pattern
EMBODIED SELF-LEADERSHIP	**EMBODIED SOCIAL LEADERSHIP**
- of short-term state	- of short-term state
- of long-term pattern	- of long-term pattern

Figure 1.4 Embodied intelligence

EMBODIED INTELLIGENCE

of pattern / of pattern
of state: / of state:

Self-awareness
>How am i?

Social awareness
>How are they?

Self-regulation
>Managing myself

Social regulation
>Influencing others

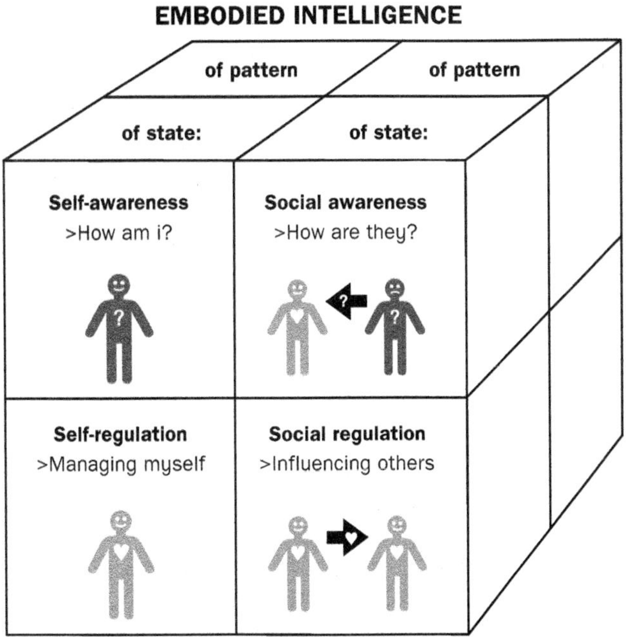

From the book *Embodiment: Moving Beyond Mindfulness* (2020), see www.embodiedfacilitator.com/book

Each aspect of embodied intelligence will be explored in detail in its relevant chapter but here's an overview:

> **Embodied self-awareness**
>
> The ability to feel one's passing state (to know how you are) and know one's long-term patterns (to know who you are)
>
> **Embodied self-leadership**
>
> The ability to both self-regulate and express oneself short term (to shift how you are), and build a new embodiment long term (to grow who you are)
>
> **Embodied social awareness**
>
> The ability to feel others' passing state (to know how they are) and guess their long-term patterns (to know who they are)
>
> **Embodied social leadership**
>
> The ability to influence how people are short term (to shift how they are) and who they are long term (to help grow who they are)

Note that embodied intelligence is radically different from bodily or kinaesthetic intelligence, which relates to athleticism, sports ability and physical movement alone.

The skills are partially independent (you can be great or terrible at any one) but also somewhat linked in a sequence. Self-awareness helps us to self-regulate, self-regulation helps us to listen, and listening helps us to lead. This is why both on face-to-face courses and in this book, I teach them in this order.

Note too that these skills will be more or less developed already according to character, life experience and past practices. A trained counsellor, for example, will likely have very developed empathy (social awareness) while a martial artist will likely have great self-regulation under pressure (self-leadership regulation aspect) and a conscious dancer great self-expression (the other side of self-leadership).

Learning and practising what's offered in this book will provide you with an opportunity to develop them all, first in the frame of self-development and then as a facilitator – the latter being built on the former.

> **Reflection**
>
> Which of these skill-sets would you say is most vital for facilitation? Which have you had explicit training in already? Which do you have a natural affinity for? If you have body practices, are they building any skills and missing any (e.g. yoga may be building self-awareness and self-regulation, but not social awareness or interpersonal leadership). Which would you pick as strongest and weakest in yourself? Please back up your answers with evidence, and ask others who know you well.

Nine tools for working with the body

One might ask what exactly one is aware of, or what one is shifting in this model; it is therefore helpful to further subdivide what we're working with into the 'nuts and bolts' of embodied facilitation. These are the basic tools of the trade and a person's ability to work with them in themselves and others defines their skill in embodied facilitation. These nine components of embodied intelligence also determine what makes a happy, healthy, flourishing human being generally! I sometimes call them 'primaries' or 'gateways', as they are primary methods – and verbal instructions should be given referring to them rather than more complex combinations for maximum clarity (techniques are built with these tools – in my lexicon) – and because any one of them opens the door to into the depths of embodiment. Each of them could be a life's study, in fact!

Let's take breath as an example. One can be aware of one's own breath – a great subtle state indicator and 'early warning' system, and you can use breath to self-regulate or express yourself. As a facilitator you will also be aware of others' breathing (very useful in, say, phone coaching for guessing the client's state), and influence it either indirectly by regulating one's own and that being mirrored – a good example of how your own embodiment comes first – or by giving the coachee a breathing exercise to up- or down-regulate themselves, for example. There are people who have studied the breath their whole lives at a level of detail that would shock you – can you identify 15 variables that could be changed in one breath, for example – and who say they are still just scratching the surface.

Note that people may be very skilled in one or two of these tools and have never used others. Systems of posture, for example, may not work much with movement and vice versa, and an expert on one may have only passing knowledge of the other. Note, too, that some tools will work better for some than others – visualisation, for example, is great for some coaches while others simply can't to grips with it at all, or it may just feel 'kooky' to them. Hence a varied tool kit is helpful, although of course we may have specialisms and favourites. For the very dedicated I would say make sure you have real expertise in one or two and passing familiarity with the rest, whereas for beginners just mastering the basics of a handful is enough.

The nine primary gateways to embodied intelligence

Of the nine tools, awareness is the most fundamental, since without awareness we can't work with any of the others. For ease of memory, you could use the acronym PRRIMAARI, but I tend to present them with awareness first – as it's necessary for all the others and defines embodied work – but aside from this there's no real order.[19]

- Posture
- Relaxation
- Respiration (breathing)

- Intention
- Movement
- Awareness
- Acceptance
- Responsiveness
- Imagery

Throughout this book, you'll be offered numerous examples of how you can easily start to use these nine primary embodied components of experience in working with your clients. Let's start now, though with just a little on each. This is just a first-take overview.

Posture (structural alignment and balance)

Stand how you choose to live. Stand for what you stand for.

– Me

From an embodied perspective, we see posture as the architecture of our being of course, and not just mechanical. We can align ourselves with the forces acting upon us, and this is not a neutral thing psycho-emotionally.[20] Gravity is perhaps the most important of these forces, acting upon us throughout our days and lives. We can structure our alignment to allow the force to be carried through our bones and into the ground, stimulating a reactive force back up again. To align with gravity, our muscles must be as relaxed as possible (they are not designed for prolonged weight-bearing) and we must provide a clear 'line' for gravity to go down.[21] Think of buildings: the walls and other support structures are vertical, and although we are not towers, the same principle applies: to align the bones to take the force and relax all muscles not involved in the essential effort.[22]

When people talk about 'good' and 'bad' posture what do they mean? Imposing some kind of platonic ideal shape? This is likely not wise, and everyone has a different theory![23] What is the best posture? Standing up 'straight'? Verticality aids alertness, but is this the best posture for sleeping? Of course not. So I ask, 'best for what?' This is a central question that I ask our students over and over again for any tool. There are better postures to get sad and angry in for example, as well as for clarity, kindness and authority.

Balance is both the result of, and a particularly important aspect of, structural alignment. The bodymind works best when it is balanced, and (as much is possible) symmetrical as a general rule, but again we could ask, 'for what'? The link between emotional and physical balancing is also fairly apparent – nobody suddenly slipped over calmly, and the emotional balancing of activities like yoga and tai chi is established (but as ever don't believe a word I say, test both of these out if you disagree).

> **Quick-win application:** Ask yourself or a client, 'Intuitively, what's the posture that's better for the thing I'm/you're doing next?' Many people will easily improve their performance this way without specialist knowledge. Another

deeper one to ask is, 'What's the posture of my/your life right now? Show me.' You can add, 'And how would you like it to be? Show me.' This is the key awareness and choice principle that I'll keep circling around in this book. This little exercise can be a profound starting place for coaching! Likewise, when working with yogis I may ask, 'Please do yoga like your life is. Note and feel that . . . [3 minute pause] . . . Now do it how you'd like your life to be.' Again, this can be huge for people to highlight their way of being and chosen lifestyle/embodiment.

Reflection: A stance for what?
Look in a full-length mirror. And then at some photos of your full body. What pose seems habitual? What is your habitual stance a posture for? In the book we will present models to explore this question but just intuitively many people can access significant answers.

Relaxation

Relaxation is perhaps a surprisingly deep aspect of embodied work. The body-mind works better when relaxed as tension inhibits both movement and feeling. Note that these are two sides of the same thing, and for some the *not* feeling is the point, despite the costs of aliveness, emotional relaxation and empathy in this. Numbing has huge consequences across the board as a coping mechanism (hence this book). Tension serves other functions in the body besides numbing emotions, such as solidifying our history and sense of who we are (unconscious embodiment)

Furthermore, living tense is like driving with the brakes on, so it takes energy. Holding on to a contraction in a pair of opposing muscles is a waste of effort that will inhibit other kinds of movement (and therefore emotion). The mind also works better when the body is relaxed yet upright (structure). I distinguish between 'dead relaxation' (a 'flop' response) and relaxation (which has movement potential and responsiveness). Relaxation is about efficient effort (mobilising the exact amount of energy and patterns of movement needed, not more), not the absence of effort. Think of an agile boxer or tiger, not a drunk guy on a sofa – the former is what I mean by 'relaxed'.[24] More philosophically, it has long been noticed that which is relaxed and pliable is alive, and that which is brittle is dead.

Many, but not all, centring techniques involve an element of relaxation, as most people could do with a bit more of it to function more effectively! Again though, 'for what?'

Quick-win application: Try out this simple trick for yourself or with a client: let your tongue hang loose in your mouth, and let your belly be soft – relax your core and let that spread to the rest of your body.[25] Say, 'aaahhh'. How do you feel? Where might this be useful in your life?

> **Reflection**
> How would your day be impacted if you were 20 per cent more relaxed today?

Respiration (breathing)

Breath is central to life itself, and at the core of nearly all of the embodiment systems that exist in both East and West. Breath is both unconscious and conscious, tremendously sensitive (hence an 'early warning device'), and hugely powerful as a tool. While there is no one right way to breathe – and different systems will tell you contradictory things – we could ask ourselves, 'what is this type of breathing for?' and learn a range of techniques, say, to up- and down-regulate[26] our state. 'Breathwork' hasn't just become popular with the likes of Wim Hof[27] and Dan Brule[28] bringing it to the masses; there is a hugely rich tradition of breathwork in yoga and other arts, as well as in Western acting and public speaking traditions. As an embodiment coach, it's certainly worth exploring!

> **Quick-win application:** Simply remind yourself or a client to breathe when you are stressed! No special breath, just a reminder! Coaches new to embodiment may be surprised how this simple 'pointing' out of aspects of embodiment can go a LONG way!

> **Reflection**
> What does your breath tell you right now about how you are?

Intention

The balance to the yin of acceptance (coming up) is the yang[29] of agency and choice: intention. Where we have conscious choice, we have freedom. Intention happens in the body and enables choice and personal leadership. It is more than just saying mentally, 'I will do this in the future'; it's a present moment bodily action – a direction. Think of reaching out to shake hands or hug someone, and notice if there is already a slight tilt forward in your body. What moves with you, or just ahead of you, is intention. Made multi-directional, the notion of 'expansiveness', 'reaching out' or 'intentional reaching' is key to some centring practices. As framed here for embodied facilitation, you can think of intention as the bridge between the purely mental aspects of activity and the more gross physical aspects. It is part of what is sometimes called (far too loosely for my liking) 'energy'.

> **Quick-win application:** Pick your intention for what you're doing now or have a client do the same. Give it a word and shape it. Cultivate a physiological sense of direction, as opposed to just floating aimlessly around.

> **Reflection**
> Pay attention to different parts of the room you're in one at a time. Notice if there's a slight tilt towards the area. What 'reaches out' to that area? Is this a reflection or an exercise?

Movement

Life breath, a central defining characteristic of life, is movement. Senior embodiment teacher Stuart Heller said, '*We move through space like we move through life.*' From when the foetus starts to wriggle we move, and when we are dead we are still. Movement one could say IS life, though perhaps more properly I should say, 'movement potential' – to include the possibility of stillness – is life.

Movement requires freedom from tension and a balanced posture, so is built on these.[30] Where our movement is chronically constricted by numbness or muscular tension (aka 'armouring'), we are less embodied and less alive. Health – both mental and physical – can be defined by the amount, quality and rhythm of movement. The latter also includes the rhythm of rest and stillness. When we feel happiest, when we are most engaged in our work and in relationships that nourish, we move! When our bodymind is working at its best, we jump with joy, run wild, dance with our partners (vertically or horizontally) and 'get a move on' at work. The entire field of embodiment is sometimes called 'movement psychology', as aside from awareness there is nothing more central to the work.

How we move is intimately related to who we are and what we're capable of. If you want to change how you are, change how you move.[31] In our teaching, I work with this in two ways that I call 'form' (top-down processing) and 'freedom' (bottom-up processing).

> **Quick-win application:** Next time you are or your client is stuck with a problem and needs new insight, move or ask them to move. Stretch, go for a walk, wriggle even; nothing fancy is necessary. See what new ideas are forthcoming. Being static usually won't help you get unstuck!

> **Exercise**
> Change how you feel yourself right now, with 30 seconds of movement.

> **Reflection: Movement pattern**
> What three words best sum up how you often move (of course, there's a situational and emotional context; but what would people who know you well

say)? Is your way of moving also a way of living? How has your dominant movement pattern served you in your life? When have you been rewarded for it? What would your life be like if you adopted the opposite pattern? What about having more range? What has been the personal or professional cost of using your dominant pattern to excess? What has been the cost of under-developing other patterns?

Awareness

The body is anchored in the here and now while the mind travels to the past and future.
– The Buddha

Awareness is the basis of all embodied work by definition, and the basis of skill in this field. It is the only tool you *must* use in embodied work. I systematically stress awareness-raising practices, especially meditation, throughout my trainings as it is so important, and I literally cannot think of one senior meditation teacher who isn't a regular and long-term meditator. Awareness is the tool that enables the other tools, and the only one included in the embodied intelligence model itself (i.e. you can be aware of your awareness!). Awareness is a profoundly human capacity, and a mystery still unresolved by science.

Quick-win application: Ask clients to notice their bodies at ANY time in a coaching process. This alone is enough to add a whole layer of insight and create much learning!

> *Reflection*
> What 'shape' is your awareness right now? Does it reach out equally in all directions? This is unlikely. How 'big' is it?

> **A particularly rich resource – awareness of sensations**
> Body awareness of sensations is your foundation as an embodied practitioner, and often what you are guiding clients towards. These are not to be confused with thoughts (e.g. metaphor, imagery, evaluation), which I also work with. A wide vocabulary of sensations[32] is helpful for embodied work, both as distinctions that actually help people feel, and to express ourselves more richly.
>
> All sensations are characterised by their:
>
> - Quality: **what**? (e.g. 'itchy', 'flowing', 'tense', 'spacious', 'bright', etc.[33])
> - Intensity: **how much**? (e.g. intensely or mildly itchy)

- Feeling tone: do you **like it or dislike it**, or neither – 'yum, yuck, whatever'?
- Location: **where** is it in the body?, what is its shape? (some sensations are global, others are not)
- Movement: **how** is it moving? (all the above factors change: we can rely upon the body to be unstable; sensation is a process not a thing; movement is necessary for all sensation)
- Immediacy: **when**? (sensation is always now, but may have a subtle sense of the past or future)

Acceptance

Acceptance: saying yes, not fighting what is, surrendering, letting go. Reality is how it is, and if we fight it, we lose every time. The universe is not broken and it has not made a mistake for you to point out. Arguing with God (or whatever you believe in) is futile.

Acceptance concerns receptivity and freely giving consent. If the 'yang' of embodiment practice is will or intention, then the 'yin' is acceptance. 'I do' is a leadership move as much as 'no!' or 'I will . . .', and without acceptance we become resentful control freaks. Acceptance of what is, is also paradoxically the second stage in changing anything after awareness, so should not be confused with apathy and is vital for coaching. Acceptance doesn't mean being passive; it means being clear. For example, Nelson Mandela accepted the reality of apartheid in order to change it.

Body hatred/body negativity is sadly part of the world still and shows a prevalent lack of acceptance for the body. In some contexts, like business, it may show up as taboos, embarrassment or immature humour.

Acceptance needs to be broken down a little more to use it, so it's cheating somewhat to call it a primary tool, but it's so vital as to be worth mentioning as if it were one. Operationalising acceptance may involve saying phrases to oneself like 'yes' and 'this is how it is right now', or just relaxing. Many people, however, will not need it to be broken down and will already have a felt sense of it, or relations like surrender (deep acceptance) or gratitude (one step further than acceptance).

> **Quick-win application:** When either you are or a client is complaining, ask what can be changed and what needs to be accepted.[34] If a client, ask them if they *can choose* to accept what they can't change. Ask them if they're *willing* to. Ask them if they will. For each part, ask them what way of sitting would help and allow them to shift posture. Ask them to say 'yes' out loud in their first language if they are willing to. If you're qualified you could add a yoga pose such as a hanging forward bend or 'child's pose' to support this process. Any kind of letting go action will be helpful though.

> **Exercise (Warning, potentially triggering)**
> Stand in front of a full-length mirror for a full five minutes looking at yourself. What parts of your body do you not fully accept or dislike? How can you give these parts of you some more love? This exercise can also be done naked, or with a considerate partner. Take care with this one and please be kind to yourself. If you could not imagine doing this, or it is a very emotional experience, you are not ready to work with another's embodiment yet.

> **Reflection**
> Are there any emotions you tend not to consider as OK? If you were more accepting of your emotions, how would your life be different? How about your energy levels? Is it OK when you are tired or wired? What about your sexual feelings?

Responsiveness

> *It is not the strongest of the species that survives, nor the most intelligent, but the most responsive to change.*
> – Charles Darwin

Bodies are not processes that happen in isolation – we always have a relational layer to our being and this is another way that we can work with ourselves. Another of the fundamental characteristics of health, efficiency and life, is to be able to respond to the environment and to be proficient at relationships. If we are functioning well, we don't just 'carry on regardless', instead we listen and reply to where we are, what is happening, and to others. Sensitivity of response is aided by relaxation and postural balance. Along with movement, this produces 'live' relaxation. This tool brings us from healthy individuals to healthy inter-dependent members of partnerships and communities, capable of effective cooperation and competition. Responsiveness could be further subdivided into a range of other somatic skills such as listening, blending and entering – all vital for facilitation.[35]

> **Quick-win application:** In order to better connect and synchronise with a person or group of people, take three breaths in time with them, or take a walk with them and allow yourselves to fall into step.

> **Reflection**
> Do you tend to be more or less the same in all circumstances, or highly flexible and adaptable?

Imagery

Imagination is an embodied phenomenon, not just a mental one. The body responds powerfully to personally and culturally appropriate imagery. This can activate subtle and complex movement patterns that would be very hard to figure out through conscious control of muscles. Imagery acts as a short-cut. Using imagery can be a powerful tool for many, though it's important to note that (a) imagery does not work for some people as well as it does for others, and (b) it's wise not to confuse imagery which can be given with clear methodological instructions – what Paul Linden calls 'operational language' – with confused metaphors given as if they were instructions.

Some common imagination themes that I have found useful teaching embodiment include:

- Animals and plants (e.g. 'picture yourself with a tail', 'imagine tree roots extending from your legs into the ground')
- Landscapes and nature (e.g. 'sit like a mountain – picture it')
- Colours (e.g. 'imagine your whole body is a bright daffodil yellow')
- Foods (e.g. move like honey)
- Life stages and family roles (e.g. 'like a five-year-old', 'in a motherly way')
- Vehicles (e.g. 'like a bus, or kite, train, canoe')
- Familiar social situations or roles (e.g. 'like you were on a first date', 'like a queen')
- Archetypes (e.g. monarch, fool, warrior, etc.; or any famous person)
- Weather (e.g. 'imagine you're a storm')
- Water and electricity (e.g. 'a flowing river', 'a lightning strike')

Quick-win application: Bring to mind an activity you're struggling with in life. Ask yourself, what animal or force of nature would be best at this thing, and picture yourself as that animal. Try the thing again.

> *Reflection – tooled up?*
> Which of these nine tools have you had explicit embodied training in already? Which might you be a 'natural' in? How might working with them add to your facilitation?

Quick-win application techniques recap

1. The posture for . . .
2. Relaxed tongue and belly
3. Breath pointing
4. Pick an intention

5 Getting unstuck by movement
6 Reminder to notice the body!
7 What can't you change coaching?
8 Synched breath/walks
9 What animal/force of nature?

You'll see from these examples that even without any skill in working with the body you can open up its wisdom as a facilitator both safely and easily. Try these, you may be surprised by the whole new world that opens up, and the power of results that can be achieved just by ASKING about the body. Gaining the skills of the rest of the book will of course add to this, but I wanted to get you started to demystify 'embodiment' and build confidence in using the method.

Practices and skills learning

Learning to be, to do and about

A critical distinction for understanding embodied learning is the difference between learning *about* something, learning to *do* something, and letting *be* something. For example, learning about France versus learning French versus being French (or French-like). Learning about something relates to cognitive knowledge, learning to do something requires skills that need practise, and being is the level that comes with time, immersion and greater practise still. Embodied learning and facilitation, and I would argue any depth facilitation approach, are about skills and being, and have more in common with language acquisition, learning to drive a car, playing a sport or learning to play an instrument, than learning *about* things by way of remembering facts. Truth be told, embodied facilitation mastery is not hard in theory, only in practice.

The notion of practise

Because of the type of learning that it is, essentially what neuroscientists would call 'procedural' rather than conceptual learning, embodied learning requires practise. Much of it is about retraining our nervous system which has default habits which we easily fall into until we build new ones. Building real awareness, range and choice as a facilitator is not an overnight job, as a result. Honestly, I think most of us have done the weekend workshops and know real transformation takes more than this. Temporary high *states* at a motivational hot-coal-walking, air-thumping, psychedelic-taking, board-breaking . . . whatever . . . do not lead to more permanent traits. Highs wear off, whether drug-induced, motivational speaker – induced, or yoga – induced, and what's left is unsexy but effective daily practise.

Community – in person and online

What I've also found helps a lot to support practice is community. Many people can be very relaxed and open on a meditation or yoga retreat, only to find that when they come home, they lose this Zen. It's partly the power place but also about the people that you are around (contexts again). Embodiments are infectious and your embodiment is in many ways the sum of the people that you spend the most time with. Communities also help in less direct ways, for example, with support, encouragement and challenge. In our hyper-individualistic times, it is worth noting the importance of other people for practice. In addition to reading this book we encourage you to reach out to other embodiment practitioners. There are several groups that I host online, for example, on social media and Zoom.[36] While not a complete substitute for face-to-face community, we have found people can develop a surprising amount of connection online using the latest technologies. At the Embodiment Conference – which is online – this has become very apparent, and there's an art to facilitating embodiment online that I will refer to in relevant sections throughout the book. Most of the exercises I'll describe can be done online as well as in person.

A personal practise anecdote

I was highly invested in cognitive learning as a child but when I was in my first year of university I had a moment of clarity. A year before was the first time a theory test had been added to the UK driving licence test and I passed that easily but failed the practical three times, unlike all my supposedly less intelligent friends at school – this was embarrassing and confusing! I had already learnt the hard way that learning about people didn't make you good at human relationships and was nursing my first broken heart, and that knowing about health didn't make you healthy (I was a drug addict and an alcoholic by 17 despite knowing the literature inside out), and had read all the psychological, sociological and philosophical works on suicide in an attempt to be less depressed, but to no avail. Having read the entire library at my school I decided perhaps the answer didn't lie in a bigger library. Doing the same old thing and all that.

Ironically it was in an academic exam that I realised the idiotic mistake of my culture, education and life to that point. I was sitting an exam on health psychology and doing the stress section. Ironically I was quite stressed due to a mix of not having done any work and the amphetamines that I spooned in my morning coffee to wake up. I realised at that point that even if I did know about the subject, that wouldn't help me with my stress which was physiological not theoretical. What did help me was a breathing exercise from an aikido class I had just joined – a basic centring technique I'd now call it, and I scraped a pass. After this I spent even less time in the library and more in the aikido dojo.

Notes

1. Credit: Francis Briers.
2. Incidentally, 'embodiment' is a word that is also used in Christian theology. Confusingly, the word has several specialist meanings in academic fields too, as well as in robotics!
3. A saying of the Asaro tribe of Indonesia and Papua New Guinea, made famous by embodiment teacher, Richard Strozzi Heckler.
4. A concept of Naseem Taleb.
5. A term coined by me and by embodiment teacher Christine Caldwell independently about the same time.
6. There's plenty of research on gut biomes and neurology being conducted.
7. For example, in *Philosophy in the Flesh: The Embodied Mind and its Challenge to Western Thought* by George Lakoff and Mark Johnson (New York: Basic Books, 1999).
8. See Philip Shepherd, *Radical Wholeness* (Berkeley, CA: North Atlantic Books, 2017) and *New Self: New World* (Berkeley, CA: North Atlantic Books, 2010).
9. This area is weak in many US schools, and I would be highly sceptical of any teacher who isn't able to answer the question, 'How is your approach to embodiment culturally biased?'
10. That being said, postmodern attempts to deny bodily aesthetics entirely (the other end of the spectrum from commercial body objectification) are also unhelpful
11. Anaïs Nin, Talmudic origin.
12. https://embright.org/mandy/
13. https://www.cnvc.org
14. See Paul Linden's fun demonstrations of this on YouTube. Search 'kind power', which will get you both him and awesome Public Enemy tune.
15. Newfield Network and The Strozzi Institute work with this aspect, combining embodiment with linguistics, and I recommend both.
16. https://strozziinstitute.com
17. https://newfieldnetwork.com
18. https://www.being-in-movement.com
19. Classical tantra and hatha yoga added these tools to mindfulness to 'supercharge' the process, so there are precedents to this list. They might also include mantra as an aspect of breath.
20. Every time I use words like 'psychological', 'emotional' and even 'spiritual' AS IF they weren't embodied, I cringe now! Paul Linden often answers questions like, 'Is that physical or emotional or psychological?' just by saying 'Yes'.
21. It isn't quite as simple as this due to tensegrity (tension and integrity), fluid dynamics, gaseous pressures and fascial networks, but it's fine as a basic model unless you're a posture geek! In reality, we're more like a tent with guy-ropes or a suspension-bridge than a skyscraper or stack of blocks (compression-based strength). Look up Gary Carter, David Lesondak and Stephen Braybrook for a deeper take on anatomy.
22. Note here that I've already had to bring in the tools of awareness and relaxation – tools are only artificially separated for clarity.
23. You'll find this with breath too – there are many theories on *the* right way to breathe!
24. Note my martial arts bias here. Always note your teacher's training bias.
25. Paul Linden's relaxation centring classics – he's spent nearly 50 years simplifying and testing such tools!

26 Up- and down-regulation are terms from medical science/physiology that refer to the process of altering the response to a stimulus. In an embodiment context they refer to altering people's general arousal level and fight-or-flight response in particular.
27 https://www.wimhofmethod.com
28 https://www.breathmastery.com
29 Yin and yang (you've seen the symbol) is an ancient Chinese model that creates many useful distinctions in embodied work, so you'll hear me mention it throughout the book as a fundamental distinction. Once you take anything and make it two poles, you have yin and yang.
30 This is a good example of how these tools are deeply linked, and only separated out for ease of understanding.
31 For more detail, see the work of Rudolf Laban on 'movement patterns'.
32 See, for instance, http://larisanoonan.com/sensations-list/
33 Building a vocabulary of feeling words is a skill-set for embodied facilitators and will actually help with discernment, as we can identify more easily what we have named.
34 This is a secular version of Alcoholics Anonymous' 'Serenity Prayer'.
35 Credit: these ideas come from various aikido Sensei working with 'off-mat' aikido, especially students of Robert Nadeau Shihan.
36 At the time of writing, this includes the Embodiment Circles on Zoom and in person, and The Embodied Facilitator Course Facebook group. These will likely change but some searching will no doubt find the latest incarnation.

2 Science, philosophy and culture

Alexandra Vilvoskaya[1]

This chapter is for those of you who wish to delve deeper into the underlying science and philosophy of embodiment. For those of a purely practical bent, the first part can be skipped, though much richness will be lost. The cultural aspects of embodiment are also worth at least reflecting on.

> ***Reflection exercise: Philosophy of the body***
> What is the body to you? Complete this sentence as many times as you can in 3 minutes: 'My body is . . .'. See if there are any patterns. Reflect on how you learnt your view of the body at school and in your family. What views on the body do you find 'weird'? Which of the following do you agree with:
>
> - The body is a brain-taxi that carries my head around.
> - The body is sinful.
> - We must learn to control our bodies.
> - The body is a tool to be used well.
> - I am not my body, I am a spiritual being.
> - The body is the main way in which I communicate.
> - The body is my playground.
> - The body is a channel.
> - The body is my source of inspiration.
> - The body is my temple.
> - The body is a source of pleasure.
> - I am my body.

The purpose of this chapter

When we deal with people, every one of us embodies their understanding of what being human is, whether explicitly or implicitly. As embodiment specialists, we inevitably build our work around our own ideas regarding the role and nature of human embodiment. We use models, methods and tools that correspond to our perception of what it means to be an embodied human being. And they in turn shape our views.

To this day there isn't any definitive answer to questions such as, 'What is embodiment?' or 'How does the fact that we are all embodied influence . . . (insert your own word)?' Every specialist has their own answers to offer. The aim of this part of the book is not so much to provide an ultimate definition of embodiment, but rather to illuminate the ideas that have intertwined to shape the phenomenon we call embodiment.

What is embodiment? – advanced

In some sense, all of the history and culture of humanity can be viewed through the lens of the body. The relationship between the body and the *soul / mind / consciousness / spirit / etc.* has long fascinated philosophers, scholars and poets. Looking back on the history of people's perception of the body, it becomes evident that it has taken decades of scientific research and at least a century of philosophical reflection to reach our present-day understanding of embodiment.

In the broadest sense, the word 'embodiment' (as a corpus of ideas and concepts) denotes the fact that the body is not only a physical object that possesses external traits, capabilities and inner workings. The idea is that our experience of our body, is an aspect of our subjectivity. This experience is not just 'there' – it has value and affects various aspects of our lives (nearly all of them, in fact), whether we're dealing with workplace success, relationships or economic or political issues (you will see how this works in the examples that follow).

The latest scientific research convincingly proves that our behaviour, emotions and cognition are mostly shaped and informed by the processes of our body – the inner physiological reactions in relationship to our environment and, more explicitly, by the changes in muscle tone, breathing, posture, quality of movement, etc.

Curiously, while older texts predominantly make use of the word 'body', the word 'corporeality' appears in *Webster's Dictionary* in 1651:

> In various religions, including Christianity, corporeal existence is often called the opposite of spiritual existence, and corporeal existence, unlike spiritual existence, is often said to be contaminated with evil. The word is also often used by philosophers, especially when considering the nature of reality.

This very word was used by philosophers up to the beginning of the 2000s to describe the phenomenon of the body as subject.

According to Noah Webster, the word 'embodiment' entered the English language in 1828 and was defined as a physical representation. It has only been in the last 15 years that we have started to use it to describe a unity of body and . . . (insert your own word), and as an overall term for practices that support this growth/return.[2]

Every specialist working in the field of embodiment probably has their own definition of embodiment and you may come across a large variety of explanations. However, they all have several ideas in common:

- Embodiment is directly linked to psychology, emotions and spirituality and impacts them.
- Our embodied experience influences our life, including our social life, and predetermines a significant part of it.
- Engaging with the body (e.g. bodywork), doing body practices (e.g. yoga) and bringing mindfulness to the body help us develop and shape our life.
- Psycho-physical integrity is a scientific fact.

If we were to differentiate an embodied view of human beings from the views that were commonly held just a few decades ago, we would focus on the following aspects:

- The unity, integrity and simultaneity of subjective (felt and experienced from within) and objective (observable and variable) embodiment.
- The interdependence and simultaneity (scientific fact) of our physiological, psychological and visible embodied processes.

'If you think your body and mind are two, that is wrong; if you think that they are one, that is also wrong. Our body and mind are both two and one', said Zen Master Shunryu Suzuki, and this is clearly not an easy theme! I feel that this quote captures the essence of embodiment. If it sounds complicated, think of quantum objects that are both wave and particle. In that same way, embodiment is both material and . . . (insert your own word). When people ask, 'what is embodiment?', they are effectively asking for an answer to one of humanity's oldest philosophical questions, so it can get dense quickly!

Embodiment: scope and history

There are several key paradigms we can single out when discussing the relationship between the body and the mind / psyche / etc.

The body is an object

Historically speaking, the first and, perhaps, still the most widespread idea is that the body is an object – a thing that possesses objective characteristics and has some kind of internal structure. This objective view of the body stems from the history of medicine and the work of ancient physicians who dissected corpses – non-living objects indeed – in order to understand the inner workings of the human body.

This view of the body has been and still is useful. In fact, much medical progress in curing disease and improving the duration and quality of people's lives is as a result of this approach. Modern engineering solutions are created precisely because their calculations take the body as an object into account.

Meanwhile, the body-as-object approach has led to what we now call *disembodiment*. The body is seen as something separate that brings discomfort or suffering (and yet it can also be a source of pleasure). However, little attention is generally given to connection with the body and to its expression. Christianity has played a large role in this by frequently describing the body as a source of sin (the body that has desires). This is of course the mainstream view and it's worth noting certain esoteric mystical traditions would take the opposite stance. The Church in Europe also pushed a body-mind split for political reasons as a kind of division of territory between themselves and science : 'OK, you get the body, but don't go near the spirit if you want to live – that's our domain!' The latest advancements in technology – from cars to computers – encourage sitting and rapid information processing, both of which are numbing, as is the move to more controlled indoor environments which provide less rich and variable sensorial experiences (as opposed to being outside with rain or sun on your skin, and wind in your hair, for example – nature through change and discomfort reminds us we're alive!). The history of the past two centuries filled with wars and trauma has also contributed to the fact that people prefer not to feel or notice their bodies – as a Russian, this is very obvious.

The idea of disembodiment is commonly linked to the ideas of Descartes – he is 'blamed' for popularising the idea of the body as a machine. This is not, however, a fair representation of Descartes' views on the human body: the parts of the manuscript in which he described his ideas of the relationship between the physical and the emotional were banned from publication during the Inquisition; however, these historical details may not seem particularly significant to us today. The idea that the body is a machine, that we can study its design, ensure its proper functioning and fix it if necessary, became rather widespread and favoured in modern Western culture.

Unfortunately, disembodiment has its consequences. Perceiving the body as an object leads to objectification, which is reflected in today's cult of athleticism, youth and polished beauty. Another consequence is the rise of violent social practices, from cult practices like male and female genital mutilation ('circumcision'), to treating humans as 'cannon fodder', to the dehumanising workplace frame of human 'resources' that reduces people to machine parts.

Starting around the beginning of the twentieth century, a new perspective on the body emerged, influenced by psychoanalysis, the scientific revolution, the First World War and other cultural and social events. The idea of a mind-body connection gained popularity. Those very ideas have shaped the field of body psychotherapy.

The body as a container

In this paradigm the body is thought of as a container: inner conflicts, psyche, soul and character are expressed and revealed through the shape of the body, tensions, breathing patterns and other symptoms of the body. The body can express and make visible our inner conflict and discord.

If you would like to find out more about the evolution of attitudes towards the body in the context of body psychotherapy, I refer you to the works of Alexander Lowen, Wilhelm Reich, Lisbeth Marcher and other body-centred psychotherapists of the twentieth century. Embodiment as a modern field is built upon their work.

The primary idea shared by these various approaches is that the body is a vessel or container that reveals the tension and disharmony of the spirit. The body is like a bag with a raging cat inside, struggling to break free, or a clogged hydraulic system that displays the effects of its failure on its surface (such as rust, etc.). The most important thing that body psychotherapy has done in terms of developing the concept of embodiment is that it established the link between the inward and the outward. Moreover, it has brought about a renewed interest in the body and contributed to the popularity of Eastern body practices (yoga, qigong, etc.), as body psychotherapy itself has borrowed many ideas and concepts from traditional Eastern practices. The sexual revolution of the 1960s and the notion that tension in the body creates mental complications and therefore chronic muscle tension should be reduced are also a result of this line of thinking.

It is curious to observe how ideas of embodiment have evolved from the Freudian 'the body is a place where inner conflicts are played out' to Bodynamics' (Lisbeth Marcher[3]) 'right of the body to . . . (existence, autonomy, freedom, sexuality, etc.)' as an integral part of an individual's human rights. In other words, through the twentieth century the body shifted from being perceived as a place (what) to being an expression of the subjective (who).

The body as messenger

Performative practices and dance movement therapy moved along the same lines, acknowledging the inseparability of body and mind. To paraphrase Marshall McLuhan, 'The body is a message. The body is a messenger.'

Key ideas for this next step for understanding the body is the body as a message: through the body we learn what we need for a more holistic and healthy life. We can listen to the voice of the body and movement and discover a new understanding of ourselves.

The idea of the body as a symbol became widespread. We express ourselves and tell our story through the body and movement (see Andrea Olsen's *Bodystories: A Guide to Experiential Anatomy*[4]). We can also 'read' another person by the signs of their body – the entire idea of body language is based on this assumption.

The same ideas were taking shape in performance art. The best-known examples of this are Butoh, the modern Japanese dance, and acclaimed performance artist Marina Abramovic´. Both have reached an understanding of the body that is at the heart of the embodiment approach. Interestingly, performance art also places importance on 'others', which is an aspect that will be discussed in this book. One of the aims of a performance as an art form is to influence the viewer. My body allows me to do something not only for myself – to express or heal myself – but also for others, to influence others through my embodiment. Here is what Marina Abramović writes about the audience of 'The House with the Ocean View', her 2002 performance: 'People would come like drunks – instead of a shot of vodka they came to have a shot of this connection with the eyes.'[5]

This idea is also present in the performances of other artists who highlight the socio-economic aspect of embodiment. Take, for instance, Russian protest artist Petr Pavlensky, whose stunts such as sewing his own mouth shut, are a clear illustration of his message: 'My body is a model of society'.

The idea that you can read the body like a book or tell your story with the body proved to be significant and promising in the field of facilitation and therapy. The semiotic approach to embodiment (the body as a symbol) paved the way for art therapy, expressive practices and the opportunity to express oneself more freely through body modifications, such as tattoos, piercings and other outward forms of self-expression.

These notions became increasingly popular in the second half of the twentieth century and sound like common sense – it is hard to imagine that a mere 30–50 years ago they sounded innovative and eccentric. 'Body language' as an idea is now a part of daily life, and the success of popular entertainment shows such as 'Lie to Me',[6] and the interpretation of politicians' gestures during important interviews and debates, show people's fascination with it.

Postmodernism and embodiment

Another substantial shift in the perception of embodiment was created by the works of French postmodern philosophers and other great thinkers who devoted much attention to the body. Since present-day ideas of embodiment are guided by postmodern views, we can draw a dotted line connecting the two.

First, it is necessary to mention the works of Maurice Merleau-Ponty.[7] In a sense, he was one of the first authors to contribute to our present-day understanding of the body as subject.

Key ideas of Maurice Merleau-Ponty

- The body is emphasised as the primary site of knowing the world.
- The body and that which it perceives cannot be disentangled from each other.
- The articulation of the primacy of embodiment led him towards what he would call 'indirect ontology' or the ontology of 'the flesh of the world'.

The concept of the body-subject involves not only the claim that the body is a 'subject', but also, conversely, that the human subject is a 'body'.

The next important brush stroke on the canvas of the development of the ideas surrounding embodiment is postmodern research. The key ideas of

38 The Body in Coaching and Training

postmodern philosophers that contributed to our understanding of embodiment are:

- The experience of the body is constructed socially.
- The construction of corporeality is politics.
- There is no single correct way of describing and experiencing your corporeality.
- The body has symbolic value.

Michel Foucault primarily addressed the relationship between power and knowledge, and how they are used as a form of social control through societal institutions. He wrote: 'In every society, the body ... is caught up in a system of constraints and privations, obligations and prohibitions.'[8]

Today, the idea of the body and power over our body is widely known. The way various forms of body politics (medical, educational, marketing, etc.) shape and manipulate our corporeality has been studied in detail. For instance, feminist and gender studies have examined the politics of sexuality and reproduction that reduce a woman to her body, which patriarchal society considers a kind of childbearing machine and an object for sexual harassment. Medical sociology and medical anthropology have devoted a great deal of attention to biopolitics, which arose out of reflections on certain medical rituals and routines that turn patients' bodies into objects to serve the needs of the physician's or surgeon's practice. Science fiction, in particular cyberpunk, and socio-cultural research on the application of high-tech solutions turn to the issue of tech policies of the body – the interaction between humans and technology, AI, biotech, etc.

Pierre Bourdieu emphasized the corporeal nature of social life and stressed the role of practice and embodiment in social dynamics. He developed the bodily capital concept and the 'habitus' concept. He wrote: 'The first thing that allows me to classify a person as a hippie, a businessman, a French intellectual, a peasant, etc. is his corporeality, the way he moves in space, the way he holds his body.'[9]

There are several other names and ideas around which the philosophy of embodiment revolves. Their influence on present-day sociology and neuroscience is evident both in the development of cognitive studies and research into artificial intelligence.

Francisco Varela, Chilean biologist, philosopher and neuroscientist, developed an original yet controversial approach to cognition. This approach, which has come to be called the enactive view,[10] is aimed at overcoming the mind-world dichotomy felt by many to be a hindrance to the development of a mature psychology. In Varela's enactive view, the world and the cognitive organism determine each other: the organism selects relevant properties of the physical world, and the world selects the structure of the organism, during their respective co-evolutionary history. An important tenet of the enactive approach is in fact that cognition is embodied. This claim represents a crucial step towards the development of a new trend of research in cognitive sciences, where the cognitive process is investigated without abstracting from the conditions in which it takes place. In fact, the statement that 'the body matters' for cognition has consequences for the conception of the body and the mind and contains indications for research on the loop between perception, cognition and action.

Thomas Csordas, professor of anthropology and religion, spent decades researching religious healing, and in his book *Body / Meaning / Healing*[11] claimed embodiment as a paradigm for anthropology. While we do not focus on this topic much, it must be said that Csordas's ideas have given some serious scientific definitions of embodiment a new flavour. He writes that embodiment is 'the existential ground of culture and self' and even called embodiment 'a phenomenology of the body'. Another valuable dimension Csordas has contributed to our work is that

> *within the paradigm of embodiment . . . we are interested in a phenomenology that will lead to conclusions both about the cultural patterning of bodily experience, and also about the intersubjective constitution of meaning through that experience. A principal characteristic of embodiment is the collapse of the dualities of mind and body, subject and object. The collapsing of dualities in embodiment requires that the body as a methodological figure must itself be nondualistic . . .*

Contemporary reflections on corporeality contain two curious aspects. The first is that the idea of non-duality as a principle of understanding corporeality is being adopted both by humanities specialists (philosophers, sociologists, anthropologists) and scientists, particularly neuroscientists. They follow different paths and find themselves in opposition to each other at times, yet today they speak of the integrity, inseparability and non-duality of the body and . . . (insert your own word here).

No less curious is the fact that sociologists and anthropologists were the original 'suppliers' of these integral ideas (they were the most vocal, at any rate). In some sense, scientific research is only just catching up with the humanities as it attempts to find experimental evidence for the idea of unity and integrity and struggles to overcome the methodological problems of such research (more on that in Chapter 3).

> **Reflection questions**
> - What ideas look more familiar to you after reading this? Are some implicit even if you have only just seen them articulated?
> - What ideas do you use most often in your life or for your work?
> - How do these different implicit ideas influence your professional practice?

The seven main influences of the embodiment field

As we look at the development of the ideas and practices of embodiment, we can single out several key areas that shaped its landscape. They are the practical fields from which the images, notions, techniques, observations and language of embodiment stem.

There are seven sources and seven components of present-day embodiment (any one of which is so broad, my brevity here will miss much out).

Yoga and meditation

The idea of mindfulness lies at the heart of any kind of embodied work. The ability to notice the expressions of your body, to be aware of your breath, posture and movement, and to distinguish between the various sensations in the body is the starting point for embodied work. Furthermore, various forms of meditation are now part of the foundation of a great number of embodied practices.

The practice of yoga has a long-established tradition of body mindfulness. It is probably the most widespread and easily accessible means for building awareness of the body, especially for those influenced more by body-accepting tantric[12] traditions than body-denying transcendent ones. Not all meditation and not all yoga can be considered an embodied practice, however, if the emphasis is either just physical exercise (many modern types of 'yoga') or sees body and spirit in opposition, in a way analogous to mainstream Christianity. It should be said though, embodiment as we know it today is deeply rooted in yogic and meditative practices, which are a major influence on most, if not all, seminal teachers.

Somatic psychotherapies

Body psychotherapy and dance movement therapy[13] have contributed significantly to the development of the notions of embodiment, as have more recent embodied trauma therapies such as Somatic Experiencing. The very idea of an intimate body-mind connection first appeared and was significantly developed in the field of body psychotherapy. Today body psychotherapy is being infused with ideas of embodiment, which has produced a shift from its original view of the body as a means of expressing psychic conflict.

Bodywork

The development of somatic practices and various forms of bodywork resulted in the spread of ideas and methods that highlighted the role of changing a person's bodily state and retraining the body. The embodied work we do is often about retraining the body, where we restore natural movement and tap into new possibilities.

The martial arts

Much of present-day embodiment has its origins in the martial arts. These practices, particularly those that originated in Asia, aim not only to physically train the body, but also to build up a warrior's spirit. Managing your state, regulating your stress response, staying focused on the interaction with your partner are all practices that embodiment has drawn from the martial arts.

Western somatics

Western awareness-based body arts such as Feldenkrais, Hanna Somatics, the Alexander Technique and Bodymind Centring are now a major influence on the field of embodiment. Although some would see 'somatics' and 'embodiment' as synonyms, to me these fields, while awareness-based, may or may not have a personally transformative element, and may be simply health practices. They certainly form a connected tradition (with most having at least some Asian roots).

Theatre, performative arts and improv

Another area that has contributed to the field of embodiment is theatre. The premise of acting training (notably that of Michael Chekhov, Stanislavsky's work and other 'method' acting techniques) is that a character is born out of an expression of the body. A gesture inspires a phrase and a pattern of movement inspires a character. Improv, in turn, helps train attention and freedom. Improv comedy is also something of a 'wildcard' modern influence on the field.

Dance

The perception of dance in the twentieth century and its forms have also been a source of inspiration for embodiment. Through the exploration and development of dance and dance training, an understanding of the link between emotions, states and movement emerged. We also cannot fail to mention the role of the system for describing movement designed by Rudolf Laban that is widely used in embodied work.[14] As well as contemporary dance (which may or may not have strong embodied elements), partner dance has an embodied wing and conscious dance (e.g. 5Rhythms) is certainly an embodied practice, and gaining in popularity to rival yoga.

But is it 'embodied'?

It is important to note that despite their affinity to embodiment (and the use of identical tools), there is a difference between body practices and embodied practices. We can practise to become stronger, healthier, or to master some kind of bodily or motor skill. And that is a great goal. But we need both awareness and an aim to develop the whole person to turn this body practice into an embodied one. Just training the body is not embodiment, it's exercise, and we need both mindfulness and the self-development focus to call it 'embodiment', in our view. Bodywork and somatics focus on the body, but usually fail to enquire how this newly found sensitivity helps us address the challenges of our everyday lives.

Top down vs. bottom up – form and freedom

Embodiment is grounded in mindfulness practices, but is not limited to them: becoming aware of your state is not enough – you have to be capable of changing it. The martial arts and yoga, which although they have achieved perfection in the art of managing your state and mastering shapes (so include choice not just awareness), often do not leave room for freedom of expression. They are 'form' or 'top – down' practices, rather than 'freedom' practices (aka 'bottom up') which involve more of a process, or unfolding, model.

See Mark's book *Embodiment* for more on this.[15] Figures 2.1 and 2.2 show first just *some* of the scope of embodied practice today, and the roots discussed in graphic form.

Figure 2.1 Scope of the embodiment field

SCOPE OF THE EMBODIMENT FIELD

- Somatic psychotherapies
  - Trauma healing modalities
  - Constellations
  - Body therapy
  - Dance-movement therapy
  - Drama therapy
- Embodied parenting
- Meditation and yoga
  - Authentic relating
  - Embodied meditation
  - Conscious eating
  - Partner/acro yoga
  - Modern postural yoga
- Dance
  - Western awareness practices (somatics)
  - Conscious dance
  - Embodied partner dance
  - Group dance forms
  - Postmodern dance
- Embodiment coaching
- Embodied leadership
- Martial arts
  - Combat-orientated
  - Health-orientated
  - Performance-oriented
- Theatre
  - Embodied movement work
  - Improv comedy
  - Acting training
  - Embodied Play
  - Voice work
- Art-assisted embodiment
- Hands-on bodywork
  - Healing modalities
  - Functional work
  - Structural/postural work
- Nature connection
  - Bushcraft
  - Wilderness therapy
  - Animal-assisted work
  - Eco-therapy
  - Embodied activism
- Men's and women's work
- Conscious sexuality

EMBODIMENT

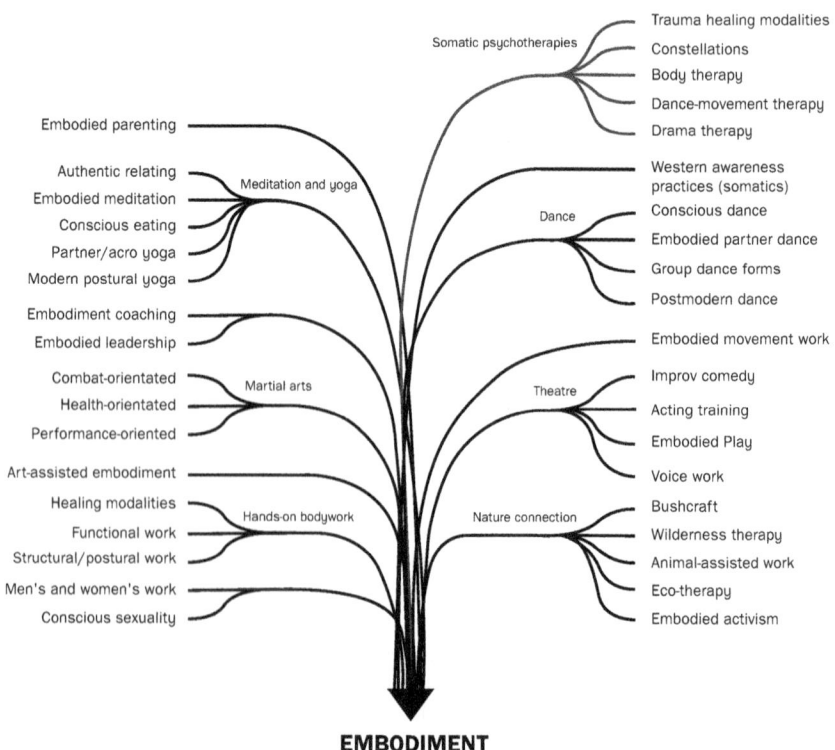

Figure 2.2 Roots of the embodiment field

ROOTS OF THE EMBODIMENT FIELD

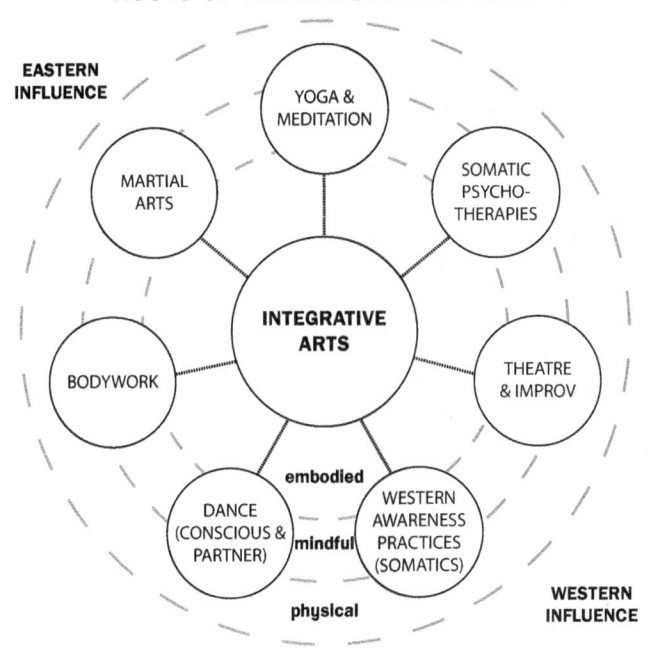

- EASTERN INFLUENCE
- YOGA & MEDITATION
- MARTIAL ARTS
- SOMATIC PSYCHO-THERAPIES
- INTEGRATIVE ARTS
- BODYWORK
- THEATRE & IMPROV
- DANCE (CONSCIOUS & PARTNER)
- WESTERN AWARENESS PRACTICES (SOMATICS)
- embodied
- mindful
- physical
- WESTERN INFLUENCE

Relation to mindfulness, body language, EQ, etc.

When someone comes across the notion of embodiment, they almost inevitably think they are familiar with it: 'Isn't that the same as . . .?', or 'Oh, it's like . . ., right?'

Sometimes such identification and connection to something they had experienced hit the nail on the head. Today, many practices and approaches rest on the ideas of embodiment. And yet, it is helpful not only to note the similarities and differences, but also to examine the premises of those practices in greater detail. This is especially important for embodied facilitators whose clients will often address such questions to them. We will explore some of these distinctive features from the perspective of the emotional intelligence model.

Emotional intelligence

The term 'emotional intelligence' became widely known in 1995 after Daniel Goleman published a book of the same name on it.[16] Goleman's model is not the only model of emotional intelligence, or EQ, though. One thing that all the models have in common, however, is their focus on the skills of noticing and managing the emotions of yourself and others.

Today, there is general agreement among scientists that the phenomenon we call an 'emotion' is an integrated psycho-physiological process which cannot be isolated from a bodily response (a popular metaphor describes emotions as our body's way of translating corporeal information into the language of the mind). The emotional intelligence model we will be using in this book is based on Goleman's emotional intelligence model with the addition of an embodied dimension (EQ can be seen as a subset of embodied intelligence, in fact). This model offers a similar set of four skills: awareness of your embodied state, managing your embodied state, awareness of the other's embodied state and influencing the other's embodiment through your own.

Body language

Body language is the first thing that comes to mind for many when we talk about how changing your posture can change a situation or influence others. The difference between embodiment and the concept of body language is its depth. Body language is what lies on the surface, like a suit you try on. It doesn't matter whether it looks good, whether it's the right size or if it's fitting for the occasion. Body language is a system of signs constructed and established within a culture. Following this metaphor, embodiment is more about choosing the clothes that are right for you at this particular moment and achieving a perfect fit. Body language does not involve a person becoming aware of their posture and movement and finding a personalised embodied solution. Embodiment, however, is just that. Another way of looking at this is that body language *expresses* who and how we are, but embodiment also *creates* it – the arrow goes both ways with embodiment.

What the science says

Another question that is often asked is whether embodiment is 'scientific' or based on science. Our culture trusts in science so it's a very natural question. And it's true to say 'yes', there is some good research and understanding that are evidence – based, but the scientific base for embodiment is not solid for now in all areas for reasons that will become apparent.

Today it is evident that science, which is based on the paradigm of objective[17] knowledge and uses corresponding tools (to quantify the results of experiments, validate the data obtained, conduct meta-analyses, etc.), faces certain methodological challenges in the study of embodiment. The challenge is in the understanding of the body and corporeality. Traditionally, scientists have viewed the body as an object, while the embodiment paradigm presupposes the subjective nature of corporeality. Although it is becoming more common for modern research to build bridges between objective knowledge of the body as an object (e.g. measuring various parameters) and the subjective experience of the body, it is unlikely that the hard problem of consciousness (the problem of explaining how and why sentient organisms have qualia or phenomenal experiences – how and why it is that some internal states are felt states) will be resolved in the near future. This very problem may serve as the foundation of the scientific substantiation of the ideas and practices of embodiment. We are greatly looking forward to this.

In 2013, a reassuring piece of research was published: it seemed to prove that simple practices or postures affect not only the subjective perception of one's state, but also objectively measurable parameters (I am referring to the research carried out by Amy Cuddy[18]). Sadly, we cannot at present consider this research proof that embodiment is a kind of 'objective reality' rather than simply a corpus of wonderful ideas and decades-old practices, or that our embodiment shapes our way of being in the world. To claim this would be premature (I will consider this case in a further paragraph).

Nonetheless, judging by the amount of available research, there is growing scientific interest in embodiment. There are at least two fields of study, embodied cognition and trauma research, which have accumulated an impressive body of scientific data that confirm that 'something along those lines does exist'. A massive field of study that deals with many of the same issues is mindfulness. We will examine several studies in order to identify meaningful scientific data that will allow us to gain a better understanding of what happens during embodiment practice as well as give us some ideas for our practice and work.

Embodied cognition

Embodied cognition is the theory that many features of cognition, whether human or otherwise, are shaped by aspects of the entire body of the organism. The aspects of the body include the motor system, the perceptual, bodily interactions with the environment and assumptions about the world that are built into the structure of the organism.

> *Our brains take their input from the rest of our bodies. What our bodies are like and how they function in the world thus structure the very concepts we can use to think. We cannot think just anything — only what our embodied brains permit.*[19]
>
> – George Lakoff

Furthermore, research in the field of embodied cognition focuses primarily on the mind (cognition) and examines empirical correlations between certain kinds of cognitive processing, sentence comprehension and types of perceptual/motor performance. Many studies have been conducted in this dynamically developing field, resulting in a collection of valuable findings. For instance, it has been discovered that people who are experiencing ambivalence move from side to side more than people who are not experiencing ambivalence. The inverse correlation – that a physical lack of stability may lead to ambivalence – has also proved to be true.[20] Or that Europeans do shift their bodies forwards and backwards when they think about the future or the past respectively.[21]

The study of the functioning of the different parts of the brain during cognitive processes (perception, decision-making, assessment, etc.) also occupies the field of embodied cognition (and that is where it converges with the field of neuroscience). A book we can recommend to those who wish to familiarise themselves with such studies is *Sensation: The New Science of Physical Intelligence* by Thalma Lobel,[22] which contains a wealth of such research (unfortunately, not all of the research could be reproduced or verified with a larger sample size, which, in turn, does not necessarily mean that the findings are false or that the hypotheses of the studies were not confirmed).

Neuroscience

There is a commonly held hope that if we thoroughly understand the processes that take place in the brain, we will be able to overcome a great number of challenges that we as individuals and humanity as a whole face. These expectations are not groundless, but there is no telling whether ultimate knowledge in this field is attainable in our lifetime.

A particularly fascinating approach is that of radical embodied cognitive neuroscience, a relatively new branch of cognitive science that looks to ecological psychology and dynamical systems theory to understand the contribution of bodily capacities to cognitive processes.[23] It is 'radical' in claiming that cognitive scientists need new conceptual tools if they are to understand the ways in which cognition depends on the body in its interaction with the environment. Embodied approaches to cognitive science stress the many and varied ways in which an animal's environmental niche offers resources for the animal to act on. The individual has bodily skills and abilities that are refined and perfected through practice for dealing adequately with the possibilities for action the environment offers. One aspect that is highlighted in this framework is the 'inseparability of emotion and cognition in the brain and the deep dependence of emotional processes on the whole body of the living organism in its practical skilled engagement with the environment'.[24]

Thus, in recent years we have witnessed a gradual paradigm shift in cognitive science. As Mark Johnson writes:

> *Western culture has inherited a view of understanding as an intellectual cognitive operation of grasping of concepts and their relations. However, cognitive science research has shown that this received intellectualist conception is substantially out of touch with how humans actually make and experience meaning. The view emerging from the mind sciences recognizes that understanding is profoundly embodied, insofar as our conceptualization and reasoning recruit sensory, motor, and affective patterns and processes to structure our understanding of, and engagement with, our world. A psychologically realistic account of understanding must begin with the patterns of ongoing interaction between an organism and its physical and cultural environments and must include both our emotional responses to changes in our body and environment, and also the actions by which we continuously transform our experience. Consequently, embodied understanding is not merely a conceptual/propositional activity of thought, but rather constitutes our most basic way of being in, and engaging with, our surroundings in a deep visceral manner.*[25]

Parallel to these developments, a view has emerged according to which the things we commonly understand as 'cognition' or 'emotions' are not predetermined, but are rather created and constructed by humans as they engage with their environment and interpret it, based on their cultural preconceptions. A vivid description, substantiation and explanation of this view are provided by Lisa Feldman Barrett:

> We find that your emotions are not built-in but made from more basic parts. They are not universal but vary from culture to culture. They are not triggered; you create them. They emerge as a combination of the physical properties of your body, a flexible brain that wires itself to whatever environment it develops in, and your culture and upbringing, which provide that environment.[26]

The way we choose to interpret the signals of the body is driven by our previous experience, determined by our culture and takes the shape of a prediction: 'In every waking moment, your brain uses past experience, organized as concepts, to guide your actions and give your sensations meaning. When the concepts involved are emotion concepts, your brain constructs instances of emotion.'[27] Therefore, the question that comes to the fore in embodied work is one that our teacher Paul Linden often asks his students: 'What do you do in your body?'

Another fruitful field of neuroscientific research is the study of mindfulness. With meditation becoming part of people's everyday lives and parlance, and new research opportunities opening up daily, the issue of what happens to the brain during meditation and how this affects the various aspects of our lives is increasing in popularity. It is evident that meditation practices have a positive effect on our health. The strongest scientific evidence to date that meditation has positive health benefits comes from two meta-analyses (analyses of data pooled from multiple studies) of meditation research. The first meta-analysis of 47 trials with 3,515 participants found that people participating in mindfulness meditation programmes experienced less anxiety, depression and pain.[28] The second meta-analysis of 163 studies found evidence that meditation practice is associated with reduced negative emotions and neuroticism, and the impact on patients of meditation was comparable to that of behavioural treatments and psychotherapy.[29]

Despite numerous studies on the impact of meditation on the brain, no definite answers are forthcoming. However, the following research is illuminating. One meta-analysis pooled data from 21 neuroimaging studies examining the brains of about 300 experienced meditation practitioners.[30] The authors found that eight brain regions were consistently altered in experienced meditators.

The eight brain regions altered in experienced meditators
- *Rostrolateral prefrontal cortex*: a region associated with meta-awareness (awareness of how you think), introspection and the processing of complex, abstract information.

48 The Body in Coaching and Training

> - *Sensory cortices and insular cortex*: the main cortical hubs for processing of tactile information, such as touch, pain, conscious proprioception and body awareness.
> - *Hippocampus*: a pair of subcortical structures involved in memory formation and facilitating emotional responses.
> - *Anterior cingulate cortex and mid-cingulate cortex*: cortical regions involved in self-regulation, emotional regulation, attention and self-control.
> - *Superior longitudinal fasciculus and corpus callosum*: subcortical white matter tracts that communicate within and between brain hemispheres.

The specific ways in which the brain regions changed varied by study (different studies used different neuroimaging measurements), but changes were seen in the density of brain tissue, thickness of brain tissue (indicating a greater number of neurons, glia or fibres in a given region), cortical surface area and white matter fibre density.

The effect of meditation on these particular brain structures appeared to be about 'medium' in magnitude – effect sizes that are comparable to the roughly 'medium' effects of many other behavioural, educational and psychological interventions.

At this stage, we need to be careful not to overgeneralise, overvalue or oversimplify what we have already learned from neuroscience research on meditation or what we could learn from it.

Posture research

As previously mentioned, great hopes have been placed on the scientific validation of the things that embodied practitioners have known for decades: that one's embodied state affects one's actions, emotions, thinking, social interactions, etc. The study conducted by Amy Cuddy in 2013 was meant to bring that into being. Media coverage and her popular TED talk[31] have contributed to the popularity of this study, which was dubbed 'power posing'. Unfortunately, in the years following its publication, researchers failed to replicate this work.[32] We could address the reasons it could not be reproduced (it seems that we are dealing with a case where researchers discovered something they did not have a methodological framework for, which significantly complicated the process of describing their experiments and the possibility of their replication). Or we could discuss the hype around this study. However, the issue of posture influencing various aspects of a person's life has become popular as a direct result of such research and has given rise to a series of other fascinating studies. They may still be in need of validation, but their findings present great interest.

Posture may to some extent affect one's self-perception. Participants who were randomly assigned to hold expanded (vs. contracted) poses – under the guise of a cover story about holding different body positions to test the accuracy of wireless electrodes – wrote significantly more self-statements than those who assumed contracted positions. Jackson et al. tested whether this finding was replicable and extended this research by aiming to characterise the process by which it occurred.[33] One hundred and twenty-eight female students were randomly assigned to hold either expanded or contracted postures. They completed surveys measuring two general classes of potential mediators ('broaden-and-build' and 'narrow-and-disrupt'), body self-objectification as a moderator, and four indices of self-concept size. Posture was not found to affect self-concept size, nor was it moderated by self-objectification. Though there was no effect on self-expansion, in exploratory analyses, assigned posture affected one of the broaden-and-build measures: psychological flexibility.

Posture can also affect one's memory and mood. Peper et al. investigated the effect of posture when sitting in a slouched or upright position on recall of either negative (hopeless, helpless, powerless or defeated) memories or positive (empowered or optimistic) memories.[34] Two hundred and sixteen college students sat in either a slouched or an erect position while recalling negative memories and then in a second step, recalling positive memories. They then sat in the opposite body position while recalling negative and then positive memories. Eighty-six per cent of the students reported that it was easier to recall/access negative memories in the collapsed position than in the erect position, and 87% of the students reported that it was easier to recall/access positive images in the erect position than in the collapsed position.

Golec de Zavala et al. have shown that yoga posture can have an effect on self-esteem (and do so more effectively than 'power poses'),[35] while Peper et al. have reported that body posture may change stereotype threat response.[36] The latter study investigated the effect of posture on mental maths performance. Participants rated the maths task significantly more difficult while sitting slouched than while sitting erect.

Attitudes towards science

Science is a way of knowing and an important one – it is, however, not the *only* way of knowing. This is apparent to most people – for example, few of us would want to select a life-partner, or even choose a job, 'scientifically'! Two common mistakes I see students make are:

- To privilege science above all else – undermining the importance of subjective enquiry in embodiment, which *by definition* concerns subjective awareness! This is disempowering and misses the very heart of embodied learning.
- To use cherry-picked science to justify existing beliefs and practices. This is a misuse of science and fundamentally dishonest. I have done my best not to come at this chapter with a 'science says we're right' approach, which is, sadly, very common. Embodiment is not a religion, and also doesn't need justifying with science! Mark and I believe that the appropriate relationship between science and embodiment is one of mutual respect and enrichment. The common ground is that both are empirical, but they are fundamentally also different and therefore complementary.

50 The Body in Coaching and Training

> ***Reflection questions***
> - How attached are you to scientific knowledge? In what ways is it great, in what ways is it wanting? Are you against science in some way[37] or 100 per cent for it?
> - Is it important to you to have any scientific base for your embodiment or professional practice? Do you use research or evidence-based data to develop your practice, or to justify it?

Cultural embodiment

> ***Reflection question***
> Is how you move and stand influenced by where you are from?

Every time we discover body reactions or habits in ourselves or others, we rarely have a firm grasp on what caused this embodied expression. When we walk without putting our weight on the back of the foot or feel a constraint in our shoulders, is it an expression of an individual habitual pattern, a reflection of our physical capabilities, a reaction to a certain relationship, to the environment or a current context (a pebble in our shoe or a shirt that is too tight)? Or is it a reflection of our cultural pattern?[38]

If we keep in mind that our embodied patterns (our personal embodiment) are the result of the interaction of a particular person with their environment, we cannot ignore our experience of interacting with our cultural environment – the cultural aspect of embodiment. 'Cultural embodiment' is the name we give to the aspect of our patterns that correlates to our experience of interacting with our current and historical cultural environment (the cultural features of the place we live, the historical experience of various communities, the peculiarities of social and professional groups, the history and narratives of families, etc.).

It's not easy to speak about cultural embodiment as it's a small, under-researched and politically loaded field. There are not too many scientists in this field because it's very socially sensitive. So the very first claim we need to declare: When we speak of cultural embodiment, bear in mind that this is not the same as a stereotype such as 'All X are Y', or 'that's because he/she is X'. A study of our own embodiment and the embodiment of others through the lens of culture may uncover the unique, idiosyncratic nature of various groups, help us experience connection and belonging and serve as a valuable resource.

Cultural studies generally approach embodiment from the perspective of body language and examine the meaning behind certain gestures, movements and facial expressions. While this is undoubtedly fascinating and may help us understand each other better, it is important to note that cultural embodiment is deeper than that. Cultural embodiment is about the embodied features – posture, movement, reactions – characteristic of members of a particular cultural group. It is the way we identify 'our tribe' (people who come from the same country or cultural group as we do) and know when we encounter someone from a different culture ('they are not like me').

A simple definition of culture is, 'how we do things around here', and this *of course* includes the body as a way to enact this.

> **Reflection exercise**
>
> Have you ever been in another country and identified someone there as coming from your own country on sight? What did you notice about them? Which aspects of their embodiment brought you to this conclusion? What did you identify as 'familiar' in their embodiment? Can you spot certain nationalities on a beach, aikido dojo or 'black-tie' event, or in another context where people are all dressed the same?

This simple exercise helps us discover how embodied cultural patterns may manifest themselves. People who travel a lot or work in popular tourist destinations often easily identify the nationalities of the people they meet. For some it is an important professional skill – identifying a potential buyer's cultural embodiment and addressing them in their first language may well boost sales.

When we spend an extended period of time living in a cultural environment, we tend to soak up the embodiment of the people around us and become a little like them. Thus, we nurture certain responses and reactions and acquire the opportunities and limitations of this embodiment, its corresponding world – view, traditions and way of thinking. This is particularly evident in our childhood experience where we follow the example of the adults around us and adopt their embodiment. These may be family patterns or geographical patterns.

> **Reflection exercise**
>
> Think of a place where you spent a significant amount of time as a child. Choose a neutral or pleasant memory to think back on. Try to reconstruct the place in as much detail as you can. Think of the people you were with (preferably the people who lived nearby, whom you met in the street or at the shop, rather than family members). Choose memories that are either neutral or pleasant. How did they move, walk, stand or sit? Try to recall some details of their posture. Try adding some of these embodied nuances to your body right now, and exaggerate them a little if necessary. Does it feel familiar? Are there situations in which you feel this way? How natural does this kind of embodiment feel for you? How are these embodied patterns manifested in your life today? What can they affect? What opportunities and limitations, advantages and disadvantages do they create for you?

In our globalised world it is vital to appreciate the cultural aspect of our corporeality. Not only does this allow us to understand each other better, but also has great practical value. Because cultural embodiment comes out when we are faced with certain situations and triggers, being mindful of this allows us to work with intergenerational and cultural trauma, gender differences and other topics.

Stereotypes (which generally communicate perception rather than fact) often take the form of statements, such as 'Russians are gloomy and dangerous' or 'Brits are stuck-up' or 'Americans are loud and overly confident' or 'Brazilians are fun', etc. Such descriptions reflect our perception of another person's embodiment, which is rooted in our habitual cultural embodiment. When we measure their embodiment against our own, it is easy to notice that they are 'different' or 'wrong'. This is unsurprising, as culture is a kind of norm. In this way, our own cultural embodiment creates an image of what a 'correct', 'normal' embodiment should look like, and subsequently affects the way we perceive different embodiments. However, if we 'try on' a different cultural embodiment, if we literally start doing what a person from another culture is doing in their body, we will be able to access the states, values, opportunities, constraints, affections and world – view held by this other culture. Exploring culture though the body builds empathy and understanding.

As we study cultural embodiment, we turn to the facts: what am I or the other person doing with my body? We describe cultural embodiment through the intention of the body, the quality of movement, the details of the posture, the tension or relaxation, the nuances of the breath and the gaze, the way one produces sounds, as well as other aspects of one's embodiment. This allows us to set aside our interpretations, stereotypes and evaluation, leaving us with the facts. At the same time, these facts give us a clearer image of how our embodiment creates our way of being, our outlook on life and an underlying logic for our reactions. They may also allow us to understand certain traditions or cultural habits better.

Very often cultural patterns are the result of the history of a group of people. When we become aware of our cultural patterns and discover their link to historical circumstances and events, we can give ourselves more choice and change things in our lives. This may refer to the historical events of a particular region or nation (or a group of people), a religious or professional community, a generation, etc.

For a long time I had to share a fridge with a friend of mine. At a certain point I noticed that we had very different approaches to food. I would always try to fill the fridge up – I brought tons of food home whenever I had the chance because I wanted there to always be food in the house. His strategy, however, was to consume the food he bought as quickly as possible, while it lasted. We grew up in the same city, but in a different year and in a different economic situation. My childhood coincided with a deficit of food in the city: we would buy it whenever it was available in the shop. As a result, I learned to jump at every opportunity to buy as much food as I could and squirrel it away because there might not be any in the shop tomorrow. My friend grew up amidst a deficit of both food and money: even if food is available today, there is no guarantee it will be available tomorrow, that's why we have to eat as much as possible now. The reaction of our bodies was the same – it was a grasping response that manifested itself in two different ways because it arose out of two different sets of social circumstances. This is an example of how cultural patterns may be not only national, but also generational, and of course other subcultures exist within any nation, and across nations, so I am not equating 'culture' with nation-state, it is just convenient to talk about nationalities.

The 'culture' of practices

We all have a certain bias that stems from our habitual embodiment. It may be the result of our personal embodiment (the patterns shaped by our personal history) or our cultural embodiment. It affects our assessment and perception, our ideas and embodied practices. It may also be a reflection of our cultural and professional embodiment.

Based on your own experience of embodied practices and your professional field, what do you find 'best' or 'most effective'? Here are several examples from our work at the Embodied Facilitator Course (EFC) that unites people of various professional and cultural backgrounds.[39]

Specialists whose embodied practice is connected to the martial arts or yoga tend to respond positively to form-based sessions and exercises that have a clearly defined hierarchy, rules of conduct and time-frame. Specialists whose embodied practice lies in the field of conscious dance (5Rhythms, Movement Medicine, Open Floor, etc.), improv or performative arts may find such sessions and exercises challenging and may experience feelings of resistance and protest. The inverse is true as well. Therapists often want to talk more about their own experience than EFC culture (which has a martial arts bias of 'just practice') gives time for, and can get quite upset and provide very clever rationalisations as to why their familiar way is better. People often experience the habitual patterns that are shaped by our culture (i.e. norms and traditions) and our practices as 'right', while everything else seems 'wrong'. On our course we use various types of practices (our aim is to give participants more range in the patterns that are available to them), which enables participants to notice their habitual embodiment and explore how embodied practices shape our embodiment and affect our preferences.

Professional 'culture'

Another aspect worth mentioning is professional preference. For instance, a strict time limit is set when participants debrief an exercise (in pairs, small groups or one larger group). This is generally well-received by business trainers and often triggers specialists whose practice involves hearing everyone out and following every detail of what they say – psychotherapists, somatic practitioners, etc. Such situations can also be used to notice the 'cultural' patterns we have acquired as a result of our profession.

Different professional cultures shape different embodied patterns. For example, we have observed that teaching (which includes business trainers) often nurtures a 'talking' pattern (the habit of assuming the role of a leader in an interaction), while therapy, coaching and narrative practice often nurture a 'listening' pattern (the habit of assuming the role of a follower in an interaction). At EFC we draw participants' attention to these professional patterns and work on giving them more range, which can be both challenging and delightful.[40]

Shadow

Another aspect of cultural embodiment which may have practical value is the issue of shadow and trauma. It is clear that various groups may find certain topics triggering and have an embodied reaction to them. These sharp emotional and embodied reactions often uncover our cultural embodiment.

When we study cultural embodiment at EFC Russia, for instance, we explore attitudes towards power. The history of Russia is full of traumatic events connected with the issue of power, so it is unsurprising that it triggers a great deal of shadow and trauma in the body. The most common reactions are 'freeze' and 'flop', a kind of passive aggressive behaviour that manifests itself in irresponsibility, fear of punishment and lack of initiative. People with a different cultural background, say, Israelis, are more likely to have a 'fight' response in the same circumstances.

More than that, every culture (both national and professional) will have its own distinctive response to the 'big three' shadows – power, money and sex. In the UK, for instance, the most loaded topic seems to be money (especially related to class), whereas sex is more of a taboo in the USA than most Europeans countries (dependent on region and subculture as ever[41]). When we discover such aspects of cultural embodiment, we can examine the effect of these cultural patterns on our lives more closely, and not be victims of them.

Gender

Another interesting cultural observation is related to gender differences (another aspect we carefully examine in our training programmes and with clients). Every culture possesses its own gender norms that shape gendered embodiment. They can be found in the intention of a person's body (inward vs. outward), how wide apart they place their feet (the famous 'man-spreading / woman-minimising'), the position of their head, the direction of their gaze, the features of their movement, etc. The embodiment of men and women in certain cultures (for instance, in Central Asia, Japan or Slavic countries) is so great that we can speak of a distinct gendered cultural embodiment in those regions. In other countries, these differences are not so noticeable, or may reverse 'traditional' patterns (particularly in The Netherlands and Nordic countries where women may well stand with a wider stance than men, for example, and interrupt more frequently in training and occupy more space verbally[42]).

Being aware of gender differences in people's embodiment and taking this into consideration when working with clients form an important competency for an embodiment specialist. At the turn of the century, a curious discovery was made regarding the stress response of men and women, which was as much a product of culture as it was of evolution, which is confirmed by an analysis of animal studies: men (males) generally display the 'fight' and 'flight' stress responses (see Chapter 4), while women (females) often display a 'tend-and-befriend' response.[43]

Note that within the embodiment world there are both radical feminists and staunch conservatives, and both positions are enriched by an embodied approach.

Trauma

Over the past few decades, our understanding of the phenomenon of trauma has improved significantly. Not so long ago, the term 'trauma' was understood as a serious event that had severe psychological or neurological consequences, and was often associated with various symptoms of post-traumatic stress disorder (PTSD). Today it is obvious that 'trauma' is in fact a state of the nervous system. One way of putting it is that it is 'a strong stress response that is constantly present in the body' that we can detect in various types of behaviour, emotional disorders, difficulties in building relationships and social adjustments, physical illnesses, embodiment, etc. In other words, 'trauma' does not necessarily refer to some specific events in a person's life, but is always connected to the body.

Historically speaking, the term 'psychic trauma' was introduced by German neurologist Albert Eulenburg in 1878,[44] while the term 'traumatic neurosis' as well as one of the first theories on the subject was penned by Herman Oppenheim in the 1880s. Based on the observations he made in 1883–1888, the young neurologist noticed that women and men suffered from nervous and mental symptoms as a result of the accidents they had experienced. In a way, technical and scientific progress contributed to the emergence of this concept: new factory equipment and the railway became the source of accidents and disasters. Railway accidents were frequent and tragic, and newspapers quickly picked up stories of the crashes and the generous compensation awarded in court – all of this created a new social context with its own idea of trauma. Railway accidents created an urgent need for doctors to comprehend and explain the rather strange set of symptoms that J.E. Erichsen had already outlined in his book in 1866[45] and other doctors had written about in medical articles. A whole range of 'nervous symptoms' was cited, including changes in thermal sensitivity, gait, reflexes, handwriting, digestion, respiration, memory, sleeping cycles and sexual potency, some of which appeared immediately after the accident while others could appear days, weeks or even months after the event.

The wars of the twentieth century, from the First World War to the events of the Gulf War, have in a way contributed to the development of research into trauma and its treatment. The consequences of the Vietnam War in particular provided a powerful impetus to the development of our present-day understanding of trauma. This process had an important political subtext: a group of Vietnam veterans, known as the Vietnam Veterans Against the War, launched a political campaign that lasted nearly ten years and which eventually resulted in the recognition of PTSD and its inclusion in the DSM-III, a classification system for psychiatric disorders. It was discovered that the symptoms of the new diagnosis were characteristic not only of Vietnam War syndrome, but could also be observed in women who had been raped, children who had been abused, and so on.

Today it is clear that a person does not have to go through a war, have an accident or be physically abused in order for their nervous system to function 'in survival and protection mode' – that is, an unbalancing of the sympathetic (excitatory) and parasympathetic (inhibitory) branches of the autonomic nervous system, and to produce bodily, psychological, intellectual and social symptoms of trauma. The above-mentioned events, however, do produce the strongest stress response and may radically change one's life. If something that directly threatens one's life and health happens, it is highly likely that the nervous system will go into survival and protection mode. States associated with a life-threatening experience are now called shock trauma. However, it is now clear that there are many more reasons why the nervous system can become unbalanced, including long-term adverse childhood experiences (known as 'developmental trauma'), such as bullying, interpersonal and social difficulties in the family, etc. Another reason can be the experience of a family before the birth of a child or cultural trauma, which can be passed on from generation to generation through the embodiment, attitudes and taboos of the people around them.

In 2016, a wave of #imnotafraid messages swept across social media in Russia, in which women – and some men – related stories of the sexual harassment and abuse they had experienced. As a result, many women sought help from me and my colleagues, saying that they felt as though this had happened to them, too, although it hadn't. As we searched for the reasons for such a physiological response and other symptoms (insomnia, anxiety, mood swings), what we uncovered were family narratives that were implicitly passed on from the older women in the family through their embodiment, reactions and words, which created such a response.

Unlike developmental trauma (the way the relationships and conditions of one's childhood affect one's adult life), which has been thoroughly studied, the study of cultural trauma and the transfer of trauma from generation to generation has only recently begun. In 2015, for instance, Rachel Yehuda[46] published her research on mass trauma survivors and their offspring. The latest results reveal that the descendants of people who survived the Holocaust have different stress hormone profiles than their peers, perhaps predisposing them to anxiety disorders. Resmaa Menakem's work on intergenerational racially linked trauma in the USA is also instructive.[47] In summary, for practitioners: it is important to be aware of the possibility of cultural, oppression-linked and intergenerational trauma, and be able to see it in a client's embodiment, and not just personal trauma.

Researchers use different models to express their ideas of what happens in the body when it is in survival and protection mode. For example, one of the pioneers and leading authorities on the subject of trauma, Peter Levine, writes that trauma is the result of an incomplete instinctive reaction of the body to a traumatic event – a flight, fight or freeze reaction. According to Levine, traumatic symptoms, such as helplessness, anxiety, depression, psychosomatic complications, etc., arise from the accumulation of residual energy that was mobilised in response to a traumatic event and found no release. Thus, the purpose of the trauma symptoms is to retain this residual traumatic energy. In order to escape this trauma, one must complete the traumatic reaction, release the remaining energy and restore the upset processes. Levine called his method 'somatic experiencing'.[48] Pat Ogden, Bessel van der Kolk, Francine Shapiro (EMDR) and others have also made a huge contribution to the understanding of traumatic processes and methods of healing.

The consensus among leading experts regarding trauma is that faced with a challenge or threat, the body mobilises its resources to protect and successfully resolve the situation. Such a reaction of the body, according to Hans Selye, is a stress response.[49] In the normal course of events, having coped with the task, the body returns to its normal functioning and restores balance to the sympathetic and parasympathetic nervous system. Yet in some situations, the stimulus can be so strong (shock injury) or so long-lasting (development trauma) that a strong stress response seems to become 'stuck' in the body: its proper functioning and balance are not restored. Physically, we will observe and feel a lasting stress response, the purpose of which is to protect the body from threat. This level of body functioning is known as 'survival mode'. It may not be in any way related to one's real current context: there may not be any real threat or danger, but the nervous system, our embodied patterns and other contributors to the stress response will continue to alert us to potential danger.

This response can manifest itself in many different forms, depending on the pattern that has established itself in our body. It can be a habitual 'freeze' response: a numbing or an urge to be 'invisible' (it's as though the person wants to hide – trauma therapists say they 'hide inside their bones'); hyper-arousal, a common form of the 'flight' or 'fight' response; or a 'lack of energy' (hypo-arousal), which is characteristic of the 'flop' response.

Today, Stephen Porges' polyvagal theory of trauma[50] serves as the foundation for understanding the physiological processes of trauma. His research has focused on how neural regulation of the physiological state influences behaviour and how these mechanisms are related to how we interact socially. The main idea is that three neural circuits form a phylogenetically ordered response hierarchy that regulates behavioural and physiological adaptation to safe, dangerous and life-threatening environments:

- **Parasympathetic** (most ancient): 'A primitive passive feeding and reproduction system creating a metabolic baseline of operation to manage oxygen and nourishment via the blood.'
- **Sympathetic** (newer): 'A more sophisticated set of responses enabling mobility for feeding, defence and reproduction via limbs & muscles.'
- **Social engagement** (most modern): 'A sophisticated set of responses supporting massive cortical development – enabling maternal bonding (extended protection of vulnerable immature cortex processors) and social cooperation (language and social structures) via facial functions.'

The autonomic nervous system (ANS) is commonly defined as the part of the nervous system that is involuntary and maintains essential functional balance. The ANS is usually divided into two complementary branches, sympathetic and parasympathetic. In the new triune theory, a third set of mainly involuntary survival functions is identified and described. This new theory recognises an additional nerve group because its actions are also involuntary and critical for survival. In addition to being a dual reciprocal action between sympathetic and parasympathetic, the ANS now becomes triune and sequential, with a regulatory hierarchy from new to old.

Being able to distinguish these reactions is important for several reasons. First, if we recognise these reactions, we can create and apply different types of restorative techniques (for example, that is how the practice of 'social centring' was invented).

Second, this allows us to use different methods more ethically and 'calibrate' their intensity. When the body is stuck in a stress response and the level of cortisol is high, we cannot learn (that is, no new neural connections are being made and therefore we cannot change our habitual pattern). Moreover, cortisol destroys existing synaptic connections. That is why it is important to regulate the intensity of the stimulus so that the client can cope with the resulting stress response.

Windows of tolerance

Third, one of the aims of an embodied facilitator is to give their client more range in choosing a course of action, which requires an understanding of the mechanisms of the trauma response. Dan Siegel introduced the term 'window of tolerance',[51] which is used to describe the zone of arousal in which a person is able to function most effectively. When people are within this zone, they are typically able to readily receive, process and integrate information and otherwise respond to the demands of everyday life without much difficulty. During times of extreme stress, people often experience periods of either hyper- or hypo-arousal. Hyper-arousal, otherwise known as the fight/flight response, is often characterised by hypervigilance, feelings of anxiety and/or panic, and racing thoughts. Hypo-arousal, or a freeze response, may cause feelings of emotional numbness, emptiness or paralysis.

The stress of a traumatic or otherwise negative event may have the effect of 'pushing' a person out of their window of tolerance. People who have experienced a traumatic event may respond to stressors, even minor ones, with extreme hyper- or hypo-arousal. As a result of their experiences, they may come to believe the world is unsafe and may operate with a window of tolerance that has become more narrow or inflexible. On the one hand, when a client tests a different kind of embodiment or practice, we may encounter a traumatic reaction, since this new embodiment does not correspond to their individual window of tolerance and is perceived as dangerous. On the other hand, allowing a client to practise in a safe environment and teaching them self-regulation skills for managing their stress response may expand their window of tolerance, allowing for more options in their choice of embodiment.

Another important thing to note is that trauma awareness allows you to create a more ethical and effective practice. In a sense, it is our attitude towards trauma (awareness, the creation of conditions under which the client develops their embodiment range) and marks the dividing line between ethical practice and the kind of practice that does not meet the ethical standards of our community. By the same token, it is of utmost importance to distinguish between real safety and the absence of a challenge. Without a challenge, there is no learning. It simply needs to be calibrated based on trauma awareness and our sensitivity to the client's feedback. A challenge that lies beyond the current boundaries of the client's window of tolerance is meaningless and ineffective.

Conclusion

Understanding people's implicit philosophy of the body, their cultural embodiment and their trauma history will hugely support your facilitation efforts. Mark will come back to these themes again in each chapter, to show you specifically and practically how they apply. For now I hope this introduction provides a solid base for the more technical applied chapters that follow.

Notes

1 Alexandra Vilvovskaya, aka 'Vilya', is Russia's leading embodiment teacher and founded The Embodied Facilitator Course Moscow as well as many other courses. She brought tango to Russia after the fall of the USSR and is an expert trauma therapist – Mark.
2 Interestingly, the idea that we either grow to, or return back to embodiment, corresponds with conservative and liberal ideas of human nature. Both have value in my opinion – Mark.
3 https://www.bodynamic.com
4 Andrea Olsen, *Bodystories: A Guide to Experiential Anatomy* (Lebanon, NH: University Press of New England, 2004). First published 1991.
5 Marina Abramović, by Laurie Anderson, *BOMB Magazine*, 1 July 2003, https://bombmagazine.org/articles/marina-abramović/
6 'Lie to Me', TV drama, Fox Network (2009–2011).
7 For example, Maurice Merleau-Ponty, *Stanford Encyclopedia of Philosophy*, 14 September 2016, https://plato.stanford.edu/entries/merleau-ponty/
8 Michel Foucault, *Discipline and Punish: The Birth of the Prison*, trans. A. Sheridan (New York: Vintage Books, 1977).
9 Pierre Bourdieu,
10 Francisco J. Varela, Evan Thompson and Eleanor Rosch, *The Embodied Mind: Cognitive Science and Human Experience* (Cambridge, MA: MIT Press, 1993).
11 Thomas J. Csordas, *Body / Meaning / Healing* (New York: Palgrave Macmillan, 2002).
12 'Tantra' here is not the same as neo-tantric sexual practices but refers to a set of transformative technologies such as breathwork, mantra and visualisation that were added to mindfulness in the Middle Ages. See scholar-practitioner Christopher D. Wallis for more on this – his book *Tantra Illuminated* (Petaluma, CA: Mattamayūra Press, 2012) is a modern classic.

13 Note the naming and classification of 'body therapy', movement therapy', 'dance therapy', etc. are complex, regionally variable (the USA and the UK, for example) and controversial!
14 See, for example, Rudolf Laban, *The Mastery of Movement*, revised by Lisa Ullmann, 4th edition (Binsted: Dance Books, 2011).
15 Mark Walsh, *Embodiment: Moving Beyond Mindfulness* (Unicorn Slayer Press, 2019).
16 Daniel Goleman, *Emotional Intelligence* (New York: Bantam Books, 1995).
17 Note the irony of using the pursuit of objectivity to prove a concept defined by subjectivity!
18 Amy J.C. Cuddy, https://www.ted.com/talks/amy_cuddy_your_body_language_may_shape_who_you_are/transcript?language=en
19 George Lakoff and Mark Johnson, *Philosophy in the Flesh* (New York: Basic Books, 1999).
20 Iris K. Schneider et al., One way and the other: The bidirectional relationship between ambivalence and body movement, *Psychological Science*, 24 (3): 319–25 (2013), https://journals.sagepub.com/doi/abs/10.1177/0956797612457393
21 Lynden K. Miles, Louise K. Nind and C. Neil Macrae, Moving through time, *Psychological Science*, 21 (2): 222–23 (2010), https://journals.sagepub.com/doi/abs/10.1177/0956797609359333
22 Thalma Lobel, *Sensation: The New Science of Physical Intelligence* (New York: Simon & Schuster, 2014). A fascinating side-note here is that for people working in robotics and AI this is very much a practical issue as early models that were used for this work failed miserably because they did not take the body into account!
23 Anthony Chemero, *Radical Embodied Cognitive Science* (Cambridge, MA: MIT Press, 2009), and the work of (2009), Lisa Feldman Barrett.
24 Julian Kiverstein and Mark Miller, The embodied brain: Towards a radical embodied cognitive neuroscience, *Frontiers in Human Neuroscience*, 9: 237 (2015), https://www.frontiersin.org/articles/10.3389/fnhum.2015.00237/full
25 Mark Johnson, Embodied understanding, *Frontiers in Psychology*, 6: 875 (2015), https://www.frontiersin.org/articles/10.3389/fpsyg.2015.00875/full
26 Lisa Feldman Barrett, *How Emotions Are Made: The Secret Life of the Brain* (New York: Houghton Mifflin Harcourt, 2017).
27 Ibid.
28 Madhav Goyal et al., Meditation programs for psychological stress and well-being: A systematic review and meta-analysis, *JAMA Internal Medicine*, 174 (3): 357–68 (2014), https://jamanetwork.com/journals/jamainternalmedicine/fullarticle/1809754
29 Peter Sedlmeier, The psychological effects of meditation: A meta-analysis, *Psychological Bulletin*, 138 (6): 1139–71 (2012), https://psycnet.apa.org/doiLanding?doi=10.1037%2Fa0028168
30 Kieran C.R. Fox et al., Is meditation associated with altered brain structure? A systematic review and meta-analysis of morphometric neuroimaging in meditation practitioners, *Neuroscience and Biobehavioral Reviews*, 43: 48–73 (2014), https://www.sciencedirect.com/science/article/abs/pii/S0149763414000724?via%3Dihub
31 Amy J.C. Cuddy, https://www.ted.com/talks/amy_cuddy_your_body_language_may_shape_who_you_are/transcript?language=en
32 Joseph P. Simmons and Uri Simonsohn, Power posing: P-curving the evidence, *Psychological Science*, 28 (5): 687–93 (2017), https://journals.sagepub.com/doi/10.1177/0956797616658563
33 Benita Jackson et al., Does that pose become you? Testing the effect of body postures on self-concept, *Comprehensive Results in Social Psychology*, 2 (1): 81–105 (2017), https://www.tandfonline.com/doi/abs/10.1080/23743603.2017.1341178

34 Erike Peper et al., How posture affects memory recall and mood, *Biofeedback*, 45 (2): 36–41 (2017), https://www.aapb-biofeedback.com/doi/10.5298/1081-5937-45.2.01
35 Agnieszka Golec de Zavala et al., Yoga poses increase subjective energy and state self-esteem in comparison to 'power poses', *Frontiers in Psychology*, 8: 752 (2017), https://www.frontiersin.org/articles/10.3389/fpsyg.2017.00752/full
36 Erik Peper et al., Do better in math: How your body posture may change stereotype threat response, *NeuroRegulation*, 5 (2): 67–74 (2018), https://www.neuroregulation.org/article/view/18396
37 This is very common in some 'alternative' communities which *only* acknowledge the problems with science (and update Facebook about it on their iPhones).
38 This is the 'contexts' model again from Chapter 1.
39 An average year may have 30 people from 15+ countries for example, with maybe 20 kinds of embodied expertise present from aikido to zumba!
40 Basically we annoy everyone, and force them to grow – Mark.
41 Actually, we have found the whole culture conversation sometimes hard to have with American students who may well have a hyper individualistic cultural frame (the USA is ranked #2 globally for this after Israel), a 'melting pot' ethos and see any generalisations as evil prejudice! Germans, too, especially Berliners, can be especially cautious around stereotypes, which is perhaps not surprising! Generally though, Europeans 'get' culture more, perhaps due to the proximity of other countries, as do most Asians and South Americans we have worked with.
42 But of course we have not had the opportunity to study the peculiarities of gendered embodiment in every country around the world, so the examples provided are limited to our personal observations.
43 Shelley E. Taylor et al., Biobehavioral responses to stress in females: Tend-and-befriend, not fight-or-flight, *Psychological Review*, 107 (3): 411–29 (2000), https://content.apa.org/record/2000-08671-001; Shelley E. Taylor, *The Tending Instinct: Women, Men, and the Biology of Relationships* (New York: Henry Holt, 2002).
44 Onno van der Hart and Paul Brown, Concept of psychological trauma, *American Journal of Psychiatry*, 147 (12): 1691 (1990), https://psycnet.apa.org/record/1991-12791-001
45 J.E. Erichsen, *Railway Injuries of the Nervous System* (London: Walton & Moberly, 1866).
46 Rachel Yahuda, https://www.nicabm.com/trauma-the-impact-of-trauma-on-future-generations/
47 Resmaa Menakem, https://www.resmaa.com
48 See, for example, https://www.seauk.org.uk and https://traumahealing.org
49 Hans Selye, *The Stress of Life* (New York: McGraw-Hill, 1956).
50 Stephen Porges, https://www.stephenporges.com
51 Dan Siegel, *The Developing Mind: How Relationships and the Brain Interact to Shape Who We Are* (New York: Guilford Press, 2012).

3 Embodied self-awareness: waking up to yourself

Know thyself.

– Inscription on the Temple of Delphi[1]

PART 1: SELF-AWARENESS – STATE

> **Opening exercise: How are you (really)?**
> How are you? No, really. Don't just say 'fine' or give a one-word label, really take time to feel deeply – how are your energy levels, emotions, overall sense of yourself? How do you know how you are? Get granular and specific. What's it actually like to be you right now? Get more global. How 'close' can you get to the experience? Take a good minute to feel and inhabit. Then answer honestly.

Promise

If you spend a few weeks working with the techniques in this chapter you will dramatically enhance both your state awareness, and awareness of your personality patterns. This will give you a huge boost as a facilitator.

> **Opening reflection questions**
> - Are you body aware now?
> - How deeply?
> - How finely?
> - Do you know how deeply and finely is possible?
> - For what percentage of the day would you say you're 'in touch' with your body?
> - Are you generally aware of your emotional state before others are?
> - When are you most and least body aware in your week? What supports this and what doesn't?

What is the skill-set and how does it help facilitation?

It all starts here. By definition, embodiment is about awareness. Self-awareness is also the basis of good facilitation, so if you only read one of the skills chapters make it this one. All other skill-sets are based on this one – if you're not self-aware, you won't know when to self-regulate, for example. Moshe Feldenkrais said, 'You can't do what you want until you know what you're doing.'[2]

An embodied facilitator needs to develop self-awareness over two time-frames – the first refers to what could be called mindfulness skills. This skill-set involves tuning into sensations and developing the various aspects of embodied mindfulness:

- The quantity of awareness itself – being aware of more
- Sustainability of body awareness – how often are you only 'in your head' vs. connected to yourself more fully?
- Sensory clarity – the level of detail of that awareness
- Concentration – the ability to direct and sustain awareness on one thing
- Depth of body awareness – as body awareness grows, new possibilities open up, including deep body systems and unearthed aspects of emotions and intuition
- Equanimity – being able to just 'be with' the body – though this crosses over with our second embodied intelligence skill-set (Chapter 4). Some would go so far as to say body awareness also contains not just the quality of acceptance but also kindness, or even love, inherently.

My own experience is that the level of body awareness that is possible just keeps deepening. After 25 years of practice I am amazed by just how little I was feeling previously, as each new stage of possibility opens up. Sometimes I remember simple specifics like not being able to feel each toe individually (for most people who wear shoes, the foot starts to map as a kind of 'clump'), not being able to feel my pulse in any part of my body by placing my attention there (I only realised this was strange when at a doctor's appointment I told her my pulse rate without having to use the usual finger on wrist method and she acted surprised), or how ragged my overall attention was on my first meditation retreat. Sitting with complete beginners now, whose distraction I can feel viscerally (imagine being in a small room with a toddler who's eaten too much sugar, it's like that), reminds me that despite my limited skill after much effort to overcome my ADHD, I've at least made some progress! In addition, I get greater and great pleasure from tuning into the body with each passing year, a product of greater clarity and less reactivity. The journey as an embodied facilitator, then, is becoming aware of more, more subtly, and being able to sustain that in a pleasant way.

I should also add that we're all human and you never 'arrive', as in, 'now I am embodied'. I still get embarrassed that as an embodiment teacher I have so many moments when I'm clearly not body aware and this has consequences. Sometimes I see my 'nerd-neck' while sitting at the computer or realise I am in dire need of a toilet break all of a sudden when deep in work! You'll see a gradual trend in body awareness with long-term practice but this is not a cure-all, and there is no perfection.

Relationship to other skill-sets

Self-awareness is the most important skill-set because it is the necessary foundation of all the others – for example, you need to know you're stressed before you can centre and reduce that stress (self-leadership).

How to develop your embodied state awareness – overview

With just a little practise, people can relatively quickly dramatically enhance their ability to tune into their bodies. The bad news is that in a disembodied and disembodying world, it requires ongoing effort to maintain and enhance 'gains'. High levels of skill of course, also require work.

How to develop your embodied state awareness – practices

I highly recommend that if you're serious about benefiting from what's on offer in this book that you start some of these regular practices to build body awareness. If you choose to develop just one skill-set, make it this one, as the others will at least to some degree follow as a result.

If possible, developing this skill with others is even more helpful. The importance of social support applies to all skill-sets generally.

Daily check-ins

Set an alarm to go off five times a day (easy on modern phones) and check-in with your emotions and energy level each time. Stop and feel for a full minute and then label your embodied state as accurately as possible (building your embodied vocabulary is a useful secondary skill). Instead of being initiated by a phone alarm these sensory check-ins can also be linked to things you do regularly, like when you go through a door, go to the bathroom, wash your hands, make coffee, and so on. Most of us are just moving too fast, and are too distracted to feel, and while with practise you can tune in 'on the run', stopping for a moment really helps!

Journaling

Take five minutes at the end of your day to review your embodied states throughout the day. Think back and feel the resonance of each one.

Journaling is a remarkably effective self-awareness practice with a strong evidence base. Given the speed of modern life, perhaps the efficacy of spending even a little time reflecting is not surprising.

Meditation

There's a reason why every senior embodiment teacher that I've met meditates daily – it's the premier awareness-raising and concentration-enhancing practice. I often think of it as the 'base' of embodiment. Mindfulness and meditation instruction is now readily available, so rather than spend much time on it I'll simply recommend some types:

1 *Mindfulness of breathing* – although a classic concentration meditation, be careful not to exclude the rest of the body when doing it, which would actually be dissociative! I recommend making the belly the main focus and the impact of the breath on the whole body
2 *Body scanning* – again, a classic, for concentration, feeling numb areas, and for overall body awareness
3 *Embodied 'heart' meditations* – classic Buddhist meditations like *'metta bhavana'* (aka 'loving kindness' / 'universal friendliness' meditation) to develop states of friendliness, compassion, etc. can be done in a fully embodied way

Note that most meditation schools teach people to meditate *on* the body, but truly embodied meditation is *with* or *through* the body, *inhabiting* it if you will. This may sound like a subtle distinction and is indeed hard to explain without the experience – people often just 'drop in' after some years of meditating on the body. The feeling is of getting closer to the body rather than of separating from it.

Whatever technique you choose, pay careful attention to posture, as this makes any technique more body-based, together with the attitude of *how* you meditate, as this will be the embodiment you are actually practising. Meditating while lying down, sitting, standing, walking and eventually while doing simple chores is a nice 'practise gradient', and each of these fundamental positions of life should be practised to some extent to ensure best transfer to daily life.

If your aim is to build body awareness, abstract visualisation meditations and chants are generally to be avoided, although any kind of meditation can be made more embodied. If you have so much trauma that meditating on the body is especially uncomfortable or anxiety-provoking, then sound meditation is useful (e.g. with a bell), though this is a warning sign that embodied facilitation is not for you yet, and trauma healing should come first.

Feel your feet

How are your feet? Be curious about how your feet feel (more accurately, how you feel in your feet). How do they really feel right now? – not how they should feel. And avoid just making a mental image of your feet – instead, notice how they really are right now.

Try moving your attention from one foot to the other – notice what that's like. What parts are contacting the ground? If you were standing in sand, what shapes would you leave?

Now try other parts of your body. Move your attention around like a spreading ivy or glow – staying present and curious. Can you direct your attention or is it more often 'grabbed'? Who is in charge of the attention? What is the quality of it? What happen to parts of the body when you apply attention? Be like an alien explorer in what is familiar and make it extraordinary again – simply by paying attention.

Hello, yes and welcome

When meditating with the body, I recommend trying these three frames – you can say them out loud or internally, but what is important is to approach yourself with their attitude: hello, yes and welcome.

Numbing less

As well as developing practices to increase body awareness, a complementary approach is to reduce numbing. The following are reliable practices:

1. Sit less and move more in daily life
2. Heal your trauma
3. Give up addictions, and minimise mental 'mega-stimuli' such as social media and porn
4. Spend more time in nature
5. Slow down
6. Quieten down (speak less, and be around less speech)
7. Be around more beauty, and allow yourself to experience pleasure more deeply
8. Spend more time with body-aware people (including children), cultures and animals
9. Reduce your screen-time
10. Reduce your consumption of advertising

Some of these are life paths, so this is not a shallow list. And I also fully appreciate that there may be practical barriers to many of these, and you may have to prioritise and 'pick your battles'. It's worth noting that embodied training generally may inspire you to go 'against the stream', to use a Buddhist phrase, of how society operates and this is a kind of loss as well as a joy. I have seen many colleagues over the years give up drugs, change their clothes and footwear (I still find it hilarious to see a coach attending an Embodied Facilitator Course (EFC) in high heels; I joke that the staff team should be sponsored by Vivobarefoot shoes as so many of us wear flat shoes, in contrast), move to the countryside, change their primary relationship or alter dating habits, radically alter their diet, change how they parent, and generally shift lifestyles as what was once normal becomes intolerable. They often don't need 'discipline' to make changes, they just become natural and obvious with a deepening relationship to the body. Embodiment leads to real and far-ranging changes that's for sure – but be warned, don't practise what is in this book if you want your life to stay the same!

> **Exercise: Drinking water**
> Drink some water or other fluid and notice how far into your body you can follow the sensation. Working with sensations that gradually diminish like this is a great way to improve sensitivity of body listening. Doing this with cold fluid when you are hot is especially easy, and it can also be done when swallowing food.

Eating and sex

Mindful embodied eating generally is a fascinating and deep enquiry for those interested in embodiment, as food is so core to our being and survival – for example, to be and to eat are the same word in Russian! Noticing not just when you eat as an awareness exercise, but how you pick foods, how you enjoy them, how hungry you are before eating them, if emotional needs are mixed in (they usually are) and how satisfied you are after eating, all are examples of embodied food enquiries. As much nutrition and dieting advice is very disembodied and top-down to the point of being body-denying, 'tuning in' / 'no diet' approaches to eating such as those of Charles Eisenstein and Beyond Chocolate (a UK group) are enriching.[3] This was a blind spot for me for years![4]

Everything I've just said about food also applies to our other 'lower chakra' needs of sex and physical intimacy. Although beyond the scope of this book, for serious embodiment practitioners, this is an area worth exploring, but be careful of charlatans and abusers in this field in particular, as well as any trauma you may have in this area. All I'll say for now is that although to recognise that the body is about much more than sex is often vital to losing this reductionist association and making the work more accessible in more conservative contexts, the truth is that embodied work requires that you be in contact with your own sexuality, in whatever form that may be. To deny sexuality is to deny the body. Also, that embodied facilitation of all kinds does access sexuality – usually in a way that enlivens and enhances people's sex lives. Very often in fact students mention positive benefits in this domain even though I only teach them embodied coaching skills and only mention sex in passing. Opening up the body does open up sexuality, and this means that those working in this area need to be well boundaried and encourage this in coachees – students can get very flirty with each other after a few days of embodied work as their body is enlivened I've noticed! – and also be aware of the potential for triggering sexual trauma issues.

68 The Body in Coaching and Training

Talking to yourself – body listening

As well as simply tuning into and being with sensations of the body, with some methods you actively dialogue with the body as a source of wisdom. While beyond the scope of this book as these methods are somewhat 'advanced', I do use them in coaching and they are worth exploring. Eugene Gendlin's Focusing[5] is the most famous example, but there are a number of systems. I give a light example of this type of work later in the book and here is one below.

> **Exercise: Self – coaching with simple body listening**
> Spend ten minutes or more meditating with the body. Now ask your body a question relating to a challenge you have. It could be very simple or a deep enquiry like, 'What's my life purpose?' Approach your body gently like a shy animal that you wish to befriend. Do not demand. Be patient. You may feel, hear, intuit or see a response.

Conscious movement methods

I recommend that in addition to still or very simple movement awareness training (meditation) that all embodied facilitators take up a more complex form of mindful movement. This might take the form of:

- Awareness walking (informally in nature)
- Hatha (slow and gentle) yoga[6]
- Feldenkrais
- Tai chi / chi kung
- Alexander Technique[7]
- Conscious dance (e.g. 5Rhythms or Movement Medicine)
- Conscious bathing / showering / receiving massage (*note*: pleasure is the friend of body awareness as it calls us back home!)
- Mindful chores / gardening

It's possible to make anything an embodied movement practice really, though some activities like yoga have features or a support culture that make them ideal. This list, by the way, is far from exhaustive.

Picking practices

All practices have different pros and cons: Feldenkrais, for example, tends to have quite mentally demanding sessions (called ATMs) which are nearly an hour long and difficult if you don't like doing things slowly and without effort, but can be learnt virtually easily as all the instructions are verbal and it doesn't require athleticism. Many sessions are also free online and can be done at home. A conscious dance class, on the other hand, can only be done at specific times and places (until you get the idea of dancing on your own), costs money (but not as much as one-to-one bodywork), and could be an introvert's hell – but maybe more fun if you love music, moving faster and you're a social type.

Picking a practice is a very individual thing and I'll return to how to pick them later, but it should meet the following criteria:

- It should be able to build the skill you'd like to build. This is the starting place
- You should feel drawn to it and it be attractive to you (so doing it will not be a chore)[8]
- It should be challenging to some degree so that you're growing
- It should be readily accessible (time, cost, geography, etc.)
- It should have a high-quality non-abusive teacher you 'click' with, and a supportive community to learn alongside

Often it's better to have the 'wrong' practice that you can actually get to, and that has a good teacher and crowd, than one you can't make it to where the teacher is unethical and the other students unpleasant. Try things out and find what works for you, then *commit* and stick with it. Find a way to love it above all, but don't rely upon initial enthusiasm. Coaching students on this is a big part of EFC so there's lots I could say, but ultimately it comes down to these simple factors.

Aware of what?

People talk about body awareness as if it were just one thing – but what are you becoming aware of in the body? Where in the body is your focus? Now for beginners *any* kind of sensate tuning in is fantastic, and for most of my business coaching clients just realising they are, say, exhausted, stressed or angry is a good step, especially when these things are really very obviously emanating from the outside! As we go further into this work, however, it's worth having finer distinctions.

Bonnie Bainbridge Cohen, who is frankly a legend and one of the top embodiment teachers, uses an approach that explores different body systems, such as muscles, skin, connective tissue, bones, and so on, as do others. I have noted that I feel totally different after the yoga classes of four local teachers who teach relatively similar poses, but have students focus on different systems. While hard to put into words, I often feel stronger and more active after the 'muscular' class (note again the embodied English), more solid after osteopath yoga teacher Pete Blackaby's bone-centric class, more sensual after John Stirk's skin-oriented class (rare in yoga), and more unified and 'sticky' after Gary Carter's fascial yoga class (fascia binds everything together in the body). I have noticed this also doing different types of body work (again, some are more about different systems), and even during dissections depending upon which layer we were cutting through, so the effect happens with other bodies as well as our own. What we pay attention to matters!

Other embodiment teachers work less with systems and more with levels of the body, e.g. the top third, middle portion or lower portion, which have different qualities. Still others use 'centres', which sometimes simply means places to orientate and lead from (e.g. Judith Blackstone) and at other times is used more esoterically like the famous chakra system (of which there are many somewhat contradictory ones). Wendy Palmer[9] uses a very practical 'head, heart, hara (belly)' model, and I've found that meditating on, or moving from different chakras, does have an impact, even if I'm sceptical of some of the more esoteric explanations as to why.[10]

In coaching, working with different systems and centres has four main applications:

- To become aware of habitual embodied use
- To develop more range and therefore freedom and effectiveness (you'll find this 'awareness and choice' principle again and again in this book, it's really all I teach)
- As an insight and problem-solving tool – 'what does the heart say about this compared to the head?', for example
- To get systems or centres 'talking', and become more integrated

> **Experiments: Systems and centres**
>
> Go for a walk or do a simple embodied practice that you already know well – e.g. a familiar yoga sequence – focusing for half the time on one body system and half on another. Visualise it until you can feel it if that's hard. Note how you feel different for each and if thinking, perceptions, emotions, etc. change. Which is most familiar / habitual? How does this impact your daily life?
>
> For the next exercise (and I wouldn't do these two back-to-back), think of a challenge in life that you'd like some insight into. Become aware of first the head (easy for most), then the heart area, then the lower belly. For each centre take some breaths (or for the head, imagining doing so), and walk for a few minutes from this area letting it subtly lead, just a few millimetres ahead of the other two (Monty Python impersonations are not necessary). Lastly for each centre, tune into it as best you can – feeling and visualising, and ask for insight around the issue. If you can make a decision integrating their input, that would be ideal, but it is not required.

Form, freedom and yoga addiction

A useful distinction in embodied work is top down vs. bottom up, or 'form' and 'freedom' practices as we like to say at EFC. Form practices involve imposing an order, discipline or structure such as practising a set type of meditation for ten minutes or a yoga pose; freedom practices, in contrast, involve listening to the body and going with the unfolding process. Both have advantages and disadvantages and different uses. Free process-oriented practices like most conscious dance are also a great way to grow body awareness, but excessively strict form practices will actually reduce it, as will excessively intense ones such as a lot of modern urban yoga. Such practices force feeling through intensity so have addictive and actually numbing properties, as the more subtler sensations of the body are drowned out. Excessive freedom practices, on the other hand, can lead to a chaotic ill-disciplined boundless quality popular amongst new agers, certain cultures and people of my personality type!

The 4-elements model

The 4-elements model, which will be introduced later in the chapter, can be used as an emotional map and as a way of paying attention. Mostly, however, I use it for long-term pattern recognition.

> **Facilitator case study: My story**
>
> So if there's hope for me, there's hope for anyone. Growing up as a British man in a working-class farming community, my emotional vocabulary was limited to 'fine, angry, hungry and horny' – and the last two aren't really emotions. I was therefore fairly shocked when I started hanging out with urbane therapists and eventually emotional-hyper-literate West-Coast American embodiment teachers, and realised that there were more emotions! Now, years later, I surprise myself with the specificity of embodied states I can describe, though I try and sound normal when around my old friends, and will still likely swear between the nuisance poetry of subtle sensation. I am also somewhat sad when I see the limited ability of people I grew up with and help them out as best I can. There's a very definite and learnable skill-set in both feeling and naming emotions (and these two both support each other).

Relationship to other skill-sets

Different things work with different clients and one size does not fit all. With that in mind, sections like the following are just guidance for you to be creative with.

How to develop embodied state awareness with clients – overview

As with so many aspects of embodied facilitation, your own state and trait are the foundation – because resonance and modelling are more important than technique (see Chapter 8 on excellence). How *you are* impacts others most. Presence calls for presence – being aware of yourself subtly encourages others to do the same. Simply asking with genuine curiosity and kindness from this 'base' directs people back to their experience. A key 'how' here is to gently point people to their experience, not to force it in their faces. Slowing down and starting from a relaxed, trusting, learning environment help a lot. People need to feel safe because if their threat-detection network is engaged, interoception is near impossible.[11]

Another good rule is specificity, where you help people 'divide and conquer' their experience. Clients will be able to feel more if you make things more specific for them, as with some of the techniques below, for example, and paradoxically by limiting responses. Instead of just asking 'how are you?', ask 'is your mood more up or down?', for example, when someone tells you they are stressed, and ask 'where?' or 'how are you doing that?' to help them be more precise. It's important to delve beneath gestalt evaluative language like 'I feel stressed' to get to the specifics. Embodiment is all about '*how* we are', and asking clients 'how are you doing that' is often a good move. This also reframes body action as being done by the client not to the client, and so is empowering and more accurate than conventional language. You don't really *get* angry, for example, more accurately you *do* anger; and moving this action from the unconscious to the conscious is what this work is all about.

How to develop embodied state awareness with clients – practices

One-to-one techniques

- **Your own state** and longer-term embodied presence[12]
- All those things listed in your own practice: daily check-ins, meditation (though this is best taught by a qualified teacher), journaling, etc.
- **Asking clients to say 'I'** instead of 'you'. Using the first person is surprisingly helpful in getting them back in touch with themselves but is a challenge at first for many!
- **Touch** also calls forth awareness in people (but see the recommendations on this). Asking people to **self-touch** (i.e. 'put a hand on your chest or belly') is better than asking to touch them, and online is necessary of course
- All of the recommendations from Chapter 4 because when people have calmed down and regulated their state, they can feel more

> **One-to-one client case study – Anekke**
>
> *Anekke was an up-and-coming 'hot-shot' executive on a management fast-track course in The Netherlands that I worked with for several years. Despite a high IQ, technical expertise beyond her 28 years and proficiency in several languages, frankly she was irritating people left, right and centre, and I was asked to work with her one-to-one. Because she didn't know how she was most of the*

Embodied self-awareness **73**

> time, she both did not look after herself and was fast approaching an early burnout, and also didn't realise the mood she was bringing to meetings, or the tone in which she spoke to colleagues, which was often abrasive and not helpful. While she was sceptical of 'that soft skills stuff', she acknowledged she had an issue that was holding her back, and so was willing to give it a try. I would ask her how she was and she was playfully 'banned' from saying 'fine'. It would frustrate her that she didn't know what to say at first but this actually motivated her, as she didn't like not being good at things. I set her the daily check-in task and she decided herself to take this to her tennis club where she would check how she was after each game in a match. After a few months doing this, something in her started to shift and she answered group check-ins proudly. In one break she confided in me, 'my boyfriend likes your course' and smiled, which I guess meant the emotional availability was also showing up relationally too. She still keeps in touch years later and describes this simple intervention as 'life-changing'.

Group techniques

- **The Pause:** even a very short pause – perhaps three seconds, while asking people how they're doing can be very helpful in garnering awareness. It interrupts the busyness. For more open groups, a 1–5-minute simple 'landing' can be used. My own company's staff meetings nearly always start this way
- **The three-word check-in:** I regularly ask groups several times a day how they are and ban 'fine', 'good' and 'OK'. This can be established in business meetings as normal procedure and becomes no big deal soon enough
- Asking for **thumbs up**, down or middling is helpful for getting a quick group mood check
- **Arm-raising:** having groups show their energy levels by holding their hands high or low is helpful.[13] You can also get people to hold up fingers for how they gauge their energy level (or anything else) out of ten. These physical gestures mean most people take part rather than just the most extroverted, and you can use this technique with large numbers of people at once
- **Walking in the room:** one of my favourite simple practices to get people feeling is to get them moving – the two go together. Walking is a good place to start as it's not too weird[14] This procedure is seen by many prominent embodiment teachers as a general 'go to' that can be used for different purposes – for integration, to mix groups up, to change the mood, for creativity, done fast to simulate busyness, etc.
- **Group massage:** this is for the most open-minded groups (it wouldn't have been OK with most corporate groups I have worked with until *well* into a training, if ever). Asking them to do simple body work with each other can be a great way of helping them feel – for example, classic shoulder-rubbing massage circles

- **Make a noise:** often when working online with more open groups I will have them make a noise about how they feel. This can be quite fun. Interestingly people can often verbalise how they feel before they have a word for it, so it helps brings things to awareness.

> **Group client case study: Group work – the librarians**
>
> One of my first ever organisational clients was a group of librarians at a major British university. I remember thinking the job might be difficult as they were all highly cognitive academics. The manager reported to me that meetings were unproductive and that people often argued, 'from the head', denying obvious emotional entanglements with the subjects at hand. I instilled in them the practice of a pause and three-word check-in before meetings started and they all found this helpful for getting a better sense of each other and what mood each of them was in, which might impact the meetings. As well as making things more productive, they also reported that the organisation had become more 'human', and warmer bonds between colleagues had formed. They were still using this technique together with centring the last time I saw the manager, ten years after I first worked with them. She had forgotten my name and every other thing about the one-day training we did but I didn't mind – core useful practices are what I try and leave behind, and often only the simple ones stick from short trainings.

Virtual considerations

When people are sitting down staring at a screen, they tend not to feel, so getting them moving is useful! As is breaking the glazed-over, 'being entertained' attitude that is not conducive to embodiment with interaction. I rarely ask people to sit without moving for more than 20 minutes in fact. Most of the awareness-building activities here are fine for online though, with touch and massage obvious exceptions.

Trauma considerations

Trauma will be addressed further later but for now I'll just state:

- Trauma can lead to chronic tension and dissociation, both barriers to feeling
- Traumatised individuals may find feeling the body unpleasant or overwhelming, so teach self-regulation with body awareness (see Chapter 4)

Having ways to bring people into the present moment by instilling awareness of sight and sound as an alternative to the body can be helpful, until better self-regulation is achieved. For example, the classic, 'name three things you can see that are green, and four sounds that you can hear now'.

Cultural considerations

Cultures differ widely in how much people are willing to reveal themselves and this needs to be taken into account. Confessional USA vs. most Asian countries, for example, where 'face' is a big deal. Northern / Eastern vs. Southern Europe too. There is some truth behind the clichés of expressiveness, but, as ever, watch out for sub-cultures (e.g. regions or ethnic groups) and crass generalisations. Note that people from less expressive cultures may have intimate self-awareness, it's they just might not want to talk about it!

Interestingly, too, areas of the body may have quite different meanings in different cultures – the feet or the top of the head, for example, may be sacred or profane. Similarly with different 'centres', while some similarities exist, the heart or gut, for example, may have different associations.

PART 2: SELF-AWARENESS – TRAIT

Reflection questions
- What three words do you think best summarise your habitual way of being? What three words summarise your public reputation? How would a friend describe you in three words? How would an enemy?
- What are your top three strengths? Can you flip these to related weaknesses? – or work the other way around if self-critical!
- What is the unhelpful thing you keep doing? What are you bored of in yourself? How might these be embodied?
- What way of being do you really have to focus on to shift into or out of?
- How regularly do you get feedback from others as to your patterns? How do you know that your self-perception is accurate or not? How can you test your opinions about yourself?

How to develop your own embodied pattern awareness – overview

As a facilitator, it's hugely important to know your default mode – our own historical unconscious 'operating system' to use a computer analogy, or the canvas we are painting all our work and life upon, to use an artistic one. We all have a way of being that formed in our early childhood – and that we took on from our culture – that was a kind of solution to the problems we were facing at the time, but now stays with us, maybe even *defines* and limits us. Our systems are 'conservative', 'sticky' or 'lazy', in that they preserve what worked *well enough* in the past.

Critically our patterns are usually invisible like the smells of our own house, or the taste of your own mouth. We all just feel . . . normal. Mindfulness does not reveal patterns as we habituate to them.

The space between this 'conditioned tendency'[15] and what actual non-historical reality calls for, dramatically limits our effectiveness. When we act from the past, the present isn't impressed nine times out of ten, but what we don't know can really hurt us when it's running the show! We may get away with it at times, but we are not in complete charge, and are caged in our own conditioning.

The good news is that there are four reliable ways to expose embodied habits:

1. Careful mindful observation (though because we have habituated to our patterns and they work over a long time-frame, just feeling isn't enough)
2. 'Trying on' various options and noting which ones don't feel strange. This might be experiencing four archetypes, five rhythms, several MBTI types (or other personality test types like DISC) or whatever; and seeing what 'fits' and is comfortable and 'at home' vs. what is unfamiliar[16]
3. The third method is feedback, which can be more or less direct. Because we can't sense our own habits directly, sometimes it helps to be shown/told them!
4. The last is deviation. When we try and copy a form such as a yoga pose, the 'mistakes' we make are insightful, as they are not really mistakes at all but habitual patterns asserting themselves[17]

> **Exercises: Arm crossing**
>
> Cross your arms. Did you *choose* to place the one on top? Likely not. Now cross them the other way. It feels weird right? I have asked thousands of people to do this around the world and for 99% of people it will feel deeply strange having the other arm from usual on top, even though (handedness aside) these two positions are functionally identical. The same experiment can be done with crossing legs and intertwining fingers. This shows how even emotionally neutral bodily patterns are deeply ingrained, unconscious and revealed by what feels strange and what we feel at home with but weren't aware that we were doing.[18]

This idea will be extended to far more significant patterns (e.g. being open or closed, more 'yes' or more 'no' – even our whole personality) in this chapter. Just as crossing your arms one way is habitual and therefore feels 'right', so too do far deeper behavioural and emotional habits. We could even say that this is our character and many identify strongly with their adaptations. This has been termed the 'bureaucracy of habit' by master embodiment teacher Stuart Heller,[19] and I find it humbling if a little disturbing that personalities are essentially habits no different from accents, or the way new contact-lens wearers keep adjusting their non-existent glasses!

Promise

By the end of this section you will have all the tools you need to accurately identify your own long-term embodiment (traits).

What is the skill-set and how does it help facilitation?

This skill-set is knowing your default operating mode that is consistent across contexts, or to put in another way – to be aware of your embodied character.

For facilitators it is utterly necessary for us to be aware of our own strengths, weaknesses, biases and perspective, before we can work safely, let alone effectively with others.

Relationship to other skill-sets

Self-awareness is the basis of self-leadership, and this underpins our social awareness and leadership. Before we can develop ourselves we must know ourselves, and we always see and lead others 'through' this.

How to develop your own embodied pattern awareness – techniques

Being copied

This is one of the most straightforward and effective ways I know to build awareness of a person's habitual embodiment. With its origins in theatre training I believe, it is now widely used by different embodiment schools.[20] Although there are various ways to do it either standing or sitting that I use online, I prefer a walking version where possible.

Have someone observe then copy your walk. Make sure they understand the reason for doing so and are not mocking you, as they are likely to exaggerate a little. A skilled body observer would be best but even a child can help with this, as we're all natural mimics. Observe them 'do' you, and ask: 'who is this person?' You could reflect on what 'they' are good at, how they find love and safety, or what it would be like to be married to / in business partnership with them. You can also ask your mimic how it felt to be 'you', how their perception and thinking changed. Interestingly, they will often feel an increase in empathy for you and can use your modelling to build their own range: 'Steal from your partner! We're all good at something as we've practised it!' I often say. But that's for a later chapter!

As when we hear our own voice on a recording, many people experience a 'cringe factor' as the gap between reality and fantasy is closed. Please do be kind to yourself doing this exercise, as like all self-awareness building it takes courage to move from comforting fantasies to seeing reality.

The 4-elements preference model

There are many systems of working with different types of embodiment, and attempting each possibility in any of them and noticing what is familiar present a great way to reveal your patterns. I have used many on my courses over the years, sometimes offering embodied versions of established models that clients are familiar with, like DISC or MBTI,[21] but usually these days I work with a 4-elements model as this is intuitive to most people.[22]

The 4-elements is a classic model found in many cultures worldwide. Now, through Carl Jung's influence, it forms the basis of many psychometric tests.[23] It gives us a versatile system for looking at many aspects of embodiment from short-term states to long-term dispositions. It can be applied to culture, music, places and facilitation styles, to give just a few examples. The model is not about putting people into boxes (we are all a complex and partly situational mix; and I avoid saying anyone 'is' an element), but about having a system of understanding preferences. We use the elements as convenient, common-sense shorthand for complexity. It is one of the central models of this book. It is useful to have a map of different ways of being embodied so that we do not miss possibilities and can more easily understand ourselves and others.[24]

The model is used to highlight strengths and weaknesses in coaching clients and in coaches I train, and as a way of helping them shift modes when flexibility is required. With groups it can be used to better understand internal team differences, see team biases, appreciate culture, and see where a different emphasis on recruitment may be needed (e.g. if everyone the MD has hired are like her, or if one element is totally missing from the company). There are many applications; essentially it's a great language for understanding and applying embodiment.

I use the elements as convenient common-sense labels – I am not of course suggesting they exist as literal physical elements, as people in medieval times may have done! Four is a small enough number of aspects for most people to get to grips with, and the intuitive labels means they are readily grasped. They can then be combined for more complexity if needed, such as 'He has an earth and fire preference'. I have also worked with embodied versions of other existing systems such as OCEAN, MBTI (Myers Briggs), DISC and the Enneagram, but prefer the 4-elements model for its intuitive simplicity. This model provides a non-judgemental language for discussing differences, improving communication and helping facilitators not only understand themselves but also empathise and work more skilfully with others. The felt empathy is a major advantage of embodied typology methods as you 'step into' other preferences, rather than just learning *about* them. As one elderly husband said to his wife on a training, 'Ah, now after 40 years I get you!!! I just thought you were like an alien! It was so interesting to do and see things your way!' The other major plus is that we are not just understanding our own preference or have clients do this, but are giving options we can actively step into. Rather than seeing character as a permanent, set-in-stone personality, we see it as simply a set of habits. Being shy or extrovert is a lot like being right- or left-handed: yes, you may have been born into it and, yes, you may always be that way, but it's also a lot about practice and you can master other ways of doings things, as I did when I broke my arm once!

Table 3.1 shows some of the specifics of how the elements are embodied. Further 4-elements tables can be found in Appendix 2.

Table 3.1 How the elements are embodied

Element	Shape	Yin / Yang	I, We, It	Primary/relational direction	Dominant emotion + relation	Movement types (Laban system)	Breathing
Air	none	yang	all / none	up away from	joy excitement disengage	float stillness light indirect disintegrated sudden free	upper chest in mouth / out nose fast 'light / inspirational'
Fire	triangle	yang	I	forward towards / against	curiosity anger engage / challenge	thrust + movement light direct disintegrated sudden free	chest in nose, out mouth emphasise in-breath fast 'heating / growling'
Water	circle	yin	we	backward receiving	awe fear receive / accept	flow + movement heavy indirect integrated sustained bound	lower back in mouth, out nose emphasise out-breath slow 'flowing / sighing'
Earth	square	yin	it	down standing ground	sadness despair resist	hold ground / sink stillness heavy direct integrated sustained bound	belly in nose, out mouth slow 'steady / grounding'

How to self-assess

Self-assessment is always tricky as we are blind to what we are blind to, and people may well have some weird ideas about their combination of elements. I used to like to think I was 'down to earth' just because it sounded nice and in alignment with my values, for example!

In order to identify your preferred element(s), have a go at embodying them in movement instead of just thinking about them. Really 'try them on', as you would clothes, or taste them from within. Time five minutes at least for each element, and note if you want to stop some early! For each of them, ask yourself:

1 Does this feel familiar or unfamiliar?
2 Is this longed for or are you sick of it?

The first question is the critical one for identifying your own patterns, so do not confuse it with the second. For example, I may *love* water but it isn't my main pattern! Most people have two primary elements (air-earth and water-fire, which can in fact be seen as polarities) and if you want to be all of them, that's air, and if it depends who you're with, that's water!

Situational factors exist of course; for example, I note that after a long flight, earth is more appealing, and when I'm stressed, water feels good. We are partly contextual as discussed in Chapter 1, so even where and when you do this may impact your 'results' – so if you do it just the once, don't have your conclusions tattooed on your forehead just yet! That being said, most students I've seen who engage with the movement work (get off your butt, reading about it won't cut it) are fairly accurate and maybe 80 per cent hold the same conclusion after a year of exploring it. Remember it is just a map, so embrace it if it's useful for examining your embodiment. Stuart Heller and Ginny Whitelaw are both excellent on the elements too, though their systems are far from identical.

Embodied Yoga Principles (EYP)

The EYP system uses archetypal postures to reveal patterns, using the familiarity and deviation principles noted already. Many videos on YouTube show the 26 poses, some of which are displayed in Figures 3.1–3.6: enthusiasm, self-care, taking space, yes and no (standing versions – they can also be done while sitting).

Getting feedback

Volumes have been written on getting feedback, so I won't say much now except that it is very valuable to ask people what they see in how you move and stand. Of course this should be framed as a service to us and body prejudices

Figure 3.1 Self-care pose

Figure 3.2 Enthusiasm (aka passion) pose

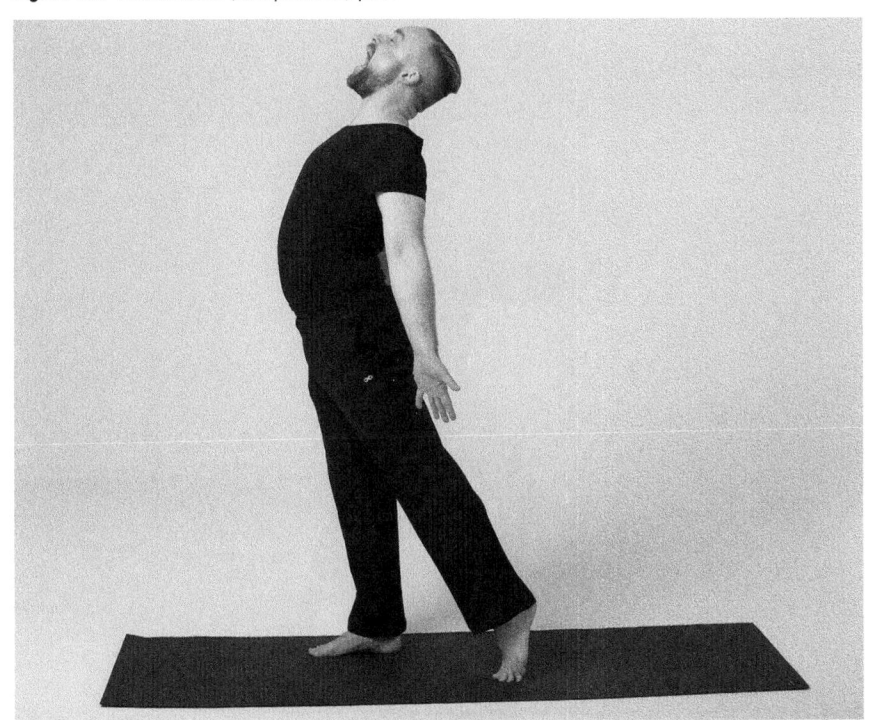

Figure 3.3 Taking up space pose

Figure 3.4 Entering pose

Figure 3.5 No pose (seated variation)

Figure 3.6 Yes pose

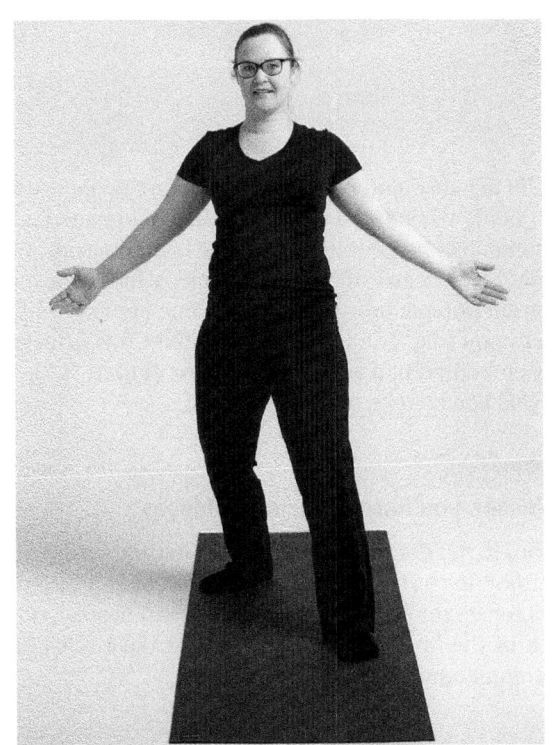

Figure 3.7 Contexts of embodiment

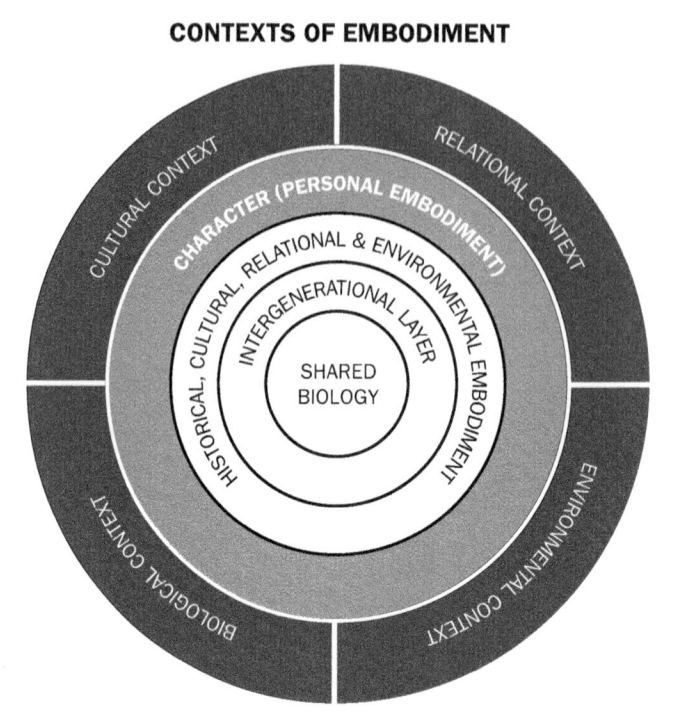

CONTEXTS OF EMBODIMENT

(e.g. 'you are jolly because you have a larger body') be ignored! Personally I'll ask more open people whenever I can and I find as long as I'm pleasant about it, the embarrassment some people experience is minimised.

It is likely you have heard of '360 feedback', which is a means of getting takes from different perspectives and not just one person or persons in a similar relationship to you (e.g. employees). Remember this principle is important as we're always embodied in a relational context (Figure 3.7), so to reveal the character level this needs to be triangulated on.

Noting what classes you hate / parts of classes

A very simple way to get data on your habits is to go try a range of movements and notice what you love and what you hate! You may adore the flowing part of a dance class for example, like a pig in s**t, and despise the staccato part. You may be sick of the linear karate, or long for the circles of Gaga dance.[25] This says something about you.

My own embodied story

By the time I did the copying walk exercise as part of a coach training with the Newfield Network in Amsterdam, I had had quite a bit of feedback from people, but seeing someone else 'do' my walk was quite shocking. There was a way in which it 'hit' me seeing it embodied by another that words could never do, and it was a real wake-up call. I was quite hard on myself while watching them – which I've since learnt is quite typical for people doing this exercise – thinking, 'OMG, what a cocky git!!' I face palmed a lot despite having done a range or more cognitive psychometric tests by that point and had some hard 'talkings to' from teachers that I respected. Painful as it was, something I really needed to work on was exposed, as was a great strength when my partner said, 'I felt like I could do anything as you!' – and I was like 'well; yeah . . . obviously . . .'.

Another instance of seeing my patterns was in creating Embodied Yoga Principles. Spurred on by a number of yoga teachers studying embodiment with me and asking for yoga-specific practices, I set out to create a set of poses which embody a range of archetypes so people could explore embodied range and their own depths, easily and in a modern postural yoga class. What I found was that I quickly thought of, or invented, many 'yang' ones like the warrior, entering and taking up space poses, but was less quick to find yin ones like the vulnerability, openness and receiving poses. Teaching the eventual full set of 26 – after colleagues helped me to add to my blind spots – it was obvious which were uncomfortable subjectively, and which I kept 'getting wrong' objectively, so I not only practised these more, but shifted my general personal yoga practice around to get more in touch with my 'yin' side more generally. Over several years of practice they became more and more comfortable and I started getting the feedback that it was showing up in my life. I received glowing compliments, such as 'you're a bit less of a pushy jerk now, Mark'. Most people put this down to getting married or just maturing. However, it's hard to identify the influences with long-term practices, as, like me, people's lives change in many ways – but I think the practices should at least take some of the credit. I also notice over a shorter time-frame – for example, when I do them each morning for a week – the influence that this has.

I've had many exercises like this over the years doing embodied training and I tend to find that I 'spiral' around certain issues, meaning they are never exactly 'fixed' by embodiment, and I still have my deepest favourite aspects of embodiment (I could even call this a 'soul'), but my range has clearly grown over the years, as have the level and subtlety of mistakes with harder aspects. Honestly, as an embodiment teacher it can be a bit embarrassing when I default back to really old habits – usually when stressed, hungry and tired – as there's a kind of pressure to be perfect in personal growth fields, both internally and as projected by students. But I try and find the balance between allowing myself to be human and still a work in progress, and having built enough range to have integrity.

Facilitator case study: Tango trainer!

I've been training for many years at high levels in the corporate world, and am trained in many schools of coaching. I think of myself as a well-rounded person but despite being fit I realised that this was not the same as being at home in my body. For this reason I decided to add embodiment to my tool-kit! The key thing I soon found, however, was that it's about working on yourself, not so much getting yet more tools.

One of the more pronounced shifts for me came when I took on tango as a practice. It gave me greater range as a facilitator as I learned to both push and hold at the same time. This proved particularly useful when working with large groups, entrenched audiences and clients. Prior to that, my (unconscious) embodiment would lean towards more yin but my practice developed a more rounded (and wiser) yang. I developed a more determined, clear push simultaneously with a clearer, compassionate holding.

– Glenn Bracy, Coach and Trainer, Valencia, Spain

Facilitator case study: Becoming not a nice coach

When I came to embodiment two years ago I was disillusioned, burning out and dreaming of doing more soulful work in the world. I had a decade-long Buddhist practice and a lot of 'personal development' under my belt, however, I quickly discovered that working intelligently through the body had been the missing piece in real, lasting change. EFC[26] was not easy, I was confronted with my habitual patterns of 'niceness' and timidity in ways I had previously managed to avoid.

As part of the course I committed to six months of daily practices to build more 'fire'. I did karate twice a week, lifted weights and practised EYP postures daily. It opened up a whole new way of experiencing myself and my body. To my surprise I started being able to say 'no' to people clearly, to send food back at restaurants, to make direct requests of my lover. These incremental changes really changed the way I showed up in the world. Eighteen months later, I now run my own embodiment coaching business. I help women make this same journey – from conditioned 'niceness' to satisfying wholeness, from abandoning themselves to be 'good', to standing bravely in control of their own lives. It's beautiful, necessary work which lights me up. I still use practices from EFC most days – they keep me honest and evolving, enabling me to lead by example and get s**t done. There is simply no way I would have been able to achieve all this without embodied practices.

– Erika Chalkley, Coach, Norfolk, UK: www.yourrighttobe.com

How to develop embodied pattern awareness with clients – overview

One of main jobs of an embodied facilitator is to gently expose clients' habitual patterns so that they can become aware of their bias, and build range if something is not working for them. Obviously, clients have to want to look at themselves to do this kind of work. Most people will understand quite intuitively that their default way of being is embodied, though they likely won't have this word for it. Most successful people are also curious about themselves, and often 'so what do you see?' is one of the first questions I get asked by people when I explain my job!

How to develop embodied pattern awareness with clients – techniques

One-to-one techniques

Walking, standing and sitting-mirroring and comparisons

A simple technique is to show a person their walk, usual sitting position or stance. This must be done with permission and made clear that you are not mocking them, of course. You could also have them compare two walks or poses and ask which feels most familiar. While a system or 'map' like 4-elements can be used, you can also just pick two that highlights a pattern that you'd like to have them see.

Video recording

Video is another way to raise awareness, and easily done on a phone these days. Again, consent and then service intention are key.[27]

Embodied feedback

So here's how I recommend giving feedback:

1 Observe the client and both look keenly and feel your own empathic mirroring – this will give two strands of 'data'.
Check in with any biases you may have. Remember there is no 'clean' place to stand and we are always observing embodiments through our own embodiment. If you are a very watery person, for example, even a moderately fiery person may seem *very* fiery. Knowing your cultural bias and that of your client is also vital ('no, he's not miserable, he's just Russian so won't smile unless there's a joke', for example), as is having done ample shadow work[28] so you are not simply projecting. While by definition we cannot be

aware of our shadow, we can note how it might impact us. I always check any feedback with a colleague, for example, where I feel a client is triggering, or if I find myself always saying positive things about them. A two-trainer mode is best for transformational work for this reason.
2. Get permission and say why you would like to give feedback – for learning. Double-check with yourself there isn't even a hint of another motive, such as revenge or a means to please them.
3. Say what you see factually if at all possible, separating out observations from evaluations from your own feelings and intuitions, which you can offer after. All these are useful but don't mix them.
4. Approach the feedback as a mutual enquiry process and with curiosity, not as an expert who knows best – remember, you've likely only seen them in very limited contexts. Ask them what they think too!

Exaggeration

'The body learns through exaggeration and contrast', Wendy Palmer says, and I find asking people to exaggerate their patterns makes them more obvious, and can be a very helpful strategy. This takes what they've habituated to and makes them felt again.

If a client rushes a lot, have them rush *more*; if they lack confidence, have them really take this on; if they are overly nice, have them be *super* nice, and so on. Obviously, great care is needed with abusive patterns, and as ever calibration is key to effective embodied facilitation. The art of 'what's enough, what's too much, and what's too little',[29] as with most things. This being said, letting people burn in the fire of their own neurosis a little is tough love, as it will have them really 'grock'[30] it.

Distinction coaching

Often people will be stuck in a habitual way of being as they have conflated two things as one. In this way they will keep 'choosing' a bad option as they can see no better option. For example, the classic 'unhealthy yang and yin' pattern at the heart of our culture, which misperceives power and love as opposites, rather than two sides of the same thing. This means many people will equate being brutal with being strong, as they feel it's better to be nasty and not weak; and others being compliant / weak with being kind, as they would rather lose and be victims than be nasty. False choices lead to bad lives.

Embodied distinction coaching is where a facilitator helps a client make a new distinction in the body, turning a false polarity into four options. For example, showing them how they can be strong *and* kind (as opposed to strong or kind).

> So a bipolar option like:
>
> 1. Strong but violent
>
> vs.

Embodied self-awareness

2. Kind and weak

is converted to seeing four options:

1. Strong but violent[31]
2. Kind but weak
3. Violent and weak (obviously not desired)
4. Kind and strong – the desired new one!

This enables a new way of being, and the embodiment of all can be practised, with an emphasis on the new desired one, to embody this distinction. Other confusions I work with regularly to separate out the component parts and give new options include arrogant vs. confident (or humble vs. unconfident), fast vs. rushing, boundaried vs. aggressive (another basic yin-yang one) and fun vs. chaotic. This is one of the more advanced techniques in this book (though to many it sounds simple), but a real go-to for me. Giving new options for new freedom through the body can be profoundly helpful.

Client case study: One-on-one

I once coached a wonderfully cynical middle-aged Yorkshire yoga teacher who thought all self-care was narcissistic and self-indulgent. This meant she did not look after herself well, and as she aged, this was having real consequences for her health. We teased this out in our first session, and I had my suspicions early on when she said things like, 'I'd like to rest after work BUT (that's often a magic word), I don't want to be one of those Instagram girls in the bath with the rose petals who think so much of themselves' [imagine this in the voice of Jon Snow from Game of Thrones]. We then took on this embodiment (to some hilarity and disgust), before more seriously exaggerating her pattern of essentially self-abuse through not resting.[32] Carefully obviously and not for long, but it did bring tears to the eyes of a woman who rarely wept ('ya bastud, ya made me cry!' she said), which hit home the seriousness of what she was working on under the jokes. Next she came up with a more humble, non-narcissistic self-care pose, which was very close to the one we teach from EYP (I could have just given ours, but prefer it when clients self-generate embodiments as it makes them stickier). She really enjoyed this and committed to taking it on as a practice. We also looked at some bodily 'markers' to act as warning lights when she had gone into self-abuse mode and linked the new self-care embodiment to some specific behaviours (time gardening, not in a rose bath mostly), and added some more usual coaching accountability structures.

Group techniques

EYP – familiarity and deviation

One of the nice things about EYP is that you can use it with quite large groups to explore an issue. I have worked with 400 people whilst keynoting the British ICF convention, around 500 at a yoga festival, and 1,000 or so in a Russian university auditorium. The basic method is very simple – show a pose, and then highlight all the ways they have gotten it 'wrong', revealing their patterns. If you do a YouTube search of 'no pose', for example, you will see a number of ways people unconsciously alter the pose, showing up their patterns around boundaries. This is the deviation principle.

The familiarity principle is even easier, just have people do a pose and ask them if they feel at home in it. Stress you don't mean if they literally do this pose of course. If you contrast two very different poses, most people will be very clear which is more habitual as a way of being.

Quick and dirty 360 feedback

360-degree feedback is quite widespread, such as where an employee will get feedback confidentially from people that they manage, from managers and from peers. This can even be extended to friends and family. The idea is to 'triangulate' on who they are, though also seeing contextual differences can be helpful.

Whole companies and online platforms can spend weeks doing a 360 for a person but I find that a text message to 20 people from different sides of life (easy on most modern phones) works well enough. Have clients ask, 'Please describe me as a person in three words; it's for a feedback exercise for a training', or similar, adding anything they think would be helpful. I find most people messaged will respond within an hour or two and positively enough that clients do not feel bad; in fact, many will find the vulnerability and what's essentially appreciation of the exercise very touching. (In the UK, it is typical for one word of the three to be sarcastic, like 'you're smart, kind but a bit of a loser' . . . because we have vulnerability issues.) Answers can also be grouped by theme and elements to see patterns – for example, 12 instances of 'confident', 'brave' and 'ballsy' could be grouped as a cluster and all labelled as 'fire'. If answers are mostly complimentary (usually the case), they can also be flipped to see the less helpful side with reflection: 'kind' could become 'sometimes too nice', 'brave' could become 'foolhardy', and funny could become 'uses humour to not feel'. Once when I did this I easily found four groups by using Post-it notes that I gave unique labels to and was able to see positives and negatives in.

The embodied training aspect is then to ask how the qualities identified live in the body. They can be exaggerated, contrasted, danced, played with, etc. In this way habitual modes become more easily identified and stepped into and out of.

Embodied self-awareness 91

The 4-elements model for client self-awareness

The model of the elements we introduced in the section on self-work is *excellent* for working with groups because it is:

- Effective
- Simple and intuitive enough for those new to embodiment to easily pick up[33]
- Fun – see any video of me teaching this to see how anarchic it can become
- Builds empathy for differences[34]
- Shows group dynamics like tension between a watery HR department and a fiery sales team, and can support communication between them

I use art for leadership training, team-building and communication training among other things. It has many uses.

Teaching it first requires you to go deeply into each element yourself over a period of time, building your own range – again, just reading about it isn't enough. People intuitively sense if they are psychologically safe enough to 'go there' or not depending on the ease with which a facilitator holds each element. It is also your own body that really teaches the element not what you say (see Chapter 6). I would suggest that people proceed with care teaching the elements, though 'lite' versions of it can still work well. I often do a very low-intensity chair-bound version with less flexible clients, for example, at least in the first instance.

Safety note: While teaching fire, people can become emotionally triggered as it may seem 'aggressive' and be scary, so make sure people have an easy 'out', do not try and force people to do things, and calibrate intensity as ever. The silliness of air is where people risk physically hurting themselves as they mess around, so watch out for this too. Have an agreed stop sign like spreading hand-raising – this is when the trainer raises a hand and the trainees copy this and stop.

Credit: Stuart Heller, Ginny Whitelaw

Here's a few more questions to help you teach the elements. See the elements tables in Appendix 2 too.

Post-exercise reflections

- Which one or two elements were most familiar? (your preference(s) maybe?)
- Which preference reminded you of particular situations or relationships? (you may embody one or more at work or with your partner, for example)
- Which felt unfamiliar to you?
- Was there one you were sick of? (maybe it's time to build range)
- Which do you long for? (it may be lacking from your life)
- Which do you find annoying or inauthentic? Which do you admire in others or even fall in love with, but don't 'feel like you'? (it may be an actively repressed type – shadow)

- How have your dominant preference(s) served you in your life?
- Was it your primary strategy for finding love, safety, belonging?
- What's your best guess at your preference (one or two elements)?
- What are the strengths of your preference?
- What are the risks of your preference?
- Where in your life are you 'seeing everything as a nail when all you have is a hammer', and using the wrong tool for the job?
- What has been the personal or professional cost of using your dominant preference(s) to excess? What has been the cost of under-developing other types?
- How will your life be if you keep your preferences as they are now for the next ten years?
- How can you manage the risks of stronger preferences and develop weaker ones?

Relational reflections
- Think of a relationship you have with another person. What preference do you express predominantly with them? Does this serve you?
- What preference do you most often have conversations in? How's this working out for you?
- How do you like people to communicate with you?
- Think of a work project that you've completed. Did you use all the types in it? Was there a cost to missing one out?
- What preference do you express as a facilitator (if you are one already)?
- What is the elemental mix of your culture (past and present)?

Credit: Stuart Heller, Ginny Whitelaw and various shamanic models have influenced my understanding of the four elements.

Client case study: Group work
I once did a four-hour team-building with an international aviation engineering company. People came from all over the world to a large hotel conference room in Spain, overlooking the Mediterranean. With the help of an assistant I took 100 people through the elements model.[35] *I had been briefed by a beleaguered HR manager that there was a lot of communication misunderstandings and tension between departments and countries, and guessed this would help. They wanted something more useful than just*

a 'jolly' (just fun), but something lively and upbeat as a break from dry accounts and sales reports. I arrived in time to have lunch with the group, and sat in on a few sessions to get a feel for them. The group was highly educated but not overly self-aware, intensely driven but friendly, and as busy as most groups I work with.

After some basic walking-in-the-room awareness-raising activities and some centring for their obvious stress, I explained why we would be moving around in weird ways. With most groups, if you give them a compelling reason linked to their goals and in their language (I picked up a few buzz-words they used earlier), they will try unusual things – even weird things. I explained to them matter-of-factly the purpose of working with the elements, and gave clear instructions before we started moving around the room. The group kept their shoes on but most loosened ties and took off jackets. As they 'got into it' I was able to calibrate the session to go a little deeper into each element than I would with some corporate groups. Frankly, it seemed it was a nice break from endless PowerPoint presentations for them.

What came out was quite interesting, as not only did it give individuals a clear sense of their patterns and how they liked to communicate, but helped them understand colleagues. National office characteristics came out (the watery-earth Dutch team and the NYC fire squad, for example!), as well as issues between departments – the earthy accountant team and the airy marketing people had some good conversations, for instance. The company also quickly adopted the elements for use in recruitment – there was an issue with a CEO hiring his own type repeatedly, for example (a classic), and as always teams need to be balanced.

The embodied shadow

Some potential aspects of our embodiment are not just underdeveloped but actively denied and repressed (and therefore likely projected onto others). We could use the Jungian term 'shadow' for this, and this is held in place by various bodily tension patterns. In one sense, the body *is* the unconscious. Many body therapy practices for surfacing the unconscious exist but are not within the scope of this book, and best done with guidance. That being said, some of the lighter and safer ones are provided below to give you a taste. I highly recommend you take the time to go deeper into this area yourself as you develop as an embodied facilitator, as in the long term it's often shadow that holds people back. Shadow work with another is a useful supplement to the core 'awareness, range and choice' model here, because it gets at what is kept out of our own awareness, and that we will never see on our own, let alone have the chance to inhabit.

> **Shadow embodiment reflection**
>
> While by definition we are not aware of hidden parts of ourselves, we can spot our over-reaction (positive or negative) to people who embody them. Our *reactivity* points to shadow.
>
> - Did you find yourself quickly judging any of the elements as soon as they were presented, e.g. thinking 'bloody wishy washy water people!!', or 'fiery just means aggressive! I hate such AGGRESSIVE PEOPLE! I am NOT like that!!!' Are there any types of people who annoy you as soon as they walk into the room? Who bothers you more than anyone else? Who do you irrationally dislike?
> - Do you tend to fall in love with a particular type of person? Do you tend to idolise a particular type of person, wishing you could be like them but not really seeing it as possible?

Virtual considerations

Much of what I've described here can be done online: mimicry exercises, 4-elements and EYP, for example. While groups may get it quicker and go deeper in person, this is not always the case. Most people are getting used to online meetings, and may feel safer in their own homes, and I have been surprised as to the depth of many online courses as I teach more of them. As in person, the concept of the 'container' is key – and if people are checking their mails during trainings, or a spouse keeps popping in, then this may not be the same as on a retreat away from it all. For transformative work like embodied facilitation, solid yet caring boundaries are essential.

There is also an art to using platforms like Zoom – see Appendix 1.

Trauma and awareness

Trauma can lead people to have a rigid and distorted self-view as a way of establishing psychological safety, e.g. 'I'm always a nice person and people like me', or 'I'm a tough guy, nothing can hurt me'. Self-awareness-raising activities can therefore be threatening as the gap between reality and self-assessment is closed. This is worth taking into consideration.

Cultural considerations

How we assess ourselves is always viewed within a cultural context. A fiery person who grows up in Russia, for example, may not assess themselves as such, but someone just a bit watery may really notice it against this cultural backdrop. Each culture will pathologise some embodied preferences (try being fiery in Sweden, for example) and lift up others (earth and water are far more accepted to stay with the Swedish example – in general, of course, as ever).

Principles used in this chapter

One thing I'm quite proud of in the EFC approach to embodiment is teaching principles. I have mentioned a few already, including:

- Awareness and choice (or primary principle)
- Familiarity
- Contrast
- Deviation

If you can pick these up from the numerous examples in this book, you will have something more than a bag of techniques, you will have a way of making sense of all the techniques, refining any that you come across, and of generating your own creatively to suit your exact facilitation circumstances. More on principles later.

> *Reflection / discussion questions*
>
> What are your strengths and areas of development? How are these embodied? How is your level of self-awareness along two time-frames (and how do you know you're right about this?)?
>
> Reflect upon these. This could involve drawing, dancing or discussing it with a friend.

Notes

1. Often attributed to Socrates.
2. Israeli Moshe Feldenkrais is one of the founders of the Western somatics movement and has a huge influence on many arts, though his sophisticated method is sadly not widely known – that is, outside of Israel and certain specialist circles.
3. See https://charleseisenstein.org/courses/dietary-transformation-from-the-inside-out/ and https://www.beyondchocolate.co.uk
4. Embodiment teachers tend to have odd blind spots generally I've noticed, where mindfulness isn't applied to some areas of their life that are somehow 'off limits'. Therapy and gentle community encouragement (rather than shaming or an expectation of perfectionism) often help and people 'fill in' the gaps over time if they are open to this. Overcoming resistance is often a humbling process too *for me*!
5. See, for example, Eugene Gendlin's book *Focusing*, first published in 1978 (revised and updated 25th anniversary edition, London: Rider, 2003).
6. The word 'yoga' has come to mean almost anything and even distinctions made may be confusing! 'Hatha', for example, historically meant 'forceful' but now usually means a more gentle approach – but not always! If in doubt, go watch a class before you take it up.

7 Australian Mathias Alexander was another early founder of the Western somatics movement.
8 It might feel like a good 'arranged marriage' though – meaning it's not exactly 'love at first sight', but passion later is a possibility, or it may just be an intuitive obsession that you dive into! 'Fall in love with it' is my best advice to anyone starting a practice, and this fuels people where discipline does not, though discipline is also necessary over the long term. It is key these two things are in balance.
9 http://www.leadershipembodiment.com/
10 Note that embodied practice doesn't require faith, only to try things. Scepticism (but not cynicism) is fine as it's primarily experiential.
11 See Stephen Porges's polyvagal model. Porges is excellent and accessible on trauma too. https://www.stephenporges.com
12 'Presence' has many definitions including in some cases all of embodied influence (Chapter 6), but can also be taught of as the long-term impact of body awareness practice.
13 Note: do this with thumbs up and to the side or it can look like a load of Nazi salutes!
14 'Walking or wheeling' is a very simple addition if wheelchair users are present, as exactly the same principle is at work.
15 Richard Strozzi-Heckler, *The Anatomy of Change* (Berkeley, CA: North Atlantic Books, 1993).
16 A fun demonstration of this familiarity principle is to ask a group to take their shoes off, and then have one of the group close their eyes and try and identify their own shoes from smell alone. Holding everyone's shoes to their nose one at a time, they would find all the other shoes 'yucky' but their own totally fine. We can identify our habits by our discomfort with others through comparisons.
17 We use this as part of the Embodied Yoga Principles system after I observed that in many yoga classes, people with different personalities made very different 'errors' – for example, less confident people did not extend their arms fully in warrior 2 pose, while more confident ones over-extended them.
18 I sometimes do a second part of this exercise where I bet people £100 that they won't be able to stop themselves crossing their arms, hands or legs (or some other habitual body gesture) for the rest of a training session. I gradually 'catch people out' and eliminate them from the game. So far nobody has won the money, and most don't last an hour, which shows how hard it can be to stay aware of patterns and change them using mindfulness alone. Embodiment is necessary as nobody can be vigilant for long! I have found long-term meditators with a high level of body awareness last the longest, so their training must have had some impact!
19 https://www.walkingyourtalk.com/
20 Actors must reveal their unconscious patterns so that they do not 'infect' the roles they take on, in that it may or may not be useful, and there are a number of systems of acting training that are essentially embodiment in nature.
21 These are two classic personality tests used a lot in business if you have not come across them. There are hundreds of others, ranging from the strongly validated OCEAN to ones published in magazines! They are all just ways of understanding differences. Ginny Whitelaw's FEBI test (https://www.youtube.com/watch?v=_5X7Ermc6eg) even has an embodied component, and Dylan Newcombe is excellent on this topic.
22 I say 'a' model as there are many versions of this literally stretching back to prehistory and it is used by some shamans even. Try this version and discover that others you may know are not wrong, just different.

23 It inspired Jung, whose students pioneered systems that led to the MBTI, which in turn influenced modern academics' OCEAN model, for example.
24 Note that there are variations such as 5- and 6-elements models, and many different perspectives on the four elements, but please put any maps you may have come across already aside now to best absorb this version.
25 A free-flowing dance form from Israel.
26 The Embodied Facilitator Course – our flagship coach training.
27 Given a choice between mirroring and video, I'd actually use the low-tech option as our own image has a way of entrancing being with over-familiarity.
28 'Shadow work' refers to deep therapeutic work with the unconscious on what we repress. When an embodiment is not simply out of reach as yet, but actively kept as such, it can be the turn of a therapist not a coach, though on longer courses we do embodied shadow work.
29 I think it was Richard Strozzi-Heckler that I first heard stress this angle.
30 *Grock*, a wonderful somatic word meaning to fully and viscerally get something on a deep emotional felt level. It may come from the name of a famous Swiss clown but the internet isn't sure!
31 Actually, being strong and violent is more difficult than being kind and strong, literally and physically as well as on other levels, due to the nature of strength . . . but that's another conversation.
32 Note the exaggeration principle at work here.
33 In a corporate groups session I usually devote 60–90 minutes to the four elements.
34 This aspect of embodied preference models / typologies is very different from simply giving everyone a piece of paper with their own style on and verbally explaining that of others. By stepping into the shoes of colleagues, people have a felt understanding of what it's like to BE another type of person! I've even heard married couples, together for decades say, 'Oh, *that's why* she does that!!!' or something similar.
35 I advise having at least one other trainer for 'crowd control' if there are over 20 people when doing embodied work.

4 Embodied self-leadership

The best gift you can give someone is to get yourself together.
— Wendy Palmer

PART 1: SELF- LEADERSHIP – STATE

Opening exercise
Think of something a little stressful (not traumatic) and notice what you do in your body as you think of it. Notice specifically what you do as a reaction. How would you reduce that reaction and create a new response?

Promise

If you spend a few weeks working with the techniques in this chapter, you will be radically better at the two skills above (noticing and managing stress), and able to teach these vital life skills to clients, as well as other forms of state management.

Opening reflection questions
How good are you at self-regulating yourself? Do people generally say that you're 'calm and collected', or more upbeat or even volatile? Can you wake yourself up, or calm yourself down easily, without external means such as drugs and music? How do you 'get yourself together' under pressure?

How expressive are you? Can you express all emotions or just some? Consider happy, sad, angry and scared as just four basic ones.

Further reflection exercise: Good and bad days?
What is the difference between you on your best and worst days (by your own values and definition)? Or good and bad moments within a day if you prefer.

When have you been most 'centred' and how would you describe what this is? What was the difference between those good and bad times, not externally in terms of events but in terms of:

- Your awareness?
- Your physiology?
- Your breathing, posture and muscle tone?
- Your relationships?
- Your happiness?
- Your task effectiveness?

Here's another one to ponder: What if there were a piece of technology available which could improve literally anything you do? What if it were free, took very little time to learn, measurably improved performance across a huge range of tasks, reduced stress, and improved individual well – being, performance and relationships? What if there were something always available and good for your health that could improve every aspect of life? Happily, such 'technology' does exist – it's a set of embodied techniques known as 'centring', an important aspect of self-leadership.

What is the skill-set and how does it help facilitation?

The category of 'self-leadership' is about change ('grow' not just know, or perhaps more accurately for state, 'shift'). Embodiment concerns not just awareness but also choice. Embodiment is not about being a passive victim of your states, but stepping up as a leader[1] and being able to influence and develop them. For example, when you are tired or stressed as a trainer, is that it? Or can you alter this, waking yourself up or calming yourself down? It is hugely practical and empowering to be able to shift how we are, so as we can better adapt to life. Everyone can do this to some extent of course, but most have not dedicated any real time to developing this skill since they were a child. Likewise, teaching clients the skills is a massive pragmatic victory for them; actually a profound world – view shift.

States can be altered with quick-win self-regulation techniques. Two important kinds of state change are up- and down-regulation – waking yourself up and calming yourself down. Doing these in yourself of course enables you to not only feel better as a facilitator (we've all been stressed out by a 'difficult' participant, or been half-asleep coaching after lunch) but also to impact others, who are more influenced by your embodied presence than by your words (Chapters 5 and 6 on listening and influence are based on the work in this chapter). Aside from work benefits, self-regulation has profoundly positive effects on our well – being – nobody is healthy when stuck in fight-flight-freeze, as well as our relationships – think of the last thing you regret saying to a partner or friend, I bet you were in a reactive mode and not regulating your state effectively.

The other side of regulation is expression (enabled through up-regulation) and if we are not to be dull grey, lifeless human PowerPoints, this embodied skill is necessary to develop.

> **Facilitator case study: Centring to defuse a volatile moment in the training room**
>
> I was facilitating a team of 30 in a pharmaceutical company – it was difficult work establishing priorities for the coming quarter. There were differing opinions in the room, to say the least. Klaus, a department lead, was annoyed and was taking it out on me as the facilitator. I was feeling exposed and attacked. He and I were in a very visible standoff. And then, by pure chance, my centring reminder vibrated on my watch (I'd been learning this form of state regulation to manage stress). I wiggled my toes, took a breath, unfolded my arms and looked around the room. I said, 'What's going on here, folks? It feels like there is a lot of frustration.' People nodded and acknowledged there was but that it was a necessary difficulty to get to what's important. Klaus nodded too, our head-to-head potential conflict melted away. By lunch we had agreed the priorities and were working on how to achieve them. I'm sure that without centring at that point – and now with more training I do it habitually – I would not only have 'lost' Klaus, but also my authority with the group, and the day would not have been a success.
>
> – Piers Carter, coach, UK

Relationship to other skill-sets

To lead yourself you must first be aware of yourself. As Stuart Heller says, '*We are the first system we must learn to manage.*' Chapter 3 is very much the foundation of this one. Have you ever heard, for example, a clearly angry man shout, '*I'm NOT angry!*' or a child that can barely keep their eyes open claim not to be tired? In both cases they are likely not lying, they are simply not aware of their state, and so don't know they need to take action to change it!

Furthermore, unless we are well self-regulated, it is hard to listen and to lead. Imagine you slip over and suddenly experience a fear response – can you listen at that moment? Or when deep in grief yourself, do you have the energy to hold space for another? Likely not. Likewise, how influential are you when panicking? Does being angry or afraid show authority? Or do warmth and calm?

How to develop self-leadership in yourself – overview

We all need to manage ourselves and unless we're toddlers, we already have some skill in this area. The ability of the average adult, however, is pitiful compared to what is possible with just moderate practice. A good place to start is centring.

What is centring anyway?

'Centring'[2] can refer to specific techniques that involve focusing attention on the centre of gravity of the body to bring you into a specific state, but I use the term here more generally to mean any body-mind techniques used for self-regulation, and for reducing the fight-flight-freeze response specifically. More colloquially, we could say that it's a set of techniques that bring us back into balance. Centring to me means techniques which create a positive foundational state from which any further action can be engaged in with greater awareness and choice. Often, these techniques involve reducing arousal levels and the famous 'fight-or-flight' reaction (aka 'down-regulation'), as this is often helpful in a stressful world; but centring also includes techniques for regulating ourselves to greater alertness and stimulation (up-regulation), and techniques for shifting state without reference to arousal level. More on fight-flight and related terms later.

Creating any desired change to your state could also be called 'centring' in a very extended sense though, and I don't use it quite as broadly. More colloquially, centring is about getting your s**t together! As I suggested in a previous exercise, I'll sometimes introduce centring by asking people to compare how different they are on their best days and their worst days – a very different way of being for most! I will then suggest that centring can be thought of as a way to have more good days and less bad days!

In models of embodied preference (e.g. four elements or yin and yang), the 'centre' can be seen as the balanced midpoint. From this midpoint we can respond skilfully. It can be viewed as a physical place – a person's literal physical centre of gravity just below their navel in the middle of their body if they are standing upright (perhaps surprisingly low to those from Western cultures that are literally 'uptight'). In traditional oriental systems, it is known as the *hara* (Japanese) or *dan tien* (Chinese), and is important for many Asian martial, meditative and health disciplines.

Facilitator case-study: My story – a centred life?

Centring has been an integral part of my life now for over twenty years, since I first learnt it on the mats of a university aikido club. It was one of the first aspects of embodied learning to make an impression on me as a practical technique due to its obvious efficiency, and it quickly improved my life. I have also used centring to stay calm (OK, calmer) in various extreme locations and unusual circumstances. It has saved my life more than once too.

One of the biggest early illustrations of centring's gifts for me came under sad circumstances; my closest friend from university, Rachel, had a sudden psychotic break and committed suicide. I sat with her parents, sister and with shared friends from university. I centred many times there and at the service, being a rock for those who needed me while never losing touch with my grief.

This really showed me the power of centring, and how it can be of real benefit through the really hard times of life and not just for the special circumstances of aikido.

While my approach to centring has become more nuanced, teaching simple centring techniques remains a mainstay of even short workshops of almost any kind. An early client at a local government department commented that she had used it to stay calm in a severe earthquake while on holiday in China some years after being taught it, and I have heard feedback from numerous humanitarian aid workers I have trained pre-deployment or in the field in areas of starvation, torture, mass-rape and war, of how it has helped them stay safe and sane. Some of their stories are too horrible to share here, but centring was useful for these people on the sharpest edge of what life can offer. I used it while in Afghanistan with military helicopters flying overhead, scared for my life a number of times, when teaching peacekeeping soldiers in Sierra Leone, and while inside a crashing car rolling in a bean-field. As the car rolled and crushed, and fragments of glass showered around me in slow-motion like hard snowflakes, I thought, 'Well, f**k it, I might as well centre now.' I did, and walked away with only a few scratches and bruises . . . much to my own and the emergency service's surprise.

On the brighter side of life, I centred before popping the question to my now wife Daria – who I met as my translator while training Ukrainian psychotherapists in centring incidentally – and when I watched in awe as she walked down the aisle so that I might better remember it. Also, when I held my barely alive niece in hospital less than a day old after a traumatic premature birth, and told her through my body it was all going to be OK (it was, she is ten now and in great health).

More mundanely, I hear nice things from coaches on how the 'quick-win' of centring has helped them get quickly to the heart of issues with clients, and see its impact directly with my own coachees. With 'hard-nosed' sceptical corporate groups it works well to demonstrate that embodiment works, and open them up to other unusual things.

I can remember many other circumstances where centring has helped, such as after learning such-and-such a dictator wanted me dead in Ethiopia; while having to take 'Hamas breaks' in a stairwell during a workshop in Israel, under frightening (if ineffective) rocket-fire; when my girlfriend and I were living and working in the violence-soaked slums of Brazil and she told me she was beaten regularly by her father and needed help; when getting sober and walking past a pub 'dry' for the first time; when I gave my father's eulogy; when men with AK47s pointed at me and shouted in African languages I didn't understand; when having dinner with an Egyptian minister (pre – Arab Spring) and his Cleopatraesque wife and realising I'd accidentally encouraged them to have someone killed who was bothering my then boss. Ooops – don't worry, we centred and said while it was terribly nice of him to offer we'd rather have the person left alive.

> What is most gratifying is seeing centring help people in day-to-day circumstances. Where centring most often helps me is not in big dramas, but in the little stresses of rows about chores at home, in traffic, managing too many e-mails, waiting for a delayed train again, an annoying text or comment online. Centring can help us with the thousand little victories that make a life. The thousand little leanings to kindness and wisdom that make a friendship, career or romance. While it's the war-stories of centring and naming famous past clients like the House of Lords (I very briefly trained peers before a trip to the prisons of Iraq) that tend to grab people's attention – so excuse me for sharing a few colourful ones here – the real beauty of centring is felt day to day.
>
> I have taught centring to thousands of people around the world, and EFC students over the years who have reached many thousands more. Online videos of centring that we've created have had close to a million hits and with much positive feedback. I think of centring as a positive virus spreading and improving life.

I, we and it of centring

Centring involves ways to alter how you feel, what you are capable of, and what types of relationships you are predisposed towards ('I', 'it' and 'we' benefits). Centring involves methods, and creates results, that are subjective, objective and intersubjective, involving the body-mind, behaviour and relationships.

Master centring teacher Paul Linden offers the following excellent definition of centring:

> Centering is the antidote to the distress response. It is possible to prevent or overcome contraction by deliberately placing the body in a state of freedom, balance, and expansiveness.
>
> The centered state is a state of wholeness and integrity. It can be described in different ways. Speaking in structural language, the state of integrity is one in which the musculoskeletal system is balanced and free of strain. Speaking functionally, this state allows stable, mobile and balanced movement. Speaking in psychological terms, this state involves reaching out into the world with a symmetrical, expansive awareness and intentionality, while simultaneously staying anchored in internal body awareness. Speaking in spiritual terms, this state is an integration of the body states of power and love. Speaking in ethical terms, this state creates an awareness of and concern for the effects of one's actions on the wellbeing of others. Whatever terms we choose to use, they refer to one and the same mind-body state. For some reason, it is easy and automatic for human beings to drop into the distress response, but centering needs to be learned and practiced, and it needs to be engaged in voluntarily and deliberately. The key to centering lies in developing and applying body awareness.[3]

Some self-leadership basics

Fight-or-flight – overview[4]

The fight-or-flight response – also called the hyperarousal or acute stress response, and sometimes extended to 'fight-flight-freeze', and more rarely 'fold' (collapse) and 'fawn' (aka placate[5]) are added – is a physiological reaction that occurs in response to a perceived harmful event, attack or threat to survival. Animals react to threats with a general discharge of the sympathetic nervous system, priming the individual to fight or flee. More specifically, the adrenal medulla (on top of the kidneys) produces a hormonal cascade that results in the secretion of adrenaline (catecholamines, especially norepinephrine and epinephrine). The hormones oestrogen, testosterone and cortisol, and the neurotransmitters dopamine and serotonin, also affect how organisms react to stress (but not all in the same direction). This is an unconscious and involuntary process. Our higher functions are often still aware, giving us an excruciatingly frustrating experience whereby we are aware of what we're doing, but we can't stop it.

If we are too stressed or reactive, our neocortex – the part of our brain capable of creative thinking and self-reflection – goes more or less 'off-line'. We suffer from what is called an 'amygdala hijack' in which a lower part of our brain, also known as the reptilian brain, takes over for our safety. In this state we are ego-centric and not able to give others a sense of connection. Centring is a way back to our normal selves from this, but when we're so triggered that we're deeply in the fight or flight mode, the 'amygdala hijack' has kicked in and for a little while we are not able to influence our behaviour through centring – which we likely won't remember to try anyway.

If unable to fight or take flight, or exposed to enough stress, people will freeze. While there is often a very small faux freeze response before fight or flight, this is more of an orientating pause, and true freeze involves extreme traumatic or extended stress as someone becomes overwhelmed and 'shuts down'. There is at first a 'hyper' high-tension freeze that eventually can develop into a 'hypo' collapse, which is a medical emergency. If you have ever frozen up when speaking in public, for example, you may have tasted the start of a hyper freeze response.

People sometimes use the terms fight, flight and freeze in one breath. Note that they belong to two different levels of (perceived) threat. Freeze kicks in when fight-flight has not worked or is not an option (being physically stuck, for instance). Freeze is a shutdown of the system for energy and life preservation in the face of being overwhelmed, and heart rate and breathing slow dramatically.

Stress traffic lights

A system I like for understanding this is the green, yellow, orange and red lights model, adapted from Stephen Porges, who describes the underlying neurology as the involvement of different nerves – the dorsal and ventral vagus nerves somewhat famously now.

Green = rest and digest: social engagement and learning both probable. Useful for facilitators

Yellow = activation: social engagement possible and learning probable. Useful for facilitators but not sustainable

Orange = fight-flight engaged: limited social engagement and learning possible. Very limited uses for facilitators

Red = freeze: social engagement and learning impossible. No uses for facilitators

Obviously as trainers and coaches, keeping people in the green zone with centring is ideal, with some excursions into activation and excitement (yellow), but whole trainings can't and shouldn't be attempted in this zone – although some high-energy motivational speakers do this to wear people down for their marketing! You could also add a 'blue'[6] zone of lethargy where activation 'wake-up' centring is needed. If you've ever taught a group after lunch you may be familiar with this 'graveyard shift' when people are a little too much in the rest-and-digest mode!

Trauma vs. stress

While it is beyond the scope of this book to look at trauma in depth, I believe it is necessary for all facilitators, and especially those working with the body, to learn the basics. Put simply, trauma is a chronic fight-flight-freeze response, manifesting as a diverse set of symptoms. The key issue with trauma is that people have become overwhelmed, not merely stressed, and this has led to a long-term change.

Here are some of the more important things for an embodied facilitator to know about trauma:

- People may be suffering from chronic tension ('freeze' response) or numbing of the body (aka dissociation — also part of 'freeze') as a result of trauma
- Trauma-related 'hyper-arousal' (chronic fight-flight) may manifest as an inability to concentrate, anger issues, anxiety, insomnia, and a generally 'wired' state
- A mix of numbing and hyper-arousal will lead to a reduced 'window of tolerance' – nothing, nothing, nothing . . . UNBEARABLE! See the calibration principle
- The body may not feel like a safe place for someone who has trauma, as it may be associated with violation or pain. A traumatised person has their sense of safety impaired
- Trauma can lead to lack of trust and other relational issues, especially with authority figures (like facilitators), and issues with intimacy
- Trauma may lead to over-defended boundaries (defensiveness) or passivity and excessive agreeableness
- Trauma has 'triggers' which may lead to the reliving of previous experiences, including flashbacks[7]

- Trauma may lead to medically unexplained symptoms (previously called 'psychosomatic illness'). Skin and digestive issues are common, for example
- Trauma may be associated with socio-economic issues, such as poverty, gender and ethnicity[8]

And here are some basic recommendations for facilitators in the light of trauma being very common:[9]

- Apply the centring principles of consent, capacity and calibration *impeccably* as detailed below. Give plenty of choice but also offer a clear lead
- Do not assume people have had an easy life or will find the body an easy place to access
- Be aware of, on the lookout for, and compassionate towards trauma symptoms
- Build trust gradually and only do deeper work when you have it. Do not demand it, and do not take mistrust (e.g. arguing) personally
- Be aware of the ways people self-regulate or self-medicate, e.g. with food, alcohol or sex. Many residential trainings will limit these, which means people could be less regulated
- Focus on using the body as a resource to self-regulate before teaching other aspects of embodiment, so people can come back to this as needed
- If you identify a specific trigger, decide if you want to adapt to it to help an individual – it may be too big an ask so could mean an individual is not suited to a standard learning environment, or it may be no big deal
- Be aware that there are issues of gender, ethnicity, sexuality and other factors that you may be blind to, and mixed teams are often helpful. For example, I always co-teach with a woman to better address certain issues as a team.
- Be aware of trauma-related scarcity issues around content (e.g. 'Will there be notes?!' 'Can I have the slides?!') and access to you as a facilitator
- Heal your own trauma – EMDR, somatic experiencing and many types of bodywork are things that I recommend. Different things work for different people but just doing yoga and meditation is usually not enough
- Know competent therapists and refer when in doubt. People with trauma often come to coaching because it is less stigmatised than therapy, but if someone presents to you with serious untreated trauma and you are not a trauma therapist, refer them to a specialist. Know the limits of your expertise
- Julia Vaughan Smith's book *Coaching and Trauma* may also be useful[10]

Trauma resources

YouTube search 'Trauma awareness for facilitators' for more from me on this, and I would also recommend the work of Peter Levine, Irene Lyon, Paul Linden, Betsy Polatin, Bessel Van der Kolk, Stephen Porges, Kathy Kain, Babette Rothschild, Resmaa Menakem, Steven Hoskinson, Ilan Stephani and David Berceli on this subject if you'd like to go into more depth. The best quick-win accessible beginner's guide I have come across is that of Steve Haines, *Trauma Is Really Strange*.[11] My podcast also has many episodes on this subject, including a beginner's guide.

Effective treatment methods

While you shouldn't attempt to apply them if you're untrained, it is good to know that effective trauma treatments exist. Personally, I see trauma as physical, social, psychological and spiritual, so the best healing includes all these elements. Effective treatments include:

- Cognitive behavioural therapy (UK NICE guideline approved)
- EMDR – an eye movement technique (UK NICE guideline approved)
- Trauma-releasing exercises (such as Berceli's TRE system)
- Emotional freedom technique
- Somatic experiencing, NARM, Hakomi and other therapeutic approaches that include the body
- Self-help books (such as *8 Keys to Safe Trauma Recovery* by Babette Rothschild)[12]

Facilitator case study: Trauma, war and babies

A big challenge for facilitators in Israel is that most of the people that come to me really want to change but have very low trust – a common trauma symptom – because we are a traumatised society even if people don't know that! People have low trust and think it's me / the world / whatever, but it's the fight-flight being stuck in their systems.[13]

When I learnt centring I was better able to build trust by shifting into less threatening modes, and it was great for reducing my own fight-flight in the moment, which in turn reduced clients'. The 4-elements model was also helpful for better understanding how to build trust with different kinds of people – for example, water clients need more care whilst the fire ones just want action and outcomes! By bringing the body into the coaching I started getting bigger results quicker as people relaxed and opened up. This way of working is 'stress friendly' and therefore 'trauma friendly'. Likewise in my work as a doula in Jaffa, the 4-elements model helps women shift the different embodiments needed for childbirth, and centring of course is not only useful for pain but always useful in an intense traumatised place. I taught it to my son during rocket-attacks, for example, and have also passed it on, as part of bi-communal work with Israeli Arabs to enable better dialogue.

I've seen many approaches to coaching and there's many good ones, but for results, embodiment is a really good one. I was a sceptic at first (another cultural trauma trait) but I tried it and now rely upon it.

– Merav Golani, coach and doula, Tel Aviv-Yafo, Israel

Consent, capacity and calibration

These are the three basic ethical principles when teaching centring, or in fact any embodied work.

Consent means people freely and fully agree to an exercise. This may sound obvious but one should take into account power differentials (a facilitator will often be perceived as an authority figure), trauma-related patterns of agreeableness, the pressure of social conformity, and just that most people are disembodied and so are cut off from what they actually want!

Minor violations of others are so socially normal that you likely don't notice them, but this is not good enough for embodied facilitation. I have found that 90% of coaches and trainers touch without consent and need retraining in this, for example, or say things like, 'OK, I'm going to grab your arm now, OK?', and hence provide little opportunity for less boundaried people to say 'no'. Do not assume you're in the 10% because you're a nice person, it's just a habit for most. I also encourage establishing both verbal and non-verbal consent, the latter meaning that people's bodies do not react in fight-flight, such as not tensing up or withdrawing. This can be hard to explain so please YouTube search 'touch in training & coaching' to see an example of this. Another general rule I have is that a verbal or non-verbal 'maybe' = 'no', so stay on the safe side.

Making consent central, and supporting people listening to their needs in embodied facilitation, mean that you are growing agency, and re-establishing a sense of sovereignty in people.

Capacity means that people are in a state to give full consent. Someone who has just done several hours of mood-altering embodied practice (yoga or dance or breathwork, for example) may be vulnerable to sales techniques, as used unethically by some state-pumping facilitators. Children are not considered to have capacity, so parental agreement is also needed, though I would argue *both* parent(s) and child need to agree.

Calibration means we start gently and work up in small steps, re-contracting along the way, and only increasing intensity when competence and calm have been established at less intense levels. This ensures that whatever we are doing is not too intense or triggering. In teaching centring, for example, you should start with something like a tissue throw or a mildly stressful visualisation, not a grab or a shout, or thinking of an abuser. Note also that traumatised people may be more likely to 'jump in at the deep end' (calibrate badly), so care is needed.

These may all sound over-the-top but you do not know who has been badly violated in the past, and these things are best practice for all people anyway, as they maximise the safety and empowerment of embodied learning. Paul Linden, who works with abused kids, has been my mentor in these matters, and I have not only found them useful in violent environments like war zones, but also in more conventionally intense domains like business. Again, we also never know what the background of people is in our trainings, and while we may assume certain demographics are likely to have experienced poverty, racism, sexism or other things that may suggest greater care, we can never know for sure.

Ways to lead yourself!

Now we've established some essential background around this topic, let's look at some techniques!

ABC centring

ABC is a simple and efficient centring technique I developed, which works well for the majority of people. It is a 'dual' technique (meaning it can both up- and down-regulate) containing certain 'cheats', which means it is more likely to work for people than most single techniques, and I have used it for over ten years with many thousands of people. If you learn just one centring technique, this is a good one – though ultimately it's good to try several and see what works best for you.

Try the following with your eyes open:[14]

- **Aware:** be mindful of the present moment using the five senses, feeling the whole body, and especially where you touch the ground (or chair) and your breath
- **Balance:** bring balance to your posture and attention – balance your physical posture as best you can up and down, left and right, and front and back (rocking or swaying may help), and 'reach out' in all directions symmetrically (visualisation of a glowing light bulb may be useful)
- **Core relaxed:** relax your eyes and in between your eyes, relax your mouth and jaw, relax your stomach, relax your lower abdominals, then breathe deeply 'into' your belly[15]
- **Connected:** look for, or bring to mind, people you care about and who care for you, people that respect you; look for what you have in common with others present. You can also connect to your values with a simple gesture or image as a reminder

Two quick centring techniques – up-down and tense-relax

Here's a very quick centring tool adapted from Wendy Palmer:

1 Extend up the back, and relax down the front. Simple!
2 Tensing and relaxing the shoulders or the belly, and sighing (say 'ahh' audibly or silently) is another very simple and quick one.

I have included these three-second techniques to show how quickly and easily we can centre. Try them, you have three seconds from now!

Shake and settle

Some embodiment systems are wholly based on shaking, like David Berceli's Trauma Release system.[16] However, even a very quick and intuitive shake of a few seconds can rebalance people, energising those who are tired and relaxing those who are stressed (making this a 'dual' technique like ABC), or just shifting the mood. You can add a quick intuitive stretch to this (think cat not yogi) and some gentle tapping massage with a finger or a loose fist.

I use this technique a lot in training, often every 30 minutes in sitting or online training, to stop people falling asleep!

Feeling your feet

Because a lot of anxiety and stress generally has an upwards embodiment, simply feeling your feet on the ground can be settling. Becoming curious about what part of the foot exactly is touching the ground can help focus the attention, as can a visualisation like imagining the footprint you would make on sand. I like that this practice can be done any time by most people (those with no feet can feel whatever is lowest to the ground).

Categories of centring

How can 'centring' techniques be classified? Well, let's geek out a bit. Centring can have four goals, be social or not, have targets, and be grouped into three broad methods.

Centring techniques can be:

- Aimed at reducing arousal (down-regulation or hypo techniques), aimed at increasing arousal (up-regulation or hyper techniques), or both, depending on what is needed (dual techniques), or simply shift state without reference to arousal
- Done internally or interpersonally – 'intra' techniques vs. 'inter' / social / co-regulatory ones
- In response to aversion (fight-flight-freeze) or grasping (or contractive response to pleasure)
- Involve one or a combination of the following three basic methods:
  - Simple bodily centring
  - Inquiry centring
  - Values centring

To expand: centring techniques can be done on one's own, or utilising the fact that we are social animals and regulate by coordinating (more on this soon). They can be done to reduce the fight-flight response or grasping (in response to pain or pleasure). They can also involve 'simple' body-mind adjustments using the tools outlined in Chapter 1 (posture, breath, etc.), enquiries such as 'what would a little more ease be like',[17] or connecting to purpose and values, such as Richard Strozzi-Heckler's 'for the sake of what?' technique, where one asks just that. All of these methods are effective and have their place. ABC centring includes elements of all of these, which is why it can work for many kinds of people.

Expressive practices

Any practices that encourage people to 'follow the body' or 'listen to the body' develop not just self-awareness but also self-expressive qualities. This includes most of the conscious dance (aka 'free dance') world, including 5Rhythms, Open Floor and Movement Medicine, improv comedy and much theatre training. It is possible to practise yoga in this way but this is very rare in classes, which normally follow forms not feeling.

In more conventional settings, encouraging people to 'move however you feel like for a few seconds', or in more open-minded ones to 'make a noise and pull a face' or even 'make an animal noise', can develop these skills as well as 'scratching an itch' for more expressive people. This can also be regulating, as an embodied cycle is completed allowing for relaxation.

People who have, say, martial arts or typical yoga backgrounds, or who are controlling by culture or disposition, may need more of this type of practice!

How to develop self-leadership in yourself – practices

So far we have already introduced five simple techniques. You may find that one's enough but some like a bit of variety and different techniques work better for different people. To recap:

- ABC centring
- Up and down centring
- Shake and settle
- Tense-relax
- Feeling your feet

Here's a few more to play with. As ever with this book, trying them is key!

Owl eyes / ears

Peripheral vision is associated with relaxation and as ever with embodied practice, this link is bi-directional so encouraging it reduces fight-flight. Simply see how much width you can see without moving your eyes. For some, this can take practice.

Listening all around for the quietest noise you can hear also creates an expansive relaxed awareness for many.

Top – down letting go

This is really just a way of relaxing top to bottom, but with an emphasis on areas of typical tension.

Start by relaxing the muscles around the skull, then the eyes, then the tongue and jaw, then the throat, then the chest, then the belly, then the pelvic floor, then the back of the knees (unlocking them if needed), and lastly the feet.

Roots and wings

While many visualisations can be used to teach embodiment, shortcutting detailed technical instructions and skill, they don't work for everyone. That being said, I often use an image of having deep red roots, or perhaps a large purple Barney the dinosaur tail or a heavy jewels cloak to find more 'down and back' – a good antidote to anxiety.

When I am feeling 'down' – again notice the directionality of emotional language – I may visualise a helium balloon or golden thread (a tai chi classic) lifting me up, or my favourite: fluffy white angel wings!

What's true?

The truth will set you free by centring you. Ask yourself, 'what is most true right now?', and see what happens. Orientating to and speaking the truth are centring (which also means that noticing how centred you get stating something, is also a way of checking your own BS). This is a form of both enquiry and values centring.

How and when to practise centring

Centring is relatively easy to do, but you can become better and better at it with practice. Critically, it is also hard to remember to do under pressure unless you have practised it a lot too. There are several ways to go about this. First, you can develop regular centring 'rituals' linked to daily activities such as when you make tea or coffee, when you turn your computer on or off, when you go through a certain door, when you go to the bathroom, etc. This will create the necessary repetitions. In addition, it's wise to practise in a context where you can control a challenge to centre in response to, thus increasing your skill level. This might be a yoga class, a martial arts class or a cold shower. In all cases you can find the 'difficult but not impossible' sweet spot of maximum growth. Note, that waiting till you need to <u>apply</u> centring is not <u>practise</u>, your screaming kids or boss or whatever, are not a controllable, replicable non-consequential environment, which is what is required for learning and growth. To get better at centring you need repeated practise where you can scale intensity, without actually say losing your job! By all means apply centring in your life, but you need to practise to learn it.

Standing waiting practice

While we should not try to practise in situations that really matter, waiting in line, while strictly an application, is a good middle ground. Here we can feel the feet, relax the knees and belly, and notice any grasping or rushing tendency and reduce it.

How to develop self-leadership in clients – overview

The primary way in which you teach centring is through non-verbal state transmission, i.e. by being centred yourself, you pass this on. Your state becomes a 'crutch' of sorts as you help others regulate until they can self-regulate, as you teach them any techniques verbally.

Simply, you develop self-leadership by teaching others the techniques that you have been practising. Here are a few things to bear in mind when teaching people centring.

How to introduce centring

Often coaches I am teaching to work more with the body ask how best to introduce centring to a client, and some are quite nervous about this. There is no one way, but here are some general rules:[18]

- Be confident (practising it yourself and seeing the benefits helps!)
- Make it no big deal. If you present it as weird, it will be
- Connect it to what they already know, e.g. sports, yoga, whatever
- Link to how it will help them and what motivates the client – how will it help them?
- Share your own experience authentically
- Mention relevant science / neuroscience if the client is that way inclined – or hippie connections if that's their thing! More macho or sporting types may prefer the martial arts connection
- Have them try it and *prove* it for themselves (i.e. 'don't believe me')
- Have them link it to where in life they can use it afterwards

These principles apply to introducing embodied work more generally with clients too.

Top tips on teaching (centring or anything else!)

Here is a set of recommendations for teaching any embodied skills that apply perfectly to centring:

Aim: tell people what you will teach them and what they will *get* from the thing you are about to teach (or have them establish this)

- Hook – ask people if they would like to have the benefit of the skill you are about to teach, e.g. 'who would like to learn a quick and easy technique to manage stress?'
- Context and set – up – help people understand where the technique comes from and pre-empt objections. Using stories from your own life, sharing the evidence base, and relating to other things they know are prime techniques here

- Demonstrate with a volunteer
- Teach the basic method step by step using clear operational language[19] and ask if anyone needs clarification
- Give space for practice. Encourage practice not talk during this time
- Suggest a paired debrief using one specific learning question
- Group debrief[20]
- Catch (application) – ask people where they can apply the skill in their lives, offer space for a commitment to practise (raising hands perhaps) and ask how they will remember to do so

How to develop self-leadership in clients – practices

All the techniques covered in this chapter are safe for you to teach clients as long as you abide by the principles of consent, capacity and calibration. They have been selected for their simplicity, so you do not need to be an embodiment master to make them work. Some others are given below.

Exercise: Walking embodied awareness and choice

This is a simple practice of 'awareness and choice' that I often use near the start of workshops to give the idea of embodiment and get people moving in a low-key way.

Invite your client to walk naturally in the room, scanning their body slowly from feet to head, following their breath, and discovering: 'How am I right here and now?' (physical sensations, emotions and thoughts – comfortable and uncomfortable). Ask them to share their most concrete observations (what, where in the body and how) as a training into embodied awareness. Pause.

Now ask your client to resume their walk, this time asking themselves, 'How do I want to be?' and literally shaping their desired quality as a movement form, with its distinctive direction, rhythm, form and tone. Invite them to raise the intensity of their shape / movement by 50%, try out different patterns and find out which one resonates. Again, ask them to state where, what and how in their body this intention resides, and how they would describe it now.

AAI (awareness, acceptance and intention)

This is a simple technique we do many times a day on the Embodied Facilitator Course. First we ask clients to bring awareness to their state, say 'yes' to it (acceptance), and set an intention for a new one – just intention-setting is enough for a state shift to begin for most. Note the acceptance part is key, and there is the paradox that those rushing to change state without first accepting how they are will often shift less quickly.

More quick-wins

These are a handful of simple 'quick-win' centring techniques for teaching clients that require minimal skill.[21] Suggest clients:

- Notice their breath a few times a day and let it go if holding it
- Lean back onto their heels, or slow down their walk a little when rushing
- Widen their awareness to take in the whole room when wanting more confidence
- Go for a walk in a park when stuck for ideas
- Relax their bellies and let their jaw hang loose when stressed[22]
- Note what state they would like to be in. Suggest that they sit that way

One-to-one techniques

Main centring applications for coaches

There will be times when you wish to teach a client centring or have them centre in a learning / coaching session.[23] These include:

- At the start of a session to let go of any distractions or unhelpful stress
- At the start of a session to clarify the aim of the coaching
- When the coaching has 'got lost' / when the client is 'rambling' / 'going in circles'
- When you and the coachee find yourself arguing or at risk of this
- When an important decision is to be made
- At the end of a session to clarify and summarise key learning points
- Before ending the sessions, especially if going back to a stressful environment
- As part of 'homework'

There are many more of course, and don't forget to centre yourself as a coach before you start a session to get into a suitable state, during the session at any point you like, or after to 'let go' of the session before moving on.

Practising centring intelligently – a guide to the principles of centring

When working with a client you can just teach them centring on its own but often it's better to use something to simulate stress. The following 'algorithm' adapted from Paul Linden, also known as the 'centring principle', is a framework for any client:[24]

1. Apply a low-level stressor – a small version of the thing they're struggling with
2. Increase in small steps if no reaction occurs until you elicit a reaction (fight-flight or grasping)
3. Help your client identify the specifics of the reaction and frame it as their responsibility (e.g. 'what are you doing in your body?', not 'what happened?')

4 Apply a centring technique aimed at reducing the reaction, e.g. ABC
5 Help them notice the new reaction (which will be less if the centring is successful) – do not tell them
6 Alter centring approach if there is no reduction in the reaction
7 If the reaction is reduced successfully, you can – with consent – increase the stressor's strength gradually until a response occurs again and repeat from stage 3. Usually you'd move from less to more realistic as a 'simulation'
8 End with a level that is still manageable (finish on a win)
9 Set up a practice routine and reminder system to embed the technique in the client's life

Stressor progression

It's important when learning to centre or teaching it to others to use an intelligent, kind progression of intensity. What I mean by this is starting below the stress / eustress response threshold, then gradually progressing (with renewed consent with each step if leading someone else through it), until a noticeable but not overwhelming level of stimulation is reached. This is an example of calibration as previously discussed, and is a vital idea to take on board to learn and teach centring effectively. The point is not to get too far along any scale as possible right away, but to find the appropriate level to work at. You can also learn to notice subtler and subtler levels of arousal and manage them more completely. Naturally as people improve their centring skills and habituate to stimuli, however, a greater level of stress is needed, due to both habituation and increased centring skill, which is the point of it all. While you never know what will be more stressful for someone, a typical progression or stress scale I might use with a client would look something like the escalation scale below – note *the client* would choose to escalate not me, so they remain in control:

1 Tissue throwing at belly[25]
2 Tissue throwing at face (far enough back, so the throw does not to seem like a punch)
3 Tissue throwing at face accompanied by a quiet shout
4 Tissue throwing at face accompanied by a louder shout
5 Single-handed wrist grab (N.B. don't pull or push, so they can identify their reaction)
6 Two-handed wrist grab
7 Wrist grab from behind
8 Double shoulder grab from behind
9 Shoulder grab from behind accompanied by a shout
10 + various extreme measures suitable only for martial artists and military personnel it's best not to indulge here

I will then often move to more realistic triggers. For many clients, I work with verbal triggers such as giving or receiving feedback, setting boundaries, insults (though compliments are worse for some), making requests, etc. The key principle again is calibration. For example, say a client is upset by someone calling them a bad mother, I may start by stating this (with consent) very gently, once and not close up. If they can manage their response to this we could work up to being closer, more unpleasant content and in a more unpleasant tone. Content, repetition, volume, tone and proximity are all calibration factors. Simulations can also be used in place of triggering situations – for example, I once coached someone irritated by a micro-managing boss and simply standing behind the coachee looking over their shoulder as they worked was enough to trigger the pattern.

There are many alternatives for stressors to the ones cited – for example, I regularly start with an irritating visualisation such as the one at the beginning of this chapter. You can also use noises, video (YouTube is excellent for finding stressors), non-injurious pain, cold, water pistols, and so on. Safety and imagination are the only limits once you understand the deeper principle at work. This is a good example of how a flexible principle-based system of embodiment is superior to a 'cookie cutter' one.

One-to-one client case study

I once was hired by a HR department of a manufacturing company in a small town outside London to work with one of their managers who had an anger issue. Let's call her Loana. She was high performing in many regards but would sometimes 'fly off the handle', get very defensive and even shout at colleagues.

Over two hours we examined her psychology (perfectionist), self-talk (highly self-critical), cultural factors (she was Romanian), diet (she regularly skipped breakfast), sleep (minimal) and caffeine intake (high), and I gave her a centring technique to work with. Note that it is fairly typical for me to use embodiment combined with other approaches, several of which impact baseline arousal levels.

Seeing several cat-decorated items on her desk, it was clear Loana loved cats. I taught centring as a way to relax and framed it as 'cat mode' – more relaxed yet still 'predatory' (her word) and in control. 'I like cats as they are all queens and don't give a damn', she told me. I taught her centring using an online video of an irritating Romanian celebrity she had a mild dislike for, and then we moved to typical verbal triggers found in her office such as when colleagues were late in handing work to her, which we simulated.

While a fairly serious person, she clearly had a soft spot for cats so this worked great, and in two follow-up phone calls she reported that it was extremely helpful. No more anger incidents were reported by colleagues to HR.

Individual adaptation

Intermediate to advanced centring with clients involves helping them identify exactly what they do in this body (this active frame of 'doing' helps them take responsibility) and creating an individual technique to suit the client's exact response and other cultural or personal factors (like the cat thing).

The most common mistakes students make when teaching centring

Having now taught hundreds of facilitators to teach centring in-depth and thousands briefly, I've identified a pattern in the mistakes they make and have even made these into a light-hearted points system game on EFC. They are:

- Not centring themselves while teaching it!
- Starting too intensely (no calibration)
- Not supporting full consent
- Standing too close when tissue throwing
- Getting startled themselves when grabbing or shouting
- Telling their clients what they did rather than letting them notice for themselves
- Not relating the centring back to the client's real life or when setting up a practice routine

Group techniques

Teaching centring to groups is very similar to teaching individuals except it is not as easy to monitor individual differences and adapt to these.

Centring has wide applications to many types of group classes. Here are some courses you may teach centring on as a trainer:[26]

- Anger management
- Communication skills
- Conflict management
- Leadership
- Managing 'difficult' behaviour
- Presentation skills
- Resilience
- Risk evaluation
- Stress management
- Time management
- Team-building
- Almost all courses in fact, as it improves anything!

Other group state-shifting techniques include:

Tone and gesture

As a trainer I am very aware how my own tone and gestures impact a group. Authority, for example, can be better gained with palms down and tone of voice depending on patterns. Fun enlivening the opposite, and tonal variation with varied pauses will also keep people awake. Again, deeper than tricks though, one's own embodiment is what is being transmitted.

Shaking

A simple thing I often get groups to do is to stand up from sitting and give themselves a shake. Sometimes I add stretching and tapping to this. This is a great wake up and 'reset' button!

Music

There are some real pros and cons to using music. From an embodied perspective music is 'packaged mood', altering people's embodiment strongly – which is why we like it as a species! It's like ear drugs! Music can be used skilfully to up- and down-regulate groups, and shift them into many embodiments. On EFC we are very careful about the music used even in breaks, and the DJ on the team will always ask the next trainer, 'How do you want them?', meaning what embodied influence should he aim for with the music? Music also creates another shared embodied context meaning groups bond with it, as it shifts them closer together in embodiment to become a more coherent group.

While powerful, a downside of using music is that people are influenced by it irrespective of whether the shift is useful for them now; nor do they learn to make the shift themselves, which ultimately is the useful life skill. That being said, if an embodiment is outside of someone's normal range – let's say they're not good at getting angry or sad – then music can support them to go there until they have learnt to do that for themselves.

There are whole systems of embodiment which work with music, including most of the conscious dance forms for those of you that would explore this further.

Group coordination practices

One aspect of social centring that can't be done by an individual is group coordination. Because we are social animals people often enjoy group movements as a way to feel a sense of belonging that is co-regulating. Most cultures have group movement rituals or singing / chanting practices that coordinate the breathing too. While a traditional Maori haka[27] isn't necessarily appropriate for a corporate team building, just having people make some simple movements together can be very helpful for building group cohesion and alignment, as can a few aligned breaths at the start of a meeting. We tend to 'get in sync' with people when moving or breathing with them due to a phenomenon known as coherence.

On sideways state shifting

Most of the techniques described so far are about up- and down-regulation, or fight-flight and calming, because this covers many useful techniques and is a good place to start. However, some are not about activation level but about something else, which we could call 'sideways' state shifting. While creativity and confidence, say, are linked to arousal and relaxation, this is not the only factor. The 4-elements system we have introduced contains a hierarchy of arousal (earth to water to fire to air in terms of speed) but is more than this – it also provides a simple map of structure (opposite order), mood and directionality.

Dylan Newcomb is an excellent embodiment teacher whom I recommend for more complex work in states, and his 'Uzazu' system goes into great detail on this topic, which is beyond the scope of this book. One technique I have briefly mentioned so far is enquiry centring, which can also be used for sideways states – for example, 'what would a little more spaciousness be like?' – as can walking with awareness and choice.

Capacity, challenge, support

Centring is a soothing technique but often involves providing challenges to practise with. This raises an important issue about balance with embodied facilitation – capacity, challenge and support. It is the role of a good facilitator to both challenge and support people. Too little challenge and people will be bored and not learn; too much with insufficient support and they will be overwhelmed and not learn (as well as be brutalised!). Individuals and groups can only be challenged if they have sufficient capacity. This is dictated by their life circumstances, health, mood, etc., as well as the degree of support offered by the coach or training team – sometimes called 'the container'. Note that individuals and cultures vary widely in how much they habitually will challenge and support and this might mismatch the actual capacity of an individual or group. This is another fire / water or yang / yin embodiment factor in facilitation.

> **Reflection**
> What is your habitual tendency as a coach? Do you tend to be a 'kick arse' challenger or a nurturing supporter? How might this be both a strength and a liability as you teach centring and embodiment more generally?

> **Group client case study**
> I was once asked to work with a group of consultants who had very low team trust for various complicated reasons, to increase their group cohesion and confidence in each other. We worked on centring to help them communicate more

> skilfully, and discuss tricky topics without adopting a reactive mode, and also did some simple group movements they described as 'tai chi like' to sync as a group, alongside more traditional team-building work on values, as well as some fun activities. I also had pairs of consultants from the two main groups who had been merged have meetings while walking, as this helps 'unstick' issues and people naturally align steps when walking, which helps them connect.[28]
>
> While fairly resistant at first, they liked my 'don't believe a word I say, try it out for ten minutes and see if it helps' approach and all agreed that while 'a bit weird', embodied methods were 'constructive'.

Virtual considerations

Centring works perfectly well online although some triggers need to be adapted, but you can even throw a Kleenex at someone on camera and they will flinch!

Group embodied coordination exercises are especially helpful for online meetings because of participants' different environments (and perhaps time zones), and thus different embedded contexts, meaning connection is less easy. Other factors, such as altered eye contact, participants treating the screen like a portal to passive entertainment, and the absence of some 'channels' of embodied trust-building (e.g. touch), mean an increased emphasis on connection is necessary online. That said, I have been pleasantly surprised by what is possible with online embodiment conferencing.

Cultural considerations

Some cultures emphasise regulation more than others, and some emphasise expression more – interestingly, there appears to be some correlation with how warm the weather is! While large individual and sub-cultural variations do exist, Germans are not Greeks. Trauma differences I've mentioned already.

PART 2: SELF-LEADERSHIP – TRAIT

We are what we repeatedly do. Excellence then, is not an act, but a habit.
– Aristotle

The battle of Waterloo was won on the playing fields of Eton.[29]
– Charles de Montalembert

> *Reflection questions*
> Is your character fixed and permanent, or have you been able to influence it for the better in your life? If so, how have you developed yourself

over time? If you have a regular embodied practice already like yoga or karate, has it changed you as a person? How do you try and shape the character of others?

Exercise: Practice 'interviews'

Find ten people who have a regular embodied practice and ask them how it's changed them. See if they have a sense of what helped and what hindered them to use their art as a character-building practice. Be aware there's a selection bias in who picks what practice, but what they say will still be revealing.

My story – what aikido gave me . . . and what it didn't

Like most people I first picked a practice through a mix of neuroticism and grace. I was drawn to aikido both because it held the earthy discipline and sensitive listening I did not have at the time, and enough martial arts fieriness to appeal to me!

The lining up in rows, strict etiquette, uniforms and very exact forms sure did not come naturally to me, but boy did it help me! Being around older, more conservative people was also a positive influence on me – after all, it's community that really makes a practice impactful. It's hard to know how aikido has changed me over the years as I've done so much other stuff as well, but people do now comment regularly on my discipline, despite that fact that from the inside things are still pretty chaotic! I certainly believe the structure of aikido rubbed off on me and first helped me get through university, then get sober and run a business. There is also no doubt I have built a capacity for grit and determination through hard practice that now serves me across my life. I am actually of the belief that all people (especially young men) should engage in unreasonably hard training at least for a time.

What was also obvious to me as I did more and more aikido is that people's characters showed through in how they approached it. Two students could have the same teacher but develop two very different ways of doing aikido. Character leads, as well as is developed by, an art. This can be a blessing, but I also saw people becoming lop-sided caricatures of themselves, pushing a trait further and further for ever reducing gains in the other parts of their lives. I fell into this trap by getting more and more warrior-like for a while until I just appeared aggressive to most people, especially in the UK (culture matters as ever).

What I did not learn so easily from aikido were the listening and sensitivity. While aikido translated into an ability to read others (see the second part of Chapter 5), it did not make me a great listener and I had to introduce supplementary practices to get to even an average level of this, despite developing a very sensitive style of aikido. My 'airy' creative side also re-emerged in aikido (where it is usually not welcome!) and I developed a very creative playful freestyle practice.

In time I also came to realise that aikido does not develop everything, and while varying styles and teachers could offset this to some degree,[30] I realised that either cross-training or switching arts would be beneficial. To slow down, I did a year of Feldenkrais; to explore passion and sexuality, I learnt to dance tango; to fully explore my fire, I did cage-fighting for a year; to develop greater subtly of feeling, I embraced meditation; to go deeper into my playful side, I did improv; to explore expression, I took up 5Rhythms dance and to make it all relational, I got into NonViolent Communication. These days I do Systema (a Russian martial art) as a workhorse for many of the elements I've explored, and because it suits both my age and some practicalities, and yoga because I can travel with it far easier than other arts. Now, I don't expect non-obsessed coaches to explore as much breadth and depth as I have, but I hope this helps you make a wiser decisions as to your own personal practice.

Facilitator case study: Reframing a depth junkie

Developing my own range as a coach and trainer and being able to offer range for different profiles are the biggest contributions of embodied work to my practice. I was good at reaching certain people in certain contexts (as Mark would say, I was somewhat of a 'depth junkie'). I still focus on the niche of deep transformational leadership work, yet feel more equipped and confident in offering embodied practices in new settings such as high-tech companies, non-profits and to healthcare professionals, all of whom need a different style. Offering practical and safe techniques helped me to overcome my own judgements and limitations about where and how embodied learning can be offered. When you simply stand or walk differently, you feel and think differently. Simple and direct experience. Easy for almost everyone to engage safely. Helping others to see this possibility is a major gift at any stage of change and learning. And it is indeed possible!

– Özlem Lale Kaleli, facilitator and therapist, Izmir, Turkey

Promise

By the end of this section you will know how you can develop yourself through embodied practice, and coach others to as well.

What is the skill-set and how does it help facilitation?

We become what we practise. This simple truth is at the heart of what embodiment is, and how embodied education works. All of us are unconsciously embodied to have a set of habits that are our default, especially when tired or under pressure. By consciously practising something else, we can, over time, change this. Why this is so helpful to facilitators is this default leans in a particular direction that may or may not be skilful, and is also communicated to people we work with – messages that may or may not be helpful. It colours our thinking and perfection, and limits what we are capable of. By stepping into agency around this, we can be our own authors and become vastly more impactful as facilitators. It is also how long-term change happens, if we are interested in supporting this with others! People go on courses and it all sounds great but they slip back into old habits unless a new embodiment is built over time. Without long-term embodied transformation, people's defaults undo any learning – hence: 'knowledge is only a rumour until it lives in the muscle'.[31]

Relationship to other skill-sets

We must of course be aware of long-term patterns (second part of Chapter 3) to change them. It is better to change traits through practise than just states, because we don't have to maintain awareness and expend effort with traits, and they are more lasting. States will come and go, but when they are practised enough can become traits. The longer-term traits you develop have an impact of course on listening and influencing (see Chapters 5 and 6).

How to develop your own embodied patterns – overview

Practice – see below.

Practice

You know intellectual learning alone doesn't cut it. Imagine if I claimed to be a great lover because I'd read many romantic novels. Or suggested you'd be safe to ride in my car because I'd been told a lot about driving. Websites and apps don't help much either – Wikipedia has not solved the world's problems. Learning about France is not the same as learning French, let alone knowing what the quality of light is like in Paris as you drink your first coffee of the day in a pavement cafe. The reason that there's a field of embodiment in the first place is that we have forgotten some really very obvious truths about what constitutes learning.

The bad news is obvious, but it's really good news not to be bulls***ted for a change – after all the motivational talks, endless advice and shelves of positive thinking books, what we really need is practise.[32] It's how we've gotten good at anything, which we all know course. Our embodiment is what we unconsciously practise, and can become what we consciously practise. Simple. Let's stop kidding ourselves and get on with it.

The what, how, when, where, why and with whom of embodied practice

To practise effectively, it is necessary to consider the 'what', 'how', 'when', 'where', 'why' and 'with whom' of any yoga asana, dance form, martial art or whatever.[33] All of these factors can support or undermine a practice. They are always present and always impactful.

The form of a practice could be described as the 'what' – for example, the asana (poses) of yoga, the kata (movement patterns) of a martial art, or the steps of a dance. The 'what' is a framework for exploring oneself. Critically, though, 'how' they are done is the real essence of embodied work (and is actually a simple definition of embodiment). If you do a linear pose in a circular way, a loving meditation in a hateful way, a fierce move in a timid way, it utterly changes the impact. *The manner matters*. The manner maketh the man/woman... through embodiment.

The postures will be quite different when done at different times of the day, times of the year and in different environments, i.e. the 'when' and the 'where'. The same pose during morning or evening, or mid-summer or mid-winter, is not actually the same pose. Similarly, a pose done on a mountain top, in a forest, in a cathedral, or in a modern office, is again not the same pose. This is easy to miss, if you only practise in a controlled environment like a studio, which, while seemingly neutral, is not. Nowhere is.

The 'why' of a practice also matters. What is motivating a practice? What is it in service to? An asana 'performed' with purpose is not the same as one built as a performance. This is a subtle difference, but significant.

Lastly, there is always a social context to any practice. 'With whom' you are doing a practice (actual or imagined) will strongly impact it. A specific relationship (such as that with the teacher), the presence of a friend or lover, or whether you feel like you belong to a group, all will have an impact.

Take all these into account to gain maximum benefit from your practice.

Criteria for effective practise of any embodied art

What is and isn't 'practise'?[34] People argue about this but I can say with some confidence what works when it comes to practice. Practice is:

- Dedicated to transformation (the sole purpose of the activity is to develop yourself)
- Controlled / simplified (by controlling variables – e.g. time, intensity – and simplifying conditions, you can maximise learning safely)

- Ritualised (this helps create a 'container')
- Social / in community
- Reflective (time is made to assimilate and reflect – again to maximise learning)
- Recurrent (you need to keep doing it!)

We can then apply the skills of a practice in daily life (e.g. being mindful during the day, as opposed to in a formal sitting) – but do not try and replace dedicated practice with ad hoc application.

> **Reflection: Mapping your own embodied practices**
>
> What embodied practices, if any, do you engage in now that meet or mostly meet the criteria above? Perhaps you do yoga or dance. Perhaps you have a physical practice that could be turned into an embodied one. Perhaps you have an embodied one that could be optimised using the criteria above.
>
> What are your practices building? Are there gaps in your practices in terms of the map of embodied intelligence (skill-sets) or the 4-elements map (qualities), or the different tools (ways of working with embodiment)? Have you perhaps over-developed one side of yourself at the expense of others? Are you simply doing what is comfortable, compensating for other aspects of your life,[35] or perhaps going too much against the grain? Does this book inspire you to 'change course' or add practices? What life would be possible if you were to use some practice to develop yourself?

Establishing your own embodied practices after reading this book

Whatever else you do after reading this book, please either get a practice or firm one up that you have. If you are not willing to do this, please stop reading immediately, and use these pages as toilet paper. If you are willing, read on – for exactly how to develop one will become clearer as you progress.

Tips for choosing and maintaining a practice

Helping students pick and maintain suitable practices to develop their embodiment is quite a big part of what I do.[36] In a world of choice, this is key. Here are my top tips:

- What embodied capacity are you actually trying to develop? Everything else stems from this, so be clear about this
- No single practice covers all the bases. Pick your focus based upon your need, your opportunities and your desire

- Check out the teacher's ethics. Never work with an abusive teacher but accept that none will be perfect either. If you can't see human flaws, or they aren't admitted, *run!*
- The best practice is the one you can practically do. Things like class schedule and the studio's distance from your house matter
- Fall in love with your practice. Commit to it for a minimum period of, say, 3–6 months
- Pleasure is your friend. If it's always hard (after an initial post – honeymoon period), it's the wrong one
- Little and often over time is better than a lot and then nothing
- Be careful not to follow comfort alone, which will just reinforce your patterns and neuroses. If it's always easy, it's the wrong practice. Listen to your body for that deep, intuitive 'hell, yes', which isn't the same as ease
- How you do the practice matters at least as much as what it is
- Who you do it with also matters tremendously; community, practice, culture and friendships can help or hinder
- How the practice integrates into your life, work and primary relationships is what matters. Most practices are bad for this integration, so you may need to add more reflection, 'bridging practices', micro hits in life, etc.

Getting a practice 'off the mat'

My list of criteria for effective practice of any embodied art includes creating a good 'container' for a dedicated practice (p. 120).[37] This is vital. However, it's also useless unless such practice transfers into daily life. To put it bluntly, what's the point of having a great aikido throw or yoga pose if you're a useless arsehole?

Here's a list of which factors lead to maximum learning transfer to daily life:

1. Form: practise a basic posture or movement
2. Feel: establish mindfulness
3. Check: ask yourself whether it's familiar or longed for (shows habits and growth potential)
4. Notice: note deviation from the 'correct' form or method. You can also exaggerate 'mistakes' and use contrast (this also shows habits)
5. Enquire: link to life – ask yourself if more or less of this quality is needed in your life (or areas of your life)
6. Explore: ask what variation of this is needed (e.g. more peaceful or severe)
7. Integrate: discussion with and feedback from others are helpful
8. Establish: practise micro poses, subtle variations of something you've been developing that you can do without looking 'weird', to apply in daily life

Note: This is just a guide and exact questions may vary. Creativity and variations are encouraged.

Facilitator case study: Feldenkrais subtlety

Through Feldenkrais – a very slow and careful moving mindfulness practice – I am becoming more observant as I am aware of more subtleties in the way I carry myself and this influences how I perceive other people and their embodiment. It has slowed me down from rushing as a coach and also given me a grace that I wasn't expecting.

– Jon, trainer, Chicago, USA

Facilitator case study: The coach who was too nice

I've always been too damn nice! Since I was little girl I've tried to please people and not upset them, seeing myself as responsible for others' feelings. I've done work on this through years of therapy, and meditation, and this helped to some extent, but it was still holding me back as a coach. I was very empathic as a coach but couldn't be direct and was terrible with the financial side as I had a tendency to give my work away. With this in mind after identifying I had far too much water in the 4-elements model, I looked for an earth and fire practice. It was scary at first but I first tried karate. I found a nice club with a considerate teacher and gave it a go. I cried a few times at first and didn't like the shouting, but within a fairly short space of time started loving it! I also started doing 'no pose' and warrior pose from Embodied Yoga, which I like as they are quick and powerful, and sometimes some power walking with direction, pushing from the back foot. After doing these for a few months I started to notice a difference – at first occasionally and then more and more.

These days I sometimes shock myself with my better boundaries and more goal orientation. I'm still watery most of the time, but I have way more range now. I've seen that in coaching I can challenge when I need to, help clients stay on focus firmly if needed, and can ask for a fair price and charge when people miss sessions (two problems before). I can be tough and kind – great – as it was always my fear that I'd stop being a decent person if I 'toughened' up. Actually I now see that it is kinder to show some tough love sometimes! While I took up karate to become a better coach it's also shown up in other areas and I think my relationship is much healthier now that I can ask for what I want too.

I don't think I'll ever be a karate expert, though I do have my orange belt now!!! But doing it consciously for a couple of years . . . not that often . . . but very consciously when I do, it has definitely changed my coaching, and my life.

– Maria, EFC graduate coach, Norfolk, UK

How to develop clients' embodiment with long-term practice – overview

I have helped hundreds if not thousands of people develop an embodiment practice and while this is quite an individual thing, I've developed a basic method.

- First clarify what is the embodiment they want to build
- Next understand why they want to develop a practice, and increase their motivation by imaging two futures – one with the change and one without it
- Learn about the practical factors of their lives, such as time and location. These can undermine any practice
- Offer some options that will build the desired capacity and see if any appeal or they have some connections to them already. A practice that builds a new capacity will likely hold some trepidation for them, but if it is too scary – for example, suggesting improv comedy to someone who is uptight, or cage-fighting to someone who is very timid – then it will be rejected. Often a positive association like a friend who did it will be a good opening
- Ask them to make a commitment to a set number of sessions a week. How many will depend on the practice. Ideally four days a week is great (more days on than off) but for many activities and people this is unrealistic. One class a week is not enough whatever. Little and often is better than one big block if there is a choice. The commitment should also be for a minimum of 2–3 months, as this is what is necessary for habit formation[38]
- Encourage engagement with relative communities of practice (e.g. meditation groups, even if they could meditate alone)
- Provide a framework for accountability and adjustment of the original idea

How to develop clients' embodiment with long-term practice – practices

Here are three kinds of practices that you may want to help clients develop:

1 *Dedicated practices* are embodied arts such as yoga, conscious dance and martial arts. There is a wide range of them and the critical factors are what qualities they build (see elements table in Appendix 2 for some ideas) and which skill-sets are involved.
2 Many clients may not have the time to commit to dedicated practices, so you may have to design a *micro-practice* that they can do for just a few minutes a day.
3 You can also make *linked practices* by connecting an embodied practice to something the client already does, whether that be a sporting activity or a daily chore.

Further techniques

Embodied Yoga Principles

The Embodied Yoga Principles system mentioned in Chapter 3 can also be used to grow an embodiment. Each pose can be done for just one minute a day and it will have an impact, if done with full focus.

In Chapter 3 I mentioned the taking up space pose (great for confidence), entering pose (for people who need to 'get tight to it'), no pose (for boundaries), yes pose (or being more open), self-care pose and enthusiasm pose (for passion). All these can be used as client 'homework' practices. If you know yoga, you could also use a classical 'warrior 2' for focus, a forward bend for letting go, child's pose for surrender, and plank as an alternative to no pose.

The 'Yoga for Your Whole Life' channel on YouTube shows these poses and many more videos and there is an online teacher training for the serious yogis.

> **One-to-one client case study – domestic violence**
>
> *One of the most touching examples of the power of embodiment came to me in an email a week after an open workshop. At the workshop, a British woman in her thirties had started crying during no-pose practice and was clearly finding it difficult. The staff team supported her at the time and while she did not disclose her story, it was clear there was history there. We helped her get the hang of it fairly quickly though and she beamed with happiness.*
>
> *A week later an email arrived thanking us profusely, saying she had been in a violent relationship for some years but could not leave. She said this simple pose and a few days of practising it gave her the embodiment she needed to leave her abusive husband. I reflected afterwards, that sometimes you just don't know as a trainer how the work helps people.*

Group techniques

People can be encouraged to develop embodied practices as a group as long as:

- You have established what embodiment is theoretically
- They have some sense of their pattern through experiencing a range of possibilities (e.g. by the copying and 4-elements exercises described), and supported via feedback
- They have *experienced* that difference is possible (both exercises from Chapter 3 mentioned will also do that)
- You have offered a number of practices to suit different types, suited to their availability time-wise, athleticism, culture, etc.

Group client case study

A while back I worked with a local government group that complained about unproductive time meetings and low-level conflict, all pretty common in the UK public sector. The group wanted something very pragmatic right away so we worked with their meeting protocols. We established 'the pause' (centring renamed) at the start of meetings, followed by a three-word check-in, followed by three breaths in unison to coordinate. We established a new norm of not interrupting with an embodied practice of touching one's back to the chair if you felt like doing so, as interrupting has a forward embodiment, a new norm that anyone could call a 30-second centring break if things got heated, and to always end meetings with specific requests (this was a linguistic piece I taught them) and lastly appreciations.

At first this felt artificial but I chaired a fake meeting for them, then a real one but something low key (not the calibration), then a more heated one. I trained three managers to take it in turns to facilitate meetings going forward. I am told that while at first these facilitators would read somewhat stiffly from a piece of paper, eventually the practices became a culture, everyone in the department could lead a meeting within two months, and people new to the group just accepted them as the norm, quite simply 'how things are done around here'. Over time these techniques shifted the culture, and meetings essentially became practice places for good habits, and for supporting the new culture of emotional intelligence, calm and respect.

I have found that systems and culture change are what are really needed in organisations to help them change, and unless training can get these to happen, it is largely a waste of time. Note in this example we didn't just shift leaders – though culture change won't happen without that – we shifted a system and the structure of their meetings and reinforced this until it became the culture. Then culture does the heavy lifting and just needs maintenance.

Cultural considerations

The idea of practice as a way to grow character is embedded in some cultures more than others. In some countries like Japan, the idea is totally commonsensical, while others are more fatalistic and the notion of developing oneself is foreign. This is worth bearing in mind.

Principles used in this chapter

Centring principle – described in detail previously
Practice principle – the idea that what we practise we become

> **Final reflection**
>
> Think of someone you admire. Are you a different species from them, or did they merely practise something you have yet to do? What more is possible for you?

Notes

1. There are many definitions of 'leadership'. Mine begins at home as 'someone who can change themselves to influence others'.
2. Also spelt 'centering' in the USA.
3. From Paul Linden, *Embodied Peacemaking* (Columbus, OH: CCMS Publications, 2007).
4. This section was adapted from a piece by Anouk Brack from my e-book, *Centring: Why Mindfulness Alone Isn't Enough* (2017). See https://embodiedfacilitator.com/wp-content/uploads/2017/11/Centring-Mark-Walsh-ebook-v2.pdf
5. Claimed by some to be more common in women.
6. Master trauma trainer Babette Rothschild has influenced me here, herself drawing on Porges and Levine. Note also that this is not the same as Hanna Somatics' traffic light model.
7. 'Trigger' is now used widely in a loose way, but has a more rigorous meaning in trauma psychology.
8. See the work of Gabor Maté for more on this.
9. For example, there are estimates that 1 in 4 women and 1 in 6 men have been abused, and 80 per cent of people in the UK have a lifetime probability of experiencing at least one traumatic incident.
10. Julia Vaughan Smith, *Coaching and Trauma* (London: Open University Press, 2019).
11. Steve Haines, *Trauma Is Really Strange* (London: Singing Dragon, 2015).
12. Babette Rothschild, *8 Keys to Safe Trauma Recovery* (New York: W.W. Norton, 2010).
13. This is a pretty good definition of what trauma symptoms are – a chronic state of fight-flight-freeze.
14. I usually suggest practising techniques with eyes open, as this makes them more applicable to life, though if this feels too challenging, they can be done with eyes closed at first.
15. It's common for embodiment teachers to say breathe 'into' a body part – this just means moving that part or moving what can move towards that part while visualising. Obviously you can only breathe into your lungs literally, but it's a convenient shorthand for saying all that! Sadly some teachers have lost track that it is just a shorthand, so may have some odd beliefs. This is a good example of how inaccuracy and jargon can lead to odd superstitions!
16. https://traumaprevention.com
17. Wendy Palmer first introduced me to this approach.
18. From by e-book, *Centring: Why Mindfulness Alone Isn't Enough*.
19. This concept from Paul Linden means to provide instructions on method not outcome or metaphor. *Most* embodiment and movement teachers do not do this well, and my students joke that I ruin 90 per cent of dance and yoga classes for them by teaching this.

20 Note that paired and group debriefs have their own advantages, so it's best to do both.
21 Taken from my first book, *Embodiment: Moving Beyond Mindfulness* (Unicorn Slayer Press, 2019).
22 A Paul Linden classic.
23 From by e-book, *Centring: Why Mindfulness Alone Isn't Enough*.
24 Ibid.
25 This is a very safe place to start as few people have been traumatised by a Kleenex! N.B. 'tissue' is British English for a 'Kleenex' if you're American.
26 From by e-book, *Centring: Why Mindfulness Alone Isn't Enough*.
27 The ceremonial 'war dance' you may have seen at the start of New Zealand Rugby Union matches.
28 Another example of what could be called somatic coherence. When walking, almost all friends and family members will be *perfectly* in step.
29 Meaning it was the character building of school sports – at the time sports were viewed more in this light – that was responsible for the quality of the British officers fighting Napoleon's armies. Charles de Montalembert, *De l'Avenir Politique de l'Angleterre* (Paris: Didier & Co., Libraires-Éditeurs, 1856).
30 Note that because aikido is the 'home' art of several senior embodiment teachers, some of whom have trained in a very particular 'West Coast' style, many embodiment students seem to feel they should adopt it. This is not necessarily wise.
31 From the Asaro tribe of Indonesia and Papua New Guinea, popularised by Richard Strozzi-Heckler.
32 Ginny Whitelaw, Shinzen Young and Richard Strozzi-Heckler are all excellent on practice.
33 From my first book, *Embodiment: Moving Beyond Mindfulness*.
34 Ibid.
35 Practices can be enabling rather than transformational if they fulfil the function of balancing your life rather than influencing it – for example, someone who rushes most of the day but does tai chi to cope with this. Practices can also compensate for other aspects of people's lives not motivating them to change, e.g. the sensei who has no power at work but absolute authority in the dojo.
36 From my first book, *Embodiment: Moving Beyond Mindfulness*.
37 Adapted from *Embodied Yoga Principles: Teacher Training Notes*, 2020.
38 Often 60 days is cited as an appropriate amount of time to commit, however this would be daily practice. In addiction recovery, 90 days is standard for rehab, but this is an extreme example.

5 Social awareness

PART 1: SOCIAL AWARENESS – STATE

> ***Opening exercise: Just sitting with***
> Sit in front of someone. Preferably another human being also doing the exercise with you, but it can be someone on a screen, or a picture even. Start by quickly scanning your own body and getting a sense of how you are. Next bring all your attention to them for several minutes. Every minute briefly check-in with your own body and see what changes. Perhaps your mood is shifting or your activation level is going up. It may be subtle or not.

Promise

If you practise the exercises in this chapter you will have the skills to increase your empathy and sensitivity to people you work with, and get better results as a consequence.

> ***Opening reflection questions***
> How good a listener are you? Do people say this about you? Do you sometimes feel more than you'd like from others or maybe you tend to annoy people by interrupting? Can you 'taste' other people just by looking at them? Do you have to be careful who you're around as it can really impact your mood, or does it not matter?
>
> Do you also have an accurate sense of how tired and engaged a group is that you're working with? Do you know who's not paying attention in a training room even if they're hiding it? How would being twice as sensitive to others' states as you are now impact your facilitating?
>
> Legendary dance choreographer Martha Graham said, 'The body never lies', and 'the body says what words cannot'. Do you agree? When might the body lie?

Facilitator case study: My story – becoming a 'good enough' listener

I've never been a great listener! But now I'm 'good enough', especially when given a nudge to be! I'm proud to say that I can now be average at this vital life skill!

Maybe due to my personality, maybe trauma-enhanced ADHD, I was never a great listener growing up. I went on some NonViolent Communication courses in my early twenties which helped, but it sure didn't come naturally. Learning centring was a major boost for me, however, as it meant I could regulate myself to have a little more patience. Becoming more body-aware generally over the years, and practising a lot of partner arts like aikido and tango, also meant that empathy grew naturally for me as a skill.

Often my life is very fast-paced, running a business and doing too many projects, but at least I have the capacity to pause and interrupt this, then tune into my own response to someone to enhance connection with them. Aside from work benefits – a lot of clients really just want to be heard by someone, and this certainly guides skilful coaching – it's likely also saved my marriage a few times! If I can learn this stuff . . . anyone can.

Facilitator case study: Highly empathic challenges

Listening is something that has always come naturally from my earliest memories, but not initially in a very healthy or self-regulated way – it used to make me very sick actually. I only learnt to be self-managed with it through formal trainings. And only after much practice and lots of struggle. Training as an actor and then training to work hands – on with the body gave me the tools to work with it.

When I am working with a client, I often get a response in my body that I have learnt is not mine, that I can speak to – if it feels appropriate – name and work with. Or work with non-verbally if it feels like talking isn't necessary. I get physical maps or imprints of emotion, tension from injury or some other stressors, and they all can manifest in my body. The main ways I can access this is through looking (the visual field), and feeling (touch). As it happens to me automatically (it is a synesthesia), I often need to disengage it for my own health. I do this by turning my gaze away and taking myself out of people's 'sphere'. Sometimes I need to be completely separate to everybody for extended periods to manage this phenomenon.

Since doing Feldenkrais training I find I can pull up internal maps of skeletal relationships and other internal maps – fascial, muscular, etc. This is hard to describe but I can 'see / feel' them in my own body, and it is activated through touch. Over the years I've learnt to keep my sensitivity but manage to look after myself. It's both a 'superpower' and something to manage.

– Rachel Blackman, corporate trainer, embodiment teacher and bodyworker

What is the skill-set and how does it help facilitation?

Awareness of others has two main aspects or 'channels':

- empathic resonance
- skilful observation

We can become aware of the embodiments of others through empathic bodily resonance (a kind of 'tasting' via micro mimicking), and also through a more visual and cognitive process of noticing and analysing. I call the combination of those two skill-sets 'social awareness'. In an embodied context 'listening' means both feeling an 'echo' of another's body, and also being able to observe another's body and make accurate guesses about them.

More complexly one could be observing breath, posture, movement, etc. (all the 9 tools), and have different skill with each. You can also listen differently by activating different aspects of your own embodiments, which can be thought of as another aspect of this skill-set.

Being able to 'listen' effectively to others is a major aspect of effective facilitation, as it gives us both information and connection, and it guides our actions! Without this skill-set anything you do will be a shot in the dark. Relationship is only possible through this skill-set and the quality of relationship is what matters most in embodied facilitation.

Relationship to other skill-sets

Empathy and clear observation are built on being aware of and managing one's own state. Resonance with others can be mutually regulating in and of itself, as we are social animals (this is known as co-regulation), or dysregulating – think of two angry people working each other up. Nervous systems impact each other in any event, and I often think about embodiments as 'infections', in that you can easily 'catch' them if not working not to.

Empathy does not mean drowning in the states and emotions of others, but does mean touching or 'tasting' them. Empathy is a bodily resonance, and we are literally wired for this.[1] If someone has a sensitive response to others and cannot manage this (see Rachel's story), this is as unhelpful as having little empathy, and sensitivity is only useful if there's enough self-leadership to match it. Equally the better regulated someone is, the more they can pick up on, as they effectively become more sensitive measuring 'devices'. Think of this metaphor: your own embodiment is a lake, and others' states range from pebbles to large boulders being thrown into the water depending on their intensity. If the lake is still, the smaller pebbles will be apparent (meaning we pick up more), and if the large rocks do not make the water choppier, then we can sail on (meaning we are less easily dysregulated by others, even when they have intense emotions).

Social awareness is about being tuned into the states of others, which is necessary to lead them. How can one effectively influence a person or group, if you don't know where they are at? Without social awareness we are leading blind, and people will not be led by anyone not resonating with them.

How to develop social awareness in yourself – overview

There are really only two things you need to do to practise social awareness in yourself: to regulate your own state, for the reasons given above, and practise! Like any skill-set, it can be enhanced in this way.

How to develop social awareness in yourself – practices

Basic embodied listening

All that embodied listening means is to put your attention on someone as a meditation, and also track your own body as you do so. A basic practice would be to find a partner, centre, give most of your awareness to the full experience of them, and notice your own responses in the background. If you can't find a partner to work with, you can even do this while buying a coffee. People tend not to mind, especially if others are treating them as means to ends all day long! This practice is really just about acknowledging someone as human.

Naming

An extra to basic embodied listening is to name in oneself the sensations that arrive while someone else is speaking. You can also name what you see in them. Naming the observations you make can also sharpen them.

3-minute listens

If you live with a partner or housemate, set aside time to *really* listen to each other for 3–10 minutes each, without interrupting for any reason (this can be hard at first). You can start with something like, 'how was your day?', it doesn't really matter. Time it. Go for quality not length here, always aiming for deeper and better listening. Keep 'listening' during pauses.

Copying walking exercise revisited

Remember the copying exercise from Chapter 3 where we got someone to copy you to see your own embodiment? This is also fascinating from the other side, to 'try on' another's embodiment and get a felt sense for them. With time this can be done on a very micro-level just by looking at people – for example, in the cafe practice below.

A variation on this is to 'steal' other people's ways of dancing at a conscious dance class, and note what you notice. Another possibility is to try and do the *opposite* of someone else's movement, or their movement but more or less.

Cafe empathy

Sit outside a coffee shop or bar, in a place where people are walking by. Practise looking at people (don't make it too obvious!) and micro-mimicking their posture. Small changes to muscle tone, breath, the spine and the eyes should be enough. This should be very subtle. Notice how it feels to be them, even in this very small way. This process will happen anyway when you look at someone and is the basis of empathy, but here you are trying to encourage it. By making this process conscious you can also inhibit it if overly 'sensitive'.

Empathy walks

Go for a stroll in a relatively busy area and notice what happens in your body, even as you just briefly walk past different people. Some of the reaction may be empathy and some a mild fight-flight closing. This can be quite subtle, so practise the exercises above first.

YouTube and podcast practice

We are lucky enough to have a huge range of people to listen to these days at the touch of a button. You can also create 'gradients' of calibrated practice of increasing dullness and irritability if you'd like a challenge to developing your skills. Podcasts can also be useful to try and 'feel-into' the embodiment of guests without visual input.

Breath syncing

A simple way to listen deeply to another is to follow their breath pattern. This can be done while touching bodies (back to back is less intense for most than front to front), with hands on shoulders, just by observing, or even just listening. All variations will build different aspects of body listening skills.

Leader-follower (basic partner practice)

A very simple form I use a lot as a kind of 'workhorse' to explore many relational themes is to stand facing a coachee and touch palms together (though a non-touch version is fine with palms closed if that's an issue).[2] Just this part of the body is enough to reveal patterns of contact and connection (e.g. how hard people connect, if they lean on each other, how much they bend the arms, create closeness or not, etc.); however, I normally take it into a leader-follower movement, walking forwards and back. This can be used to explore leadership too (see Chapter 6) and is also a great way to feel your partner's embodiment in relationship at, say, the start of a coaching session, but here it is presented as a way to learn embodied listening.

You can use more complex forms like acro-yoga or tango, of course, but these are often less effective because although they reveal patterns equally well, the complexity of the movements and pressures means people have less mental space to spot the patterns. Sometimes, however, variations are useful to bring up certain themes and you can see other forms that I use on YouTube. As ever, the principle is the important thing here.

Hand on chest listening (aka deep embodied listening)

A classic embodiment exercise to develop deep listening is to place your hand (consensually) on a partner's chest centrally in front of their heart and have them talk about what they love. At some point apply a little gentle pressure to remind them of this area. This can be a great way to better access values and passion for the speaker too. By feeling them breathe, move and tense/relax, you can get a strong felt sense of someone.

Boring meetings and buying stuff

Excellent locations to practise deep body listening skills are places where you have spare attention and where it doesn't really matter. This could be in a very boring meeting, or when buying things day to day. On EFC there's a daily practice of doing this with the shop clerk when buying the first thing you buy every day – coffee, cigarettes, gum, whatever. This practice can be surprisingly humanising for people, usually subtly objectified as object delivery mechanisms. Ultimately embodied listening is really just about acknowledging our own and others' full humanity.

What are they not feeling?

A deep enquiry when empathising with someone is to ask what are they enacting but not yet feeling? What wants to emerge from them? This is a more intuitive practice, so be careful of projecting here or imposing your own values.

How do they want me to be?

A more advanced body listening exercise is to ask yourself how does the person you're interacting with want you to be? For example, do they want to be in charge or do they want you to be? Do they want to make you laugh, or have you be a safe, respectful or strong person? We are always 'forming' others in subtle ways.

Who's X?

A game I often ask students to play in pairs is to ask questions like, 'who's the boss?', 'who's the funny one?' or 'who's the nice one?'. I have them do this silently and after only a few seconds of pairing, answer by raising hands. All questions force a choice. This helps people feel subtle relational dynamics at work. Improv training will also do this, and should not be underestimated as a deep listening practice.

Paired movement practices

I have spent many thousands of hours in aikido, partner yoga and partner dance moving with strangers, colleagues, lovers, friends, kids in my care and students, and find this adds a whole new layer to 'listening' as a skill. Different types of paired practice will also bring out different skills – for example, 'basing' in acro-yoga (a combination of acrobatics and yoga), where someone balances on top of your feet, will help you learn supportive and trust-building skills, and I highly recommend gender-neutral dance classes as a way to learn the skills associated with both roles.

Circling and authentic movement

If you'd like more in-depth practices of embodied listening, I recommend both circling and authentic movement as places to explore further beyond these small exercises. These are essentially relational meditations where a strong focus is placed on the dynamics between people.

How to develop state social awareness in clients – overview

All the practices given in the first half of this chapter are appropriate for coaches to share. There's always a judgement call, however, as to how much is too much. Hand on chest listening, for example, would just freak some corporate groups out, while a very open group may be open to extended full-frontal hugging breath syncing – naked ... in jelly!

Essentially helping clients listen to each other means developing conditions of safety and trust. This could be with your overall manner, with centring, with ethical ground rules, making space for breaks and more.

How to develop state social awareness in clients – practices

One-to-one techniques

Simply paying attention again

One of the main techniques I use to teach listening skills is to simply suggest people pay attention to each other. I have done this in workshops with hundreds of diverse groups and usually do it for just 3–5 minutes each way in pairs.

I say something like, 'Talk about anything you like as long as it matters to you. If you're not talking, pay attention and don't interrupt or tell your own story. Just listen and have the intention just to connect. It may feel a bit weird not talking but give it a try.' Remarkably this often really helps to bond pairs, breaks down old resentments, moves people to tears and teaches the heart of empathy skills in ten minutes!

I also use the basic leader-follower form a lot with clients to help them develop social awareness.

> **One-to-one client case study: Book bother**
>
> *I remember leading the above technique with a small publishing company in a British cathedral city. The problem was a lot of arguing in 'cover meetings', where decisions on the titles and covers of books were made by the small team. People did not listen to each other, and eventually good ideas would simply be thrown out and one of the bosses would get their way.*
>
> *I taught them to centre and then did the simple attention exercise above, as well as the leader-follower, which they thought was 'fun and like dancing'. In the break afterwards, people told me they understood more about colleagues in ten minutes than they had done in the years they had known each other – even a married couple there said this! We also established a few simple ground-rules for their future cover meetings such as 'no interrupting', 'nobody speaks for more than 3 minutes' and 'breathe once before replying', to help them embed the learning and work more constructively together. They rebooked me twice that year, so I guess it worked at least to some degree.*

Group techniques

Centring conversations

Just having clients centre and then have a conversation is a profound shift for many, and they find that their listening and connection improve dramatically as a result of this.

Elements listening

The standard 4-elements exercise detailed in Chapter 3 is also an embodied empathy exercise, as it puts people 'in the shoes' of others with different preferences. This can be quite revealing for people. One can also use the elements as a 'sideways' state shifter to listen from four different viewpoints.

3-centres listening

You can listen both to yourself and to others from various centres. 'Centres' here refers to orientating points on the body, which one can shift one's perspective to. Although there are many models of this, including seven chakras (though with conventional groups I'd definitely avoid the word 'chakra'), the 3-centres model is quite simple and accessible to most people who say such things to themselves as, 'Well, my head says do it, but my heart and gut don't!' The three centres are:

- The centre of the head, in the middle of the skull, in line with the eyes[3]
- The centre of the chest roughly where the heart is[4]
- In the lower abdomen just in front of the spine in the centre of the body[5]

Note these are deep within the body, centrally aligned, not at the front.

You can encourage clients to 'tune into' these centres by bringing their attention there. Touching and moving away from them can help. Then ask participants to think about an issue or try a coaching question. It's very common, even in those new to embodiment, for very different and useful answers to arise.

The exercise above could have been introduced in Chapter 4, of course, as it shifts state, but applied to social awareness clients can listen 'from' these points too, and get different ways to connect with others: what does your head feel in connection to this person, your heart, etc.?

I have seen a similar 3-centre approach to this used by several teachers, including Wendy Palmer and Judith Blackstone.

Group client case study: Softening Russians

I've done a lot of work in Russia over the years and it's a 'low trust' culture owing to the history of trauma there. This means that groups do not bond easily and teachers cannot immediately do deep work as a result. However, over the years I have found that certain things can help. Centring, of course, is useful, as well as having people dance together early in the course. Strong gender and age patterns also need to be appreciated, helping people 'open up' to each other, and hierarchy and respect need to be more fully taken into account than in, say, The Netherlands.

Interestingly, there is a Russian tradition of 'dachas', country houses where people relax. It is noticeable that people let go far more, and more fully open up to each other, during our country retreat modules on EFC Russia, so we plan group processes with this in mind. Similarly, food also REALLY helps! This is of course true in many cultures, but in Russian the word for 'to be' and for 'food' is the same, so it's pretty core to helping people connect!

At first Russians seem unfriendly, especially to foreigners, but once you appreciate that they often simply take a little longer to 'thaw' to one another, you get to see the big and loveable Russian heart!

Virtual considerations

Proximity, touch, shared context, shared challenge, visual empathic resonance and group synchronisation, all break down barriers between people. Note that the first three of these are lost online whereas the last three can still be engaged. Note, too, previous comments about eye contact. It is possible to build a lot of embodied connection and empathy online but you have to work on it.

Trauma considerations

Trauma is toxic to listening and connection, and traumatised people may well need more support self-regulating to get to a place where they can take other's views on board and not be defensive. When empathising with traumatised people it's important not to take on their hyper-arousal, and you may find yourself feeling things *from* them that they have numbed.

Cultural considerations

In some cultures listening is encouraged and supported, in some it is even demanded and viciously reinforced, while in others (like with my own Irish background), we all talk at once! I have Israeli and Italian colleagues on the one side, and Dutch, Nordic and German on the other . . . so this sometimes makes for interesting meetings!

PART 2: SOCIAL AWARENESS – TRAIT

Reflection questions

How good are you at assessing someone's character when you first meet them? How much can you tell about a person from how they move and how they hold themselves? The late Stanley Keleman asserted; 'My particular bodily form, my particular body feeling, is testimony to my particular character, my particular way of behaving, both psychologically and physically.' In the next part of this chapter you will learn to read someone's psychology from their physicality as of course an embodied perspective is that they are inseparable.

Exercise

Take a look at someone elderly. How is their past written on their body? How does their manner reflect the life they have had? How have they formed themselves as a way of finding love, safety and belonging? Now consider a young child: Is there future there to see too? How do you know prejudices haven't slipped in?

> **Facilitator case study: My story**
>
> *I have come to 'see through people – and there's some real pros and cons to that! I think I developed the ability to body-read well in a unique set of circumstances. For seven years I travelled the globe touching many, many bodies in aikido, and also while being extremely promiscuous sexually.[6] Basically I had close intimate physical connection with far more bodies in that period than most people will in a lifetime. I was also in danger and very poor a lot of that time, so was perhaps paying more attention to people who might have been a threat than I would have otherwise done. So what, you might ask? Well, I started seeing patterns connecting how people moved with how they are as people.*
>
> *A first it really helped to touch people to get a sense of them – common sense really, but then gradually the same skill started to come at a distance for me as I could see the patterns I was used to touching. It became easier and easier for me to just look at people and have a very good sense of them. I try not to jump to conclusions of course, and see all guesses as starting points for enquiry but this skill became so refined I was employed to travel with the head of an NGO working in war zones just to give my opinion on people we met – including African dictators, spies, a princess and murderous government minsters!*
>
> *There are, however, real benefits and issues related to this skill. It can lead to very quick decision-making, for example – job interviews for my company can be under three minutes – and it's great for guessing what help students may need without having to talk to them for long. It is, however, hard to turn off and potentially invasive! While I don't consciously look at people this way without consent and the appropriate relationship, I can't totally turn it off either! This makes people more 'naked' than they may be comfortable with. Being right most of the time can also lead to jumping to conclusion and a kind of judgmentalism, so it's a mixed blessing!*
>
> *Many coaches who I have trained with have given me feedback that embodied work has given them 'x-ray specs'! They are now able to work with far more clients because they can adapt to different styles and know when to be playful (if that is their natural style) and when to adopt different practices. It is such a valuable ability to walk into a room of new delegates without having any information from HR and immediately see the company 'culture' and how best to adapt their teaching style to the type of people there.*

Promise

By the end of this half of the chapter you will be able to learn the skill of accurate body reading, and teach some basics to clients.

What is the skill-set and how does it help facilitation?

This skill is being able to accurately assess people by looking at them. Being able to see the traits of your clients helps embodied facilitators immensely. With this we can help people develop themselves as human beings, as our observations may back up their self-discovery and can be used to challenge any self-deception. It also forms the basis of any impact and influence we may wish to have on others.

Relationship to other skill-sets

We can only see another's actual patterns if we know our own patterns, states and prejudices (as this is the lens we see through), and can manage our state to be calm enough to observe well. It is also worth establishing how state is influencing our clients so we don't misread this as trait.

Pattern recognition is obviously the basis of helping clients change too. Trait recognition is the foundation for embodied influence, as we need to know what kind of people we are trying to influence!

How to develop your own embodied body reading – overview

Building this skill comes down to attention, feedback and repetition. If you wish to learn this, the first thing is to start to really look at people, look at what embodiment patterns correlate with their behaviour. This alone is huge. Touch can also help as per my story and I always advise dedicated embodied facilitators to take on a touch practice, partly to build this skill, as the information is just so much more readily available than through looking alone. Next, you need to get feedback to see if you guessed right.

Basic models

While there are many in-depth models of body reading, including classical Reichian character analysis,[7] upgrades such as the Hakomi method and NARM, and excellent modern systems such as Uzazu, these are too complex for this book. The 4-elements model we have introduced is an intuitive place to start, however, so I'd recommend using this model. Once you have practised each of the patterns yourself, it becomes relatively easy to see them. Some examples of enquiries:

- Is their breathing more fiery (chest pushing and pulling), more stable and rhythmic (earth), lighter and looser in chest (air), or more soft and flowing (water)?

- How weighty are they? Are they very low down (earth), low (water), higher up (fire) or at the top and light (air)?
- Where do they seem to be moving from? Down in the legs (earth), in the belly (water), more in the chest and arms (fire) or the head (air)?
- How do they move? Like which element do they intuitively seem?

This is one of the harder skills to learn, but will become obvious as you study the elements for yourself, and get more and more familiar with them experientially. See also Appendix 2 on them too.

Body reading scale?

Within the embodiment field there is some disagreement as to how much the guessing of character traits from people's embodiments (not simple body characteristics, but how we live in and as bodies) can reveal their character patterns. I have heard a few, very experienced embodiment teachers that I respect, such as Don Hanlon Johnson, say it's impossible, while others believe that a single observation definitely and always leads to a single conclusion. We could think of this as a scale of certainty. I tend to fall somewhat in the middle, seeing themes and suggestions from observations. Let's take the example of someone whose feet point out and not straight ahead (they're 'duck-footed'). I have seen this far more with extroverts than introverts, but it could also just be the shape of their bones (large variations exist interestingly), the fact that they practised ballet as a kid, a cultural factor, the trousers they are wearing today, and so on – so I am never quick to jump to conclusions. That said, there is a pattern that I've seen too many times to deny.

Avoiding inaccuracy, prejudice and power

Saying you can see something about someone in their body can become a kind of magic power and I've noticed that this can go to people's heads. This is to be avoided. Equally, it's easy to project body prejudices onto someone based on stereotypes about body shapes or how someone dresses, for example. Here are a few checks I make with myself to avoid this, and to generally be more accurate:

- What do you actually see in a person that leads you to a certain conclusion? What are the *facts* upon which your opinion is based?
- Are there any merely physical factors at work such as injuries or a particular body shape that could be misread? I had a student that looked very flat-chested, for example, because he was biologically missing his pectoral muscles, and know a teacher born with a fused spine who was often told he was a 'stiff' person – which he is not at all!

- Am I applying stereotypes from their body shape or clothes, e.g. 'larger people are more jolly',[8] 'people in suits are greedy', etc.?
- How does my own long-term embodiment impact how I see people? 'We see things as we are, not as they are'[9] after all. How might my 'lens' bias what I see? For example, a very fiery person will see even a moderately fiery person as watery by comparison
- What is my mood and how could it be influencing what I see?[10]
- Am I centred? If not, centre
- How might the environment, relationships and context I'm seeing this person in impact their contextual embodiment and not be a true reflection of the character level? Remember the model above – for example, if you are seeing someone on holiday with their wife vs. Monday morning at work with their boss
- What is my motivation for trying to read them? Do I benefit from a certain position or does it reinforce a long-held view – for example, 'It's obvious that my enemy is a bad person from . . .?

Figure 5.1 Contexts of embodiment

CONTEXTS OF EMBODIMENT

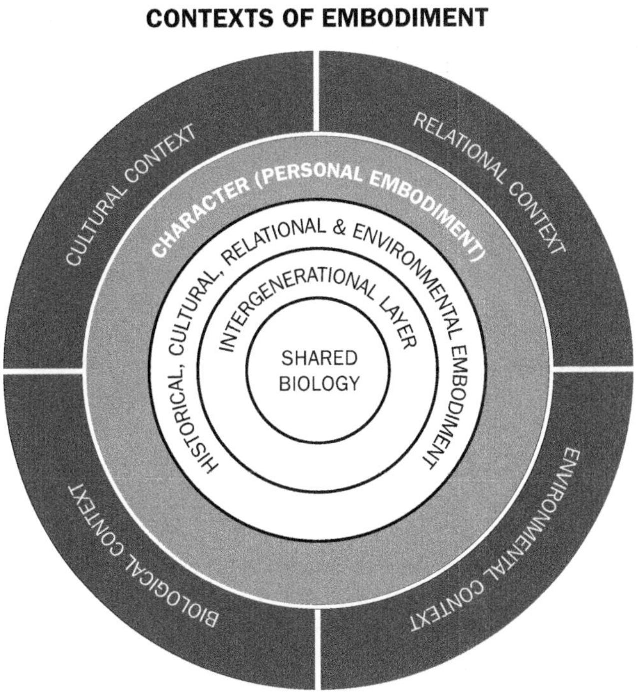

> **Exercise: A knock on the door**
> You can start body reading patterns before you even see people. Can you identify people you live with by how they move through the house? Could you identify someone from how they knock on a door? Could you make a guess about someone by how they did this before you'd seen them?
>
> Try knocking on a door using all four elements – for example, a slow and steady knock for earth. I'll let you work out the rest . . .

How to develop your own embodied body reading – techniques

Train spotting

This is a good beginner's practice. Sit in a train station cafe and watch people go by. Note the differences in how they walk. Make up stories about them. Allow yourself to project and go wild. Have fun.

Dance reading

Go to any busy partner dance class that you can. Dance with many partners, make some guesses about them and get to know them a bit afterwards verbally to see if you're correct. A favourite of mine is to guess what embodied practice people have done in the past as each leaves a certain feel. It's a bit of fun freaking people out with this if I'm honest![11]

Am I right?

This is a harder version of dance reading. Stop strangers in the street and ask if you can make guesses about them as a person. Do not just say things that would apply to anyone. Make definite, 'this not this' statements, and ask if you're right.

I did this repeatedly for some time and while it may seem strange at first, just saying you are studying body-language and most people will be interested. I used to average an 8 out of 10 for accuracy when I asked them to score me. While not scientific, this was pretty interesting.[12]

> **Facilitator case study: Embodied sales observer**
> *I pitch to HR people a lot. Often, I am one of several trainers that they are meeting for a very short period of time before they hire one. It's just the nature of my niche in the training industry. For years a problem was that I could say many different things about my work, but different HR managers would want different things. They can also just be cagey when I ask them what they'd like.*

> *These days I walk into these sales meetings, shake hands with them and have a very good but brief look at them as they sit down. Based upon the embodied pattern I see I make my pitch. For more watery types (common in HR but disguised in the business world) I stress the relationship and feelings, for fire types I just get right down to business, with earth types I slow down and give more details and say how I'll mitigate any risk, and with the occasional air types I bump into I make it fun and stress the novel and creative aspect of what I do. Having done a fair bit of embodied training now, I can see immediately what style will work and am usually right. I never lie, but do angle how I sell my work to what I see.*
>
> – Anon, trainer, New York

How to develop body reading with clients – overview

Largely this area is not something I would suggest teaching clients unless you already have expertise. That being said, I have on occasion done so with, for example, groups of HR managers, and often at least share a few basics when teaching models such as 4-elements in regard to self-development.

How to develop body reading with clients – practices

Suggesting clients pay attention to other people and simple practices like train spotting can be fine in my experience. Also, pointing out indicators of models used for self-awareness and extending this to others.

> **One-to-one client case study: 4-elements marketing**
>
> *There was one marketing agency I worked with who were completely enamoured with the 4-elements model and how it could help them better communicate with clients of different types. They described various clients to me and we fairly quickly identified their types together using not only how they described their embodiments, e.g. 'Jack always seems rushed and tense", but also their offices (e.g. water types have lots of family pics), the lengths of mails they sent, how they did business (e.g. 'Sarah likes to talk for hours before we contract'), etc.*
>
> *The marketing company then developed mail templates and sales calls, and meeting standard operating procedures based on their clients' preferences. For example, the air template for mails included colours and emojis, while the earth one certainly did not, and calls to fire people cut right to the chase, while for*

water people, there was more relationship-building upfront. They updated their customer relationship management with this information so every client was labelled with an element's best guess. While this may seem manipulative, it is worth noting that they were only communicating with clients how the clients themselves would choose to be communicated with.

You can also make requests as a customer or manager of course and state your own preferences, I always brief new providers something like this: 'Make our meetings quick and don't show me too much detail or mess around, just give me the stuff that really matters' (my fire preference).

Virtual considerations

Body reading is of course more difficult via a computer as you can't see as much. I use a large screen to help counteract this, but face-to-face is much better for this activity. It's also worth bearing in mind that computer interaction will also influence people dramatically, narrowing their focus and therefore embodiment in most cases, for example. Having said that, you can still get an OK 'read' of people online so it's not a total waste of time!

It may also sound impossible to do this kind of work on the phone but this is not the case. The breath reveals a huge amount and it is almost intimate with a good head-set how much you can hear. Often I close my eyes when listening to a client on the phone to better tune into them. I'll also ask what position they are in – standing, walking or sitting, for example – and take the same position myself.

Trauma considerations

People with issues around trust and safety may find it invasive being assessed in this way and great care should be taken in such cases. It's also important not to encourage people to identify trauma patterns that can be healed with who they are in making assessments!

Cultural considerations

Culture is embodied and either denying this, or making assumptions and generalisations in body reading from it, is a mistake. Stereotypes about what different shapes of body mean are of course culturally dependent too, and bias may stem from these – is a large belly a sign of Buddha or the sign of drinking beer, for example!?

Principles used in this chapter

Note the 'avoiding inaccuracy' body-reading principle outlined above – seeing this as a principle for body reading more generally means you have a way of using any system you learn in the future, not just 4-elements, to guess a person's embodiment patterns accurately. As ever in this book, this is my aim: not just to equip you with a tool, but with deeper principles for using any embodiment tool you come across.

> ### *Reflection / discussion questions*
> How much do you think you can tell about a person by how they stand and move? What's your position on the scale mentioned earlier? What are some of the key ethical issues and temptations in this skill-set?

Notes

1 Look up 'interpersonal neurobiology' and Daniel Siegel especially for more on this.
2 This exercise is similar to partner dance, which is used to both assess compatibility and bond couples, cross-culturally. Western/Northern Europe and the USA are unusual in that not everyone does partner dance!
3 Sometimes called a 'third eye' point, though usually this means more to the front of the skull.
4 Not as far left as most people think.
5 This is the 'hara' (Japanese) or 'Dantian / dan t'ian' (Chinese).
6 I am not boasting about the latter it was simply my lifestyle at that time and relevant here and I'm also aware that some people will judge me for this. These days I'm middle – aged, married and have calmed down! The background is relevant here, however.
7 This system was an early form of body therapy and has types with pleasant names such as 'narcissistic' and 'psychopathic'.
8 There is a long history of this, including the following wonderful Shakespeare quote from *Julius Caesar*: 'Let me have men about me that are fat; Sleek-headed men and such as sleep o' nights. Yond Cassius has a lean and hungry look; He thinks too much: such men are dangerous.'
9 Leo Rosten: https://www.brainyquote.com/authors/leo-rosten-quotes
10 As an experiment, try wrinkling your nose up in disgust, and now look at others – very likely you will see them in a more negative light.
11 Be careful of the 'magic power' power trip though that can come with this skill – it is seductive.
12 There is some science on personality and movement patterns showing, for example, that extroverts swing their arms more when they walk; see Dr Peter Lovatt's work too, but most theories out there are quite basic currently. The real experts on this stuff are animators like Pixar who have figured out how to convey personality so skilfully.

6 Social leadership

PART 1: SOCIAL LEADERSHIP – STATE

Power without love is brutality. Love without power is ineffective.

– Paul Linden

> ### *Opening exercises: Touch your knees*
> Here's an experiment I've run across the world many times that you can try. Next time you're leading a group, ask them verbally to touch their knees, while simultaneously touching your own *elbows*. Note what most people do. Assuming they are not expecting a trick, the vast majority of people in a group will either touch their elbow or at least go to do so first before correcting to the knees. In many groups, only 5 per cent will follow the verbal instruction, and never as many as 50 per cent. So what does this show? People follow the body more than words.

> ### *Exercise: Love wins*
> A related exercise can be tried with a partner. First, get in as loving a state as you can (thinking of loved ones and using a relaxed open embodiment, for example) before firing as much abusive language at your partner as they will allow (they calibrate – and be careful!) in the most loving voice you can. Note the impact. Next, get in the tightest most aggressive state you can and shout (again consent and calibration, please) compliments and loving comments. Again, notice which 'works' – the tone / volume / embodiment or the words?

> ### Bilingual dog story
> *Once teaching in a forest in Russia, a large aggressive black dog came to visit the training. I spoke to the dog in a calm, friendly yet dominant voice, inhibiting my natural fear response physically, and saying, 'Good doggy, I like doggies, I'm in charge, and I like dogs', etc. The dog calmed down and soon flopped its*

> head to the side, rolled over and let me tickle his belly – to which one of my local students commented, 'OMG, this dog speaks English!!!' Of course, the dog spoke embodiment. In a less comedic example I have used tone and body language to save my life when confronted by angry men with guns whose language I did not speak while doing humanitarian work, and have also honed this skill working with 50,000+ children – all of whom copy what you do, not what you say! 'Monkey see, monkey do (monkey ignore what you say)', I have found.

Promise

By the end of this section you will have learnt to better influence the state of others, and you will be hilarious and romantically irresistible too – okay, I've overstated those last two but it will help.

> *Opening reflection questions*
> Are you good at making people laugh easily without words? Do people tend to follow you as a 'natural leader'? Are you a good flirt? Can you easily soothe a crying child or an upset colleague? Can you enliven and wake people up with your tone of voice?
>
> These are a few of the skills we could call embodied social leadership.

What is the skill-set and how does it help facilitation?

Embodied social leadership is about how we can influence the states of other people, and how we can encourage others to develop a practice to impact their own traits.

For a facilitator it is vital to be able to calm down and wake up groups, use humour skilfully, inspire, motivate, be charismatic and generally have an impact. Some people mistake the main task of a trainer or coach as information transfer, but this means very little without social leadership skills, which are where the real value of a facilitator lies.

Relationship to other skill-sets

This skill-set is built on the last three. In order to be influential one must first listen, and to do this, one must be self-regulated, and to do this, you need to be self-aware. You could also say that a loop exists here, as leadership creates feedback for self-awareness.

How to develop social leadership in yourself – overview

'By doing everything in this book so far' would be one answer to this question, and you'll have noticed that the chapters have become shorter as we have gone along, as much of the skill-set is simply what has come before (but not entirely so) – and guess what, 'practise' would be another! I feel a bit repetitive saying 'practise' yet again, but it's really at the heart of the matter.

The beautifully brutal feedback of leadership

If you've ever tried unsuccessfully to train a dog, been rejected by a lover, or failed to get a child out the house in time for school, you know how *brutal* the feedback of ineffective embodied leadership is. People may like you, and you may be a nice person, but it will be extremely apparent whether or not you make someone laugh, inspire and energise them, turn them on, or whatever. There is no hiding from the results of our own embodied practice, or lack therefore, fed back to us by merciless social proof. Reality does not care *one bit* how good you think you are, who your teacher was or which books you've read!

What are 'charisma' and 'chemistry'?

Charisma is an embodied capacity than can be thought of as a balance of warmth and power. The balance between self-regulation and self-expression is also a part of it. Think of someone you regard as charismatic; likely they will be both friendly and authoritative, and calm without being dull. It is not magic, and all the constituent parts have been taught in this book.

What people call 'chemistry' between people is often an embodied polarity. If we take the embodiments of fire and water as poles, then we see that 'opposites attract' (as long as values are aligned). This is especially important in sexual relationships, though chemistry also matters in other domains. If your love life with a partner has flagged, this is likely why – and polarity can be shifted into as a state, or worked on as a trait.

How to develop social leadership in yourself – practices

Reviewing the embodied foundation

Sit opposite a partner and start a short conversation about the weather and notice how compelling you feel, and how compelling they seem, just to find a baseline. Next feel your whole body for a few minutes. Feeling your body and getting more present leads to presence. Chat again and observe your partner and see if this is true. Now stand up and move every part of your body, joint by joint to mobilise them and encourage expression. Chat again and notice any differences. Now centre and then see if this helps. Lastly give your partner attention, as you also feel and regulate / express your own body. How much more attractive – in the widest sense – are you both from the start? This exercise is an experiential review of the last three chapters, and highlights their impact on influence.

Leader-follower (basic partner practice) revisited – deviations and variations

The palm-to-palm lead-and-follow exercise, described in Chapter 5 to build social awareness, can of course also be used to reveal leadership patterns. All such 'simulators' reveal character patterns, and can be used to develop them. Noticing which element you lead in habitually, and choosing to practise something else, would be just one way to work with this.

You will also see deviations from the norm, revealing people's habitual leadership styles during this exercise – for example, do people tend to keep their partner very close or far, do they grab their partner's hands (could be controlling), do they lean on their partner, do they angle their hands down, etc.?

4-elements coaching – self

A nice use of the 4-elements model is to shift consciously through each of the modes while coaching. This can be done in a number of ways from the systemic to the intuitive, but the result will be the same – you will come up with more varied questions, and influence your coachee in more varied ways. Some humanistic fundamentalists may claim you should never lead a coachee but (1) this is impossible – we are always influencing via the body, and (2) most coachees would say it's part of what you're paid for as well!

4-elements coaching – client

In this variation you not only shift your own state but lead the client in shifting theirs. I often use this to brainstorm and generate new ideas when stuck on a problem. Depending on the client, you can go more or less intensely into each element. I normally start from earth and work 'up', as this feels safer for most, but this is not a hard and fast rule. The quicker version of this exercise is just to use your social awareness skill to see what they are doing already and suggest a shift to what's missing. For example, if they are a very watery person, the answer will likely lie in fire, as they have already thought of and tried the watery options.

Coachees will be amazed how many fresh perspectives they can see when they shift their bodies, and the whole process can easily be done in 10–15 minutes with a little practice. YouTube search '4-elements coaching' to see several examples.

Note: These 4-elements techniques could also be included in Chapter 4 on how to shift states for clients, of course, as could much in this chapter, as anything that will shift your own state will shift that of your coachees! Leading yourself is your primary tool for leading others.

Tone games

Tone comes from overall embodiment and has a huge impact on inflection, with upwards inflection and variation being warmer, and downwards inflection and less variation (but never no variation) being more authoritative.

There are some fun ways you can play with this, such as having someone speak words incongruently with tones (e.g. begging in a demanding voice, or speaking very forthrightly in a questioning tone), or taking it to comical extremes. Play. Explore.

Competitive moods games

Embodiments are influential, meaning that two states essentially compete to turn someone a certain way. A really fun way to demonstrate this, and to improve one's ability to influence, is to play competitive mood games. One person has to stay serious and the other jovial, or one soft and open and the other hard and closed, or one sleepy and the other wide awake, etc. The two then meet and try to 'turn' each other. This is also great self-regulation practice in holding your own state while influencing the other, and can be a lot of fun to play with.

Subtle influencers

Another interesting way to develop your embodied influencing skills is to see how little you can do to alter a partner's embodiment. Sit or stand opposite a partner and decide who is the receiver and who is the influencer. The job of the influencer is to create a change in their partner while doing as little as possible. Of course, this is excellent social awareness practice for the other person too.[1]

Clowning and improv

These are excellent practices for building influencing skills. The book *Listen! Say Yes! Commit!* by Harry Puckering and Julia Knight[2] and *Own It* by Liz Peters are excellent take the skills of improv into the training room, and aside from classes is a great place to start.

Death-matches and meditations

This first exercise is a variation on several I have seen in different places. Two people sit opposite one another looking each other in the eye, and have to express with as much authenticity and passion as they can, what they love, and why they – and not their 'opponent' – should be allowed to live. After both have spoken for a set amount of time, either an external judge or group of judges decides, or it is left to the two parties to gives themselves the thumbs up (live) or thumbs down (die). If both have thumbs up, you wait for as long as it takes. Both reading the same poem, or dancing their love and loss are variations.

Death meditations are also very helpful for putting people in touch with their own mortality, and sense of purpose, and stem from several traditions. Search 'Mark Walsh death meditation on YouTube' for one. I take my more serious students to graveyards at night to talk about their leadership, and while this is not appropriate for many groups, I will very often start trainings by half-joking, 'So by the end of today you'll be 8 hours (or whatever) closer to your death . . . so how are we going to spend that time?', to at least flag our mortality in a lighthearted way. Whether by life circumstances or through deliberate engagement, a leader must confront their mortality to gain depth.

While intense, these kinds of exercises can put people in touch with their desire to survive, their values and their passion – all of which make for compelling leadership.

> **Facilitator case study: My story**
>
> *I'm generally assessed as having a strong sense of presence and of being a good influencer, but it wasn't always that way. Now some of this is down to practice, as I've taught and facilitated for well over 10,000 hours. Although it does get easier, I still get nervous on the big stage. Not long ago I keynoted the British ICF conference, which is a fairly big gig, and I was a little anxious as despite having talked on larger stages before, 'prophets have no honour in their hometowns'! Centring, of course, helped and I used an EYP pose embodying generosity before going on.*
>
> *More formatively, working with large groups of children in my youth was very helpful. You learn that confidence and 'presence' are king, and if you can manage 100 kids in a field (I was involved in outdoor education), then a class of 20 adults is easy. Children demand that you hold their attention, and give immediate feedback when they are bored. They force you to be dynamic and develop an expansive embodiment. Likewise, you must convey both safety and authority.*
>
> *I've previously mentioned learning to listen though aikido, partner yoga and dance, and learning to lead is also part of these arts. In aikido the art of non-resistant leadership is taught, and in tango subtle and sensual direction.*
>
> *On a deeper level I would say I gained depth, an extremely important if intangible characteristic for influence, from confronting death in various ways. A strong sense of life purpose and reorienting to service away from a natural tendency to selfishness regularly have also made a difference. These things do not come quickly or easily.*
>
> *Lastly, I'd say that while humour has been a part of my character since an early age, I underestimated this as a trainer at first, and thought it didn't fit with corporate work especially. When I reintegrated it, I got better feedback about being authentic. I've now taught many other trainers and the best ones know how to be themselves.*

158 The Body in Coaching and Training

> **Facilitator case study: Little furniture lady**
>
> I once worked with an extremely smart senior executive – let's call her Agnetha – who was on the board of a Scandinavian company. She was actually referred to me by someone who followed me on social media, and who worked in her HR department. Her problem was that because of her stature and high-pitched voice, she was often spoken-over by tall male colleagues in meetings who did not mean to be sexist (a big no-no in Scandinavian culture) or heightist,[3] but just felt compelled to. Naturally she found this very frustrating.
>
> Because she was a very busy woman, I gave her just three EYP poses to do daily for one minute each: authority pose, taking up space and warrior pose. We also did some voice work together around releasing the diaphragm. This was all done on Zoom in four 30-minute coaching sessions over two months. Between sessions she practised the poses and over time built a more powerful imposing embodiment, and naturally was interrupted far less by her colleagues. Agnetha also found the poses built authority with her children who were growing much taller than her too!
>
> After I was brought in to do a leadership retreat for the company on Agnetha's recommendation. I got the social listing all wrong, miscalculated my humour, offended half of them and wasn't invited back.[4]

> **Group client case study: Wired humanitarians**
>
> I once worked with some 'fieldies' (humanitarian workers deployed to such places as disaster zones) of a major aid charity, while they were back in the UK between deployments. They were a cynical war-weary bunch and didn't seem that open to learning the resilience techniques that I had been asked to teach. There was also seething resentment among some of them, and before I could begin the training, bickering had broken out. People seemed highly traumatised and stuck in hyper-arousal states, or collapsed sinking into their chairs with arms crossed.
>
> I started by matching their pace and brusque tones, taking on a no-nonsense style. I told them what they would get and how it would benefit their work, and told them to give it 20 minutes, after which they could leave and I'd still record them as having attended. I shared some 'war stories' of my own and made some off-colour jokes. I asked them to turn their phones off for the duration as previously agreed, and had to firm up my own embodiment a few times when they tested the boundaries.
>
> Over the morning I had with them (none left after centring which I taught early as a quick-win), I softened my manner and they followed this embodied 'lead'. The humour became lighter and they shared some touching stories about stress, trauma and burnout. Several cried, and the group bonded. Towards the end I sped up the pace again and took them away from emotional depth as I knew they'd be going out the door to some potentially rough stuff and would need to be ready.

> **Exercise**
> See if you can make someone smile today. If that's too easy, make them laugh. Without speaking. Don't be creepy or weird. What are you doing with your body?

How to develop state social leadership in clients – overview

In my experience, clients really enjoy learning to be more impactful. Often this is why people come to leadership workshops and the like, and this section is often motivating work in all the other areas of this book. I have also found there are lots of really fun ways to go about teaching social leadership, based of course on the embodiment foundations laid out so far.

How to develop state social leadership in clients – practices

One-to-one techniques

Centring coaching

A very simple application of centring is to ask a client what their challenge or coaching question is. Have them centre, and then ask them again. Often the second iteration will be more constructively framed and felt as less threatening. For example, someone may go from saying, 'my boss is a total nightmare!', to 'how do I communicate better with my boss and set appropriate boundaries?'. Because this technique is safe and fairly simple, it can be taught to people to help others with.

Marry me! / give me a pay rise

One fun way to play with embodied leading is to have people propose marriage in each of the elements. Have people ham it up. It's great fun to see a *really* boring earth proposal, or crazy air one, for example! After people have got the idea 'large', we take it down to a more real-world application of this technique.[5] With more conventional groups, a slightly straighter version to start with is to ask for a pay rise.

Interestingly you can also ask, 'So which of those 4 would you marry?' and people immediately respond with such definite answers, showing how our decision-making is impacted by people's embodiment far more than by what they say. This also highlights how we like to be influenced.

In the real world you could also have people experiment with ordering lunch (subtly) in four elements, or some similar low consequence application as a way in. The basic principle here is that it's good to have a bridge between the dojo (classroom) and deeply meaningful or impactful real-life applications.

More leader-follower simulators

The standard leader-follower model is a great simulator for revealing to clients their leadership styles and giving them a safe place to work on them. Note that this form is not set in stone though, and other simulators can be created to reveal different patterns more easily or things added to the basic form. For example, you could work with how they are when someone holds them back (they walk, you hold their shoulders), when someone resists their leadership, or when someone leaves them. You can also create group set-ups, and really creativity is the only limit. The key thing is to create a situation which has a resonance that's appropriate for the topic being explored, as we're symbolic animals.

I have found that seemingly innocuous set-ups can create deeply revealing and emotional responses in people, in that we are meaning-making animals and this is embodied, so simple arrangements resonate at a deeper level. Once, for example, we did a variation of leader-follower from a handshake where one partner abruptly left, and someone who had been completely cynical and disengaged in the exercise (it was at a networking event) immediately broke down in tears. Afterwards I found out that his wife had left him that week, and even though he logically hadn't given the exercise much meaning, the symbolism came through powerfully. This was in the early days of my company and cautioned me about the power of this work and the care that is needed.

One-to-one client case study: Four-elements parenting

A yoga teacher took our year-long course and extended her earthy watery range by taking on a martial arts practice and doing some improv (for fire and air). A year later, we were at her house one evening designing a yoga initiative together. The work had gone on late, and it was time for her to put her son to bed. I had previously heard her talk about this being a struggle, and also his pattern of staying up and eating a lot of food at night, which meant he was becoming obese.

As she rolled her eyes, and went to his room for her nightly challenge, I gently suggested, 'Maybe try something new?' As we'd just been talking about the four elements in relation to ways of doing yoga, this was the obvious choice. I heard through the door as she tried in what I guessed was her usual way, only to illicit the whiny passive aggressive complaining from her son she had mentioned to me earlier. She then shifted mode and tried an air way of being silly, suggesting he stay up all night and eat everything in the fridge. 'Err mum, I'm not sure that's a good idea . . .' he stuttered. The normal pattern was broken. Then she got firmly earth and fire on his disobedient butt, and simply stated that it was his bedtime in a way that left zero room for argument. Finally, when he was well settled, she shifted to a sympathetic watery mum and kissed him goodnight.

While of course there is no magic bullet for parenting, embodied flexibility of leadership helps. Children have greater range and behavioural flexibility than most adults, so can run rings around them usually without this!

'Away' and 'towards' humour – a distinction

Humour is underrated by most. Humour allows leaders to:

- Break tension and more generally relax others
- Build rapport
- Say the unsayable, and go where dry sincerity cannot
- Create 'space' around difficult emotions
- Establish status
- Wake people up

In discussing the uses of humour, it's worth asking if it takes oneself and others deeper into connection (with oneself and others), or away from it. I call the former 'towards' humour, and the latter 'away' humour (which is a defence). I usually encourage the first in training rooms, and discourage the second. They have very different embodied flavours and it's relatively easy to show people the difference, as it's intuitive to most people once the distinction has been made.

Group techniques

Awareness and centring recap

It is fairly easy to show people how body awareness and centring make them more compelling leaders. You can also show this to a group by having three people check their phones for a few minutes while you coach another three into a centred embodiment. Then ask the group who looks the most compelling. Easy choice! You can also play with turning awareness, movement, posture, breath, etc. 'on' and 'off', to create this effect with a whole group of people at once so they can really feel the difference (contract principle again). One creates a room full of radiant charismatic leaders, and the other a really depressing draining wake! It's not subtle when a whole room of people are doing it, and people quickly learn about the power of embodied influence.

Get me across the room

A fun exercise I use is to have people pair up, and then person A tries to get person B across the room (who is instructed to be 'moderately obstinate') without speaking or touching them. You'd be amazed at the strategies people use – from seduction, to threat, to bribery, etc., and these can also be very revealing. 'Do you do that in life, too?' is a classic embodiment coaching question that I use here. People are 'holographic', meaning one part contains the whole, and patterns in one area often (but not always) reveal broader patterns.

Calm Karen down!!

Another playful one is to have someone do some star jumps[6] until they are out of breath and let them scream and shout a bit. Then, two people have to calm them down, and the activated one chooses who is the most relaxing.

'Wake Bob Up' is the after lunch variation, which is the same but with a sleepy person. Usually we suggest a no touching or shouting rule here though!

More competitive mood games

Competitive mood games with groups can be really wild. A game that I love, inspired by one devised by the Newfield Network, is to split the group up equally into four and have each subgroup occupy a different corner of the room, where they are each coached into a different embodiment. The groups / modes are:

- Action – trying to change what you can
- Peace – not trying to change what you can't
- Resentment – trying to change what you can't
- Apathy – not trying to change what you can[7]

The groups then meet in the middle of the room and try to 'win' by shifting each other's states, which often gets fairly crazy. Again, a no touching rule is good and assistants help! The roles are rotated until everyone gets to think, feel, see and interact in the four different embodiments (this is thus a great way to demonstrate the functions of embodiment too, and people will be amazed by how different the world looks 'from' each of them), encouraging state flexibility, noticing what is familiar (a trait awareness-building principle), as well as being a great training in influencing.

You could do this with the four elements of course too, but I wanted to show how the idea works with any model. This is also a good example of an exercise which builds several embodiment skill-sets.

Group client case study: Teaching medical receptionists

I once worked with a large group of medical receptionists. The UK health system is quite overloaded, and these women (occasionally men) have a fearsome reputation as 'guard dogs' (their phrase not mine) for the doctors they book appointments for. This is a bit of an issue as their job is essentially customer service, and while they have to handle many 'difficult' people daily and are sadly often verbally abused, they also meet many vulnerable people who would like a friendly face when seeking help!

The first thing I had them do was explore the distinction between being nice but a pushover vs. being kind AND strong in their bodies. I also had them prove to themselves physically that being 'a moody medical megalomaniac' (again, their choice of words) was actually weak. They used a pushing exercise for 'testing' these from Paul Linden (YouTube 'body mind spirit Paul Linden'). We also practised centring of course (repeat after me, 'if in doubt, teach centring') and we played some of the influencing games in this chapter as well as working

> with tone and embodiment while practising some things they frequently said at work, like 'sorry we don't have an appointment until next week'.
>
> I had to REALLY work on my own authoritative embodiment to handle 150 people used to being in charge, but we also had a lot of fun after we settled who was leading!

> ### Exercise: Svetlana the Russian mega bitch
>
> One of the most fun role-plays we do on EFC UK is when my colleague Vilya (author of Chapter 2) transforms into Russian oil executive and 'mega bitch' Svetlana. Coaching students then take it in turns to try and coach her, most of them failing and being crushed under her steely Slavic gaze. People try all sorts of things to try and build rapport with her and it's great training. In many Western European and Asian cultures there is little honest feedback but not here – for example, 'Why are you doing weird things, hippie?', 'You look like a puppy dog, calm down', 'You are boring me, and I am busy'. You get the idea. Now, Svetlana tones this down a bit for less robust or newer coaching students, but it's one hell of a good way to work on self-regulation and influencing skills under pressure. I hope you meet Svetlana one day. She will break you!

Virtual considerations

With the exception of touch and shared context as list builders, most of what has been discussed here is possible online. I do find it more challenging to 'body lead' large online groups where I can't see people, and I find students who I've met at least once in person carry much trust online, and that this lasts quite some time. There is a kind of 'body memory' of someone that I have hugged even once years before that makes them far easier to connect with and therefore lead. Tone, of course matters online.

Trauma considerations

Interestingly, trauma can help people more easily lead, especially by clear authoritarian styles that play into fears and feelings of lack of safety. There may also be a greater need for safety where soothing leadership is appreciated, and hyper-vigilance for any weakness or any threat from the leader. A slow development of trust may be all that is possible and relationship is required for leadership – but trauma interferes with people's ability to build relationship.

Trauma can also get in the way of people's abilities to self-regulate and listen as discussed, so can be a real barrier for leaders themselves. Because visible or subtly communicated stress is often seen as a sign of low status, being stuck in fight or flight is detrimental to being respected, and because of trauma's ill effects on connection skills, warmth is also lost. It is hard to trust a nervous, aggressive or isolated leader, and these states will be communicated which people will not enjoy. That being said, in a traumatised population, someone who is healthy may not resonate, while someone who is also traumatised may be influential. In all cases, I highly advise leaders with trauma to seek treatment.

Cultural considerations

There is so much I could say here! Cultures have very different ideas on the amounts of warmth vs. power considered ideal in a leader, as well as the physical and emotional distance around leadership, how sensitive people are to influence, gendered patterns, and a host of factors relevant to influencing others' states. Pay attention to these.

PART 2: SOCIAL LEADERSHIP – TRAIT

Reflection question
How do you coach others to develop themselves as people over time?

Exercises
1. Make a plan for a client you have (or could have). How might you help them develop a practice and stick to it?
2. Think of an embodied practice that would help ten people you know grow as people
3. Make a list of ten common client issues and think of practices to help with them
4. Think of ten embodied practices that I have mentioned in this book and link them to client issues you encounter
5. Make a list of as many practices as you can find in this book, add to it with any others that you know, and then assign an element that could be developed though each
6. Make up an exercise not in this *book* to develop each aspect of the embodied intelligence model

Facilitator case study: My story
One of my greatest joys as a trainer has been to work with students over time, to see them get to know themselves and to develop themselves. I especially love it

on our longer courses when they are confronted with their patterns (often after years of suspecting), and choose heroically to develop more range. I love supporting them as they struggle to pick a good practice, adore challenging them as their old patterns try to hijack them once they've started, and delight in celebrating with them as they stick with it long enough for it to make a difference. This is both the art and the delight of being an embodied facilitator.

Facilitator case study: Not aikido!!

I had a client, let's call him Steve, who had heard that Mark and several other teachers they respected had practised a lot of aikido. However, what they wanted to develop in themselves was not actually a great fit for the only aikido club near them. There are many styles of aikido and that of the club close by where they lived was very brutal (and Steve is 60+), while they wanted to develop sensitivity in relationship and leading. In addition to the style issue they did not get on with the teacher and found it unfriendly. They still persisted, however, as they REALLY wanted to do aikido!! It wasn't much fun.

I asked Steve to step back and tell me WHY they wanted to do aikido. Once we had gotten clear on this, and because they had skipped this stage and jumped to a practice, this took a little while, we explored other options. I suggested partner dance but this seemed to terrify him and while a stretch is useful, this was clearly 'a bridge too far'. In the end I suggested capoeira and wing chun kung fu, both of which are martial arts with relational elements. Steve had seen capoeira on the TV and thought it looked cool, so we went for that. He actually found two groups near him and did a taster with both before settling on the one that had the nicest teacher and club culture. Through capoeira he got to develop what he wanted and stuck with it for some years, I'm told. This example is quite typical in that people tend to get their practice picks 'back to front' and that style, convenience, teacher and the vibe of the group are major factors, as well as image and it being appealing!

– Peter, life coach, Newcastle, UK

What is the skill-set and how does it help facilitation?

In order to help people change long term, facilitators need to become skilled in helping clients build a practice. Without this, tricks and tips will always eventually fail.

Relationship to other skill-sets

In some ways this skill-set is straight conventional coaching but it is hard to know about practices and inspire people if you have not gone there yourself. Of course being able to observe others, traits skilfully is very helpful to know if their direction of change is a suitable one, and if they are making progress.

A note on role modelling and inspiration

It has been my experience that perhaps the best thing I can do to encourage students to practise is to set an example myself. By seeing both the work ethic involved and results obtained, people will naturally want to practise an art for themselves. The proof is in the pudding . . . and that's you.

How to develop client's embodiment with long-term practice – overview

See the second part of Chapter 4 on 'clients'.

How to develop your own practice-building skills

To effectively support others to establish practices you need to:

- Coach someone to have enough self-awareness of their own patterns to see what they might want to develop
- Motivate them to do the work to change
- Help them know enough about different practices to suggest options
- Both support and challenge them to choose a suitable practice
- Help your client set up a realistic practice schedule based on the practicalities of their life
- Help keep them on track, or alter course if needed
- Celebrate success with them!

A key aspect of this skill is to know how your personal bias might impact what you think they need and what practices may be of benefit.

How to learn about the MANY different embodied practices

There are many, many different arts out there from aikido to Zumba, and new ones get created every day! How, then, does a good embodied coach know what to recommend for what? Well, the first thing I'd say is get stuck in and try a range of them – there's no reason why everyone reading this book can't follow an online chi kung fu video or attend a virtual yoga class. Have fun exploring, and watch what you can't do. With online videos and the like, it's very easy to explore. Also talk to people! See what people do and what they get from it.

Next, learn to ask the right questions. Let's say someone says they found a tang soo do club (a Korean martial art). You could ask how it is different from taekwondo if you know that, or if there is sparring or just forms, if it's fast or slow, if it's anything like karate, and so on. You don't need to know everything, you just need to know about enough arts to have reference points, and enough experience to ask good questions. I also look for opportunities to try out new things, for example, festivals with many activities or yoga centres with different approaches.

I invite you not just to become an embodiment geek, but also to dive into your own practice when the opportunity arises. Is it really a hassle to try ten healing body work modalities over a month, for example, when you are sick or injured? Could you take a week off and do all the yoga classes in your town? That's a great little 'staycation'. Could your marriage be improved by a dance class? (*Warning*: dance classes can bring issues out!)

For those who want to go deeper, I recommend this. I like to pick an area of study for a year based on opportunity and interest, and go deeper into this experientially. At the time of writing, for example, it's covid-19 lockdown in the UK and I'm taking the chance to do online chi kung and tai chi lessons, which don't require touch. Over the years I have done many arts, and in a year you can get to what I describe as 'minimal depth' where one's learning curve slows down but you've gotten a real sense of it. You can't do everything but you can get minimal depth in a range of arts, though it does take dedication. I also recommend 'marrying' at least one art and sticking with it through thick and thin, as while returns diminish, some understandings only come with time.

In summary of much of what's in this book, your own and your client's practice should be driven by:

- *Opportunity*: what's convenient and practical in your life?
- *Desire and inspire*: what butters your muffin?
- *Necessity*: come on, let's be honest, what do you need?[8]

Clients

Coaching people to coach other people is beyond the scope of this book, but feel free to pass on anything simple and safe with credit where appropriate.

Virtual considerations

Helping people develop a practice can easily be done online. On one online course we run, for example, we ask students to try six different practices over six weeks: one meditation class, one conscious dance form, one partner dance form, one martial art, one yoga class and one improv comedy class. At the end of this they work with teachers and a peer group to pick one, and then do it for several months, with online check-ins for accountability and course correction.

Trauma considerations

Trauma can lead to unhealthy patterns of obsessive over-practice – both in intensity and amount of practice, so this is worthy of consideration. People abused by someone in power may also be either extra cautious of new teachers, or paradoxically drawn to abusive teachers. Routine is normally attractive to traumatised people as it can provide safety, and this may help establish a practice if it doesn't become too neurotic, though another trauma pattern is to constantly seek new stimulation, which is a real issue in terms of jumping around between arts and not 'digging a single deep well'. I have also observed a somewhat mysterious 'invisible hand' guiding people to healing practices, and have come to trust unusual client choices because of this.

Cultural considerations

As mentioned in Chapter 4, different cultures relate to the idea of long-term practice quite differently. In Japan, for example, the idea of a 'do' personal growth path is utterly conventional, British school sports also hold this notion implicitly (though this is somewhat class – based), and in Islam the idea of cyclical daily and yearly practice and discipline is deeply embedded. Other cultures stress spontaneity and freedom from routine far more, and you may bump into the Brazilian love of pleasure or the Italian 'sweetness of doing nothing' when supporting people with this topic.

Principles used in this chapter

Both the simulator principle and exaggeration principle have been described in this chapter. Familiarity and distinction principles are also mentioned again.

Committing to a practice

So now we come to the most important part of the book:

> *What practice would you like to commit to, to develop yourself?*

Begin with what skill you'd like to build. Maybe review the embodied intelligence model, and browse the book so far to get some ideas. Did any of the case studies resonate? What have you always known you need but always put off? Your life is ending one breath at a time, and if not now, when? Who will benefit from you getting yourself together? Who will suffer if you do not?

You could start by taking on some of the smaller practices in this book to do daily like centring in the shower or practising social awareness when buying your daily morning coffee. If you just get a couple of regular things you can do from this book, that's fine, and hell of a lot better than just reading about embodiment abstractly. You may also want to ask, how will you remember? Maybe involve a friend. Maybe link it to something else that you do. Just commit and tell everyone you have.

Maybe you're inspired to go deeper into embodiment? If so, commit to three months of doing one art, two or three times a week. Maybe you want to try a few options first, but set a time-frame for this. Maybe you want to do a coaching session on this with your coach, or talk to your mentor or spouse – whatever, but please, if you want to really get the most from this book, *pick something and get stuck in*!

What about if you're really keen and want to devote your life to embodied facilitation as I have? Well, first get a blackbelt or equivalent in whatever you are most drawn to. You will need passion to turn up four or five times a week for 3–5 years. If you've done this, do it again with a totally different but complementary art. Just knowing one thing makes you provincial and biased, and you won't see the deeper principles until you've got at least two reference points. On top of that, experience ten arts over ten years, using the minimal depth approach I described previously. Whatever your level, seek community – get feedback, support and challenge as we learn in relationship.

> **Final facilitator case study: You!**
>
> So the final facilitator case study in the book is you! Hopefully you've read this book over time as instructed. If you got enthusiastic and got this far in a half a day, then please go back and do the work, you naughty reader, you!
>
> If you've been doing the practices, what stood out? How would you describe your learning journey? What were your main discoveries? How have you started to change? How have your work and relationships been impacted?
>
> Take some time to write down your process, and see how far you've come. Chew on it. What have been critical moments and practices? Write it up as the last case study here . . . and well done!

> **Reflection / discussion question**
> With embodied training, what could you become?

Notes

1 Note, people picking up on subtle cues is a huge part of social interaction, and also the basis of 'cold reading' and social compliance that are given a more esoteric explanation. No-touch throws in martial arts rely upon this, despite what the charlatans say.
2 Harry Puckering and Julia E. Knight, *Listen! Say Yes! Commit!* (Morrisville, NC: Lulu.com, 2015).
3 A rarely named and endemic somatic prejudice that is common globally.
4 I think it's fair to include some of my failures here too!
5 This is using a key embodied principle of 'the body learns though exaggeration and contrast' – thanks to Wendy Palmer.
6 Aka 'jumping jacks'.
7 Note this is a version of the serenity prayer.
8 Shinzen Young uses a similar system for meditation.

7 Applications

Hopefully you have found this a practical book. However, I'd like to highlight some common applications of embodied work for facilitators in an easy-access chapter.

Techniques list

First up here's a list of some of the main techniques in the book. Once again, it's the underlying embodied presence of the facilitator that matters most, and his or her deeper knowledge of generative principles beyond that, but it doesn't hurt to have a handy list of techniques.

- Copying awareness-raising
- Meditation
- Basic centring
- Pleasure centring
- Meaning centring
- Enquiry centring
- Cycles work
- Embodied values and purpose work
- 4-elements (for coach and coachee)
- Partner listening / following
- Embodied listening
- Body reading
- Group embodied coordination exercises
- Walking in the room
- Free movement work
- EYP poses
- Centring coaching
- Influencing games

Common applications list

Embodiment can be used with any type of training because whatever you do, people will always have a body! I also hope you use the principles in this book creatively to apply to your own unique circumstances like my doula student, colleague and friend Merav, who took centring and 4-elements and applied them to childbirth in a Palestinian and Jewish context. Now I know *nothing* about giving birth, so this is a good example of generative use of this work!

That being said, here are some ways you can apply embodiment to common themes.

Addiction coaching

Commonly applied techniques and models: pleasure centring, EYP poses (e.g. surrender, self-care and letting go poses).

Notes: Embodied work has been part of my own sobriety for over 13 years.

Anger management training / coaching

Commonly applied techniques and models: meditation, basic centring, 4-elements (especially looking at fire and water).

Notes: I have found embodied work exceptionally helpful with angry people and usually combine it with well – being work, inner critic work and other more traditionally psychological approaches. Centring alone is a massive win.

Change management training / coaching

Commonly applied techniques and models: cycles, basic centring, embodied values and purpose work.

Notes: 'Change management' could emphasise many of the other applications given here and is a wide area, but cycles work is an obvious centre-point.

Communication skills training / coaching

Commonly applied techniques and models: basic centring, 4-elements, partner listening / following.

Notes: By helping people become centred and aware of different communication styles, you can massively improve their communication. Partner work adds an experiential element to much listening skills training.

Conflict resolution skills training / conflict resolution facilitation / embodied peacemaking

Commonly applied techniques and models: basic centring, 4-elements, partner listening / following.

Notes: Centred people who can listen rarely fight! See Paul Linden's work on this topic.

Confidence / assertiveness training

Commonly applied techniques and models: basic centring, EYP poses (especially no pose), embodied values and purpose work.

Notes: Embodiment is a clear help with this area.

Cross-cultural training / coaching

Commonly applied techniques and models: 4-elements, cycles, copying awareness-raising, EYP poses.

Notes: I am slightly obsessed with this topic due to having travelled widely and love revealing and simulating how cultures are embodied. Many people really enjoy figuring out what, say, being German is like, and stepping into another culture's shoes!

Creativity training / coaching

Commonly applied techniques and models: meditation, cycles, deep listening, free movement work.

Notes: *Any* kind of embodied work will increase creativity, even just getting people up and walking!

Dating / attraction / intimacy coaching

Commonly applied techniques and models: centring, 4-elements (especially the fire-water polarity), cycles, pleasure centring, copying awareness-raising, partner listening / following, EYP poses (the passion pose, for example).

Notes: Attraction is embodied ('chemistry'), so embodiment can be used to help people with their confidence, sensitivity and attractiveness. YouTube search 'blackbelt beauty'. There are also many embodiment teachers working with conscious sexuality.

Emotional intelligence training / social skills training

Commonly applied techniques and models: centring, elements, partner listening / following.

Notes: EQ is basically a subset of embodied intelligence, so you could use a lot of what's in this book! For some corporate clients, it's also a good introduction to the topic of embodiment generally.

Financial skills coaching

Commonly applied techniques and models: basic centring, pleasure centring, embodied values and purpose work, EYP poses.

Notes: Many of my more 'alternative' students have deep money issues and embodiment helps a lot. We have EYP poses for most aspect of finances, using centring for pricing and asking for money.

Leadership training / coaching

Commonly applied techniques and models: copying awareness-raising, 4-elements, basic centring, embodied values and purpose work, EYP poses.

Notes: This is one of my specialisms and I love teaching leadership through the body.

Life purpose coaching

Commonly applied techniques and models: basic centring, purpose centring, deep listening, EYP poses, embodied values and purpose work.

Notes: I have run several courses and coached many mentees on this topic, as it seems to be of the times. Listening deeply to the body and enticing what 'lights you up' or gives you energy form one of the main ways to get in contact with purpose, and a kind of 'somatic radar' to develop in coachees. I also use death mediations and several key EYP poses. Search 'purpose black belt' for more on this.

Parenting coaching

Commonly applied techniques and models: centring + all!

Notes: This is just a huge topic and not my specialism but please look up Jane Dancey and Kristie Seabourne who have developed embodied parenting approaches, as well as Susan Bauer's book *The Embodied Teen*.[1]

Public speaking coaching

Commonly applied techniques and models: basic centring, EYP poses (authority pose), see all under leadership too.

Notes: I have helped many people feel more relaxed and have more impact on stages of various kinds using embodiment. I hope how by now is apparent.

Stress management / resilience training

Commonly applied techniques and models: basic centring, meditation, EYP poses (especially the self-care pose).

Notes: I have done a large number of stress management workshops globally and centring is regularly assessed as the best quick-win tool. I also often look at the embodiment of acceptance and change, as the difference between them is at the heart of stress management.

Team-building

Commonly applied techniques and models: 4-elements, embodied values work, coordinated movement, leader-follower exercises, basic centring.

Notes: People connect primarily through the body, not through words. While the term 'team-building' can cover many activities, if you would like to have a team bond emotionally, understand each other's communication and connect to a shared vision and set of values, then embodiment is very helpful.

Time management training / coaching

Commonly applied techniques and models: basic centring, EYP poses, cycles.

Notes: Interestingly, even for something as apparently cerebral as time management, embodied techniques are helpful. For example, people will not make good prioritising decisions if they are not centred.

Trauma therapy

While therapy is beyond the scope of this book, it should be noted that embodied work is central to trauma therapy and many schools exist, include Somatic Experiencing, EMDR, NARM, Hakomi, TRE and more; all work with the body.

Wellness training / coaching

Commonly applied techniques and models: centring, deep listening, 4-elements, meditation, EYP poses (especially self-care and receiving poses).

Notes: A deeper approach to well–being is to tune into the body and also to expose the patterns of self-abuse that limit us. The 'no diet' movement includes embodied coaching around tuning into appetite and the associated emotions, for example.

I have also not included spiritual counselling, life-transition coaching, relationship counselling, neurodiverse coaching, diversity training generally, complexity management, ageing and endearing, or organisational development – either because these areas are largely covered by a related topic or just due to limitations of space.

> **Reflection**
> What's your specialism or an area that is especially live for you right now? What techniques in this book would be a good fit with it?

Designing an embodied workshop or coaching session

Before I can explain how I design embodied learning, there's one more major model to learn. As well as having a preference model, one must also have a model of change.

Cycles

> To everything there is a season . . . a time to be born and a time to die, a time to plant and a time to reap.
> – Ecclesiastes 3:2

To understand embodied facilitation, you must appreciate flow: the art of change and of tact. The embodied model I use to look at this is the seasons. Many models of cycles are adopted by embodiment schools and this is just one of those. One could also use a simple 'beginning-middle-end', Joseph Campbell's complex 'hero's journey', or a model from the conscious dance world.

Whatever model you use, what's key is that life is not just movement but rhythm. In the modern world a sense of natural rhythm has largely been lost, but the fact remains that the bodymind has its cycles, and we would be wise as facilitators to be aware of them. These cycles can be short or long and operate in everything we do – from taking a sip of water, to relationships, to work projects, to the course of our life. Cycles exist within cycles, making them 'fractal'.

Perhaps the easiest cycle to use – because most Western people are so familiar with it – is that of the seasons (Table 7.1).[2] I use this as a model for coaching people to become aware of how biases impact them, such as quitting work too early, finding new projects hard, struggling to leave relationships, etc.; as well as for designing my own trainings and tracking the flow of coaching.

The model can be explored with individuals or groups in an embodied way using handshakes (business-friendly), hugs or more complex movements, to name but a few ways. It's really everywhere, so your creativity is again the only limit.

Based on all cycles of nature, we can identify algorithms of cycles that apply to most (if not all) cycles of subjective experience, relationships and actions – the 3-dimensions of the 'I, We, It'.[3]

Numerous embodiment schools have their own flow model and I've been influenced by at least ten, with Richard Strozzi-Heckler's and Gabriel Roth's models being two of the first I came into contact with.

Specifics of training design

Any workshop or coaching session should have a beginning, a middle and an ending, and there should be time for participants to rest and reflect afterwards. This is the four seasons cycles model applied to facilitation. Each of the seasons

Table 7.1 The four seasons of embodiment

Season	Features	Images and archetypes	Direction	Life-stage	Simple
Spring	Starting, awakening, growing, accelerating, rising, increasing	- Blossom - Light green shoots - Conception and birth - Spring showers	up	Childhood	- Turning on / waking (I) - Greeting (we) - Preparing (it)
Summer	Fulfilling, expressing, full growth, full speed, high, maximum	- Fruit - Full green leaves - Mature animals and families - Sun	forward	Early adulthood	- On / awake (I) - Relating (we) - Do (it)
Autumn	Containing, slowing, declining, falling, less speed, decreasing	- Storing nuts - Falling brown leaves - Ageing animals - Cloud and drizzle	back	Middle age	- Turning off / sleepy (I) - Parting (we) - Stop (it)
Winter	Ending and preparing, resting, slowest, low, minimum	- No fruit or leaves - Hibernation and death - Snow	down	Elderhood	- Off / sleeping (I) - Alone (we) - Don't do (it)

Applications 177

has specific functions, some of which apply to any workshop and some of which are specific to embodiment. This is the general flow of a training:

- Shallow – deep – shallow
- Known – unknown – known
- Unconscious – conscious
- Strangers – connected – letting go
- Outer world – inner world – integrated world
- Self – other – self in world
- Abstract – personal – application
- Untrusting – trust – letting go

More specifically:

Spring – the start of any workshop or coaching session[4]

> Relationally: meeting
>
> Aims: establish and clarify
>
> Trust: build warmth and establish authority (including of all there)
>
> Emotionally: aid 'arriving' (check-ins often help), inspire, calm or energies as needed, connect to values (motivate)
>
> Boundaries: establish. Create the 'container' and establish roles
>
> Information: introduce basic concepts
>
> Embodiment specifics: differentiate between embodiment and body language / wellness, define 'embodied' (vs. mindful), explain contexts (avoid pushback), explain the embodied intelligence model
>
> Experientially: introduce idea of embodiment with a short, simple (and likely playful) experience
>
> Learning: create learner mindset and set expectations. Explain learning theory (doing and being, not just learning *about*)
>
> Ethics: establish consent and confidentiality. Also responsibility for self-care

Summer – the heart of any workshop or coaching session

> Relationally: relating / deepening
>
> Aims: keep in mind
>
> Trust: deepen warmth and keep authority
>
> Emotionally: support depth and transformation
>
> Boundaries: keep. Hold the 'container' and roles

Information: deliver core material

Embodiment specifics: explain why the body is being worked with for each exercise

Experientially: the deepest, most intense work

Learning: keep focused, give state experiences, record insights

Ethics: calibration and ensure ongoing capacity

Autumn – the last part of any workshop or coaching session

Relationally: parting

Aims: check met

Trust: loosen warmth and give away authority

Emotionally: support people letting go, encourage appreciation for a sense of completion

Boundaries: loosen / open the 'container'

Information: connect core material to other known area, offer ongoing resources

Embodiment specifics: principles of practice

Experientially: 'pepper' techniques into applications

Learning: clarify main insights. Focus on real-world application and long-term trait embedding practices. Reflection

Ethics: support people to 'land' back in their lives safely (the completion of this whole flow) and encourage them not to make sudden big decisions. Ensure physical safety leaving if still in a lettered state.[5] Encourage self-care

Winter – afterwards

Rest, reflection, further integration

Ethics: dual relationships ethics

This flow is a condensation of well over 10,000 hours of facilitation experience and I have found that students learning these models can dramatically speed up their paths to excellence. It requires some study, and is as deep as you'd like it to be!

Notes

1. Susan Bauer, *The Embodied Teen* (Berkeley, CA: North Atlantic Books, 2018).
2. Do be aware though that in some locations there may be other seasons like rainy and dry! You can always use the same model but change the primary labels to 'beginning, middle, end and ended'!
3. See Ken Wilber's Integral framework.
4. Actually much starts before you meet people in terms of aims, trust, authority, etc. Sometimes the mail or gossip that goes around before a workshop can make or break it in fact! In corporate work especially this may be 50 per cent of the success.
5. After deep work and conscious dance workshops people may be quite spaced out if you haven't 'landed' them well, so it's important they don't walk out the door under a bus!

8 Principles of excellence

I'm a geek and an unashamed snob when it comes to excellence in facilitating embodiment. It has been and remains my life's path, to keep improving in this area myself and to help others to do so as well. With that in mind, this chapter will be a good review and will 'take the hood off' much of what has gone before. There will also be some more advanced considerations for experienced embodied facilitators.

Top 7 mistakes embodied facilitators make

Let's start by summarising some of the main mistakes you could make:

1. *Fail to practise yourself, or become provincial in one practice*
   I hope it's obvious by now that your own practice is vital for teaching embodied work with efficacy and integrity, and that no one practice has it all
2. *Not be fully in service to the client*
   Often people push their own agenda of change, enjoyment or even politics when teaching – don't!
3. *Not have clear aims, or use clear language*
   In a remarkably large number of embodiment practices the point is not clear, and this can transfer into work with clients. *Why* are you doing a particular activity? Equally, clear 'operational' language is very important – this will be expanded upon shortly
4. *Not be trauma-aware* (e.g. lack of consent and calibration)
   I hope I've stressed throughout the book why this matters
5. *Ignore your own bias, or not adapt*
   A good embodied trainer knows their own type and how this biases them, and is able to adapt to different types of people, cultures and circumstances
6. *Poor flow*
   Most facilitators are not aware of their cycle's preferences so mess up flow, skipping beginnings, trying to cram too much in (I guess 50 per cent of the EFC exams I mark make this mistake) or rushing endings
7. *Lack of authenticity and fun*
   Frankly, many people in this field are pretending to be someone else and taking this stuff way too seriously

> **Exercise**
> Go to a yoga or dance class, take note of the teaching, and discuss with a colleague afterwards which mistakes the facilitator made, and where they were strong.

Verbal mistakes when teaching embodiment[1]

These are the most common verbal mistakes I see students make:

- Giving possible outcomes and metaphors, rather than clear instructions – for example, 'empty your mind' or 'have a mind like water' vs. 'bring your attention to the physical sensations of breathing'. This is known as non-operational language, as the clear method is missing and it forces people to guess what you'd actually like them to do!
- Opening instructions with 'Just . . .'. This is a common verbal tic that actually minimises the task, which may not be considered trivial by your participants
- Forgetting to ask permission when touching. Or, alternatively, asking but not really being okay with a 'no' answer. This creates compliance. The ethical way is to gain explicit verbal consent
- Using 'we' when no agreement has been reached. This is an example of 'forced teaming', as opposed to gaining consent – for example, 'We are doing X now' (also a *fait accompli*)
- 'Next you'll . . .'. This is another *fait accompli*. Again, it removes the possibility for participants to consent. Instead, you could offer alternatives, support people who choose not to follow your lead and actively teach students to say 'no'
- Using foreign, 'spiritual' or anatomical / scientific jargon, as a way of status-claiming; it often makes things less clear too
- Speaking in an annoying breathy spiritual 'yoga voice' or even a different accent. Just speak normally! More broadly, skilful use of tone matters, as this conveys your own embodiment
- Adopting 'good', 'nice' and other value judgements, which suggest certain options are better than others (assuming you don't want to do this). For example, 'nice and deep into the stretch', implying that it's somehow better to go deep than not. Value judgements may be inherent in word choices such as 'collapse the chest', which sounds harsh compared to 'flex the upper spine'!

> **Exercise**
> Go to a yoga, martial arts or dance class and want to tear your own ears off now that you can't un-know this.

So what makes a competent embodied facilitator?

In summary:

- Ethics
- Power and love embodied
- An intention to serve
- A commitment to 'do no harm'
- A community of accountability and support
- A commitment to a clear code of ethics

Personal embodied presence

- Health – this is the foundation. You don't need a six-pack or to be a vegan to teach embodiment, but you do need a certain level of health
- Embodiment! Short-term state management and long-term disposition as a result of practice. Far more important than tools and tricks is how we are and who we are
- Personal qualities across all four elements. A range of virtues is needed
- A range of micro-skills from the four aspects of embodied intelligence – awareness, management, empathy and influence
- A developed sense of rhythm (see cycles). Timing and flow are everything both in planning and in the moment

An adequate tool-kit

- Good depth and breadth with the nine embodied primary tools: awareness, acceptance, intention, imagery, posture, relaxation, movement, responsiveness and respiration
- Yang and yin tools (e.g. challenge and support, direct feedback and deep listening)
- Fundamentals of the trade (e.g. ICF core coaching competencies)
- Other relevant professional skills (e.g. sales, marketing and financial skills)

Five levels of embodied facilitation

This is another way of looking at what creates excellence. When assessing and developing your competence as an embodied facilitator, examine all these levels of focus and competence:

1. *Micro skills*: awareness and choice across all tools
2. *Techniques*: methods you have for working with self and other (this is the least important)

3 *Principles*: what makes the techniques work. This means you can adapt them to suit the situation
4 *Relationship*: people learn in relationship
5 *Being*: what underpins it all. This is why we have our own practice

Embodiment exam criteria?

When I sat down to create the first Embodied Facilitator Course in 2012 with Francis Briers, we faced a real challenge: we wanted a meaningful course with a practical exam, so that there was a real standard, but we also had students from many different disciplines who wanted to apply the work in many different ways. We had already created a principles-based course that allowed people to apply a deeper understanding of embodiment creatively, so we could not examine people on how well they copied us![2] Our solution was to find standards of excellence consistent over many great teachers that we could apply to any exam, whatever the coaching session, an embodied kung-fu class or a skilful flirting workshop! It took us a few years to refine the criteria but here they are as they exist today. In our exams they are independently measured by different raters to a high degree of reliability. While for conciseness I'm leaving out specific details here, they should also make sense from the content of the book so far:

1 Ethics (especially confidentiality, consent and calibration)
2 Embodiment (one's own – includes state and trait aspects)
3 Clear aims
4 Principle use (shown by creativity usually)
5 Tool use (i.e. they can use a range of techniques)
6 Listening (verbal and bodily)
7 Adaptation (individual, situational and cultural)
8 Rhythm (cycles)
9 Language use (operational, lack of jargon, etc.)
10 Testing (that they work empirically, not based on faith)
11 Application (that they help clients apply the work in their real lives)
12 Body leadership (Chapter 7)
13 Change the world (we would like to see them link embodied work to their deeper values and those of clients, and understand the bigger picture of how embodiment is socially impactful)

Of these trainers often over-emphasise techniques, when it's the others that make the techniques work that really matter

Note that this is not about box-ticking and they are all complex. Establishing aims, for example, could happen prior to a training and involve multiple stakeholders, discussion and enquiry, and could shift within a session, or be left open at times, so it isn't just 'tell people the point'.[3]

> **Exercise**
> Video-record yourself teaching or coaching and then assess your performance based on these criteria. Get a colleague involved if you can. Where can you improve?

Do you have a learning community?

I'll be blunt: it's almost impossible to get good on your own. The people that I see consistently getting better and better at embodied facilitation not only have a regular practice and some great mentors, but are also part of an ongoing learning community. A community can provide support and challenge in your growth, and provide very practical professional benefits. The world of embodiment is so broad that no one person can be an expert in all of it, so having people with a shared language, values and norms you trust and can go to is vital. Those without community usually not only stagnate in their learning and become arrogant, but often create small fiefdoms with dwindling ethics. If like me you are the head or founder of a community, ensure you are not the *centre* too, that leadership is distributed, and that people can challenge you, on both your teaching and ethics.

The principles of embodied education

Throughout this book, I have mentioned that what I'd really like you to take away is not just a se of techniques, but also the underlying principles behind them.[4] This will allow you to understand what makes the techniques work, so you not only can teach them more effectively, but also that can adapt them to the circumstances, and even create entirely new ones for your own unique contexts. I am rather proud of drawing these principles out from observing many embodiment approaches, and believe it to be one of the few major contributions I have made to the field of embodiment.

Here are the principles in this book laid out first as tenets, and then as the principles themselves. This is a condensed summary of much of this book, and quite advanced, so if you're a total beginner maybe come back to this section in a few years – most students I work with face-to-face take a couple of years to get them.

Tenets

1 *Context*: Our current situation, relationships, culture, disposition and the environment are all embodied. We are layered adaptations to context and history

2 *Comfort*: The body reveals what's familiar. We feel 'at home' in what we have practised
3 *Joy*: Delight reveals what's needed or longed for
4 *Holography*: The body reveals our way of being in all things
5 *Deviation*: The inability to follow a form (e.g. a set of dance moves or a yoga pose) reveals habitual patterns
6 *Guidance*: The body can guide our life. When listened to, the body gives wisdom
7 *Practice*: We are always practising, unconsciously or consciously, and become what we practise
8 *Contrast*: The body reveals and learns by exaggeration, contrast and embodied differentiation of new distinctions
9 *Relationship*: We learn in relationship
10 *Integration*: We can transfer embodied learning into daily life, by creating somatic markers[5] and micro poses,[6] and by designing a practice routine
11 *Process*: The body is a process and it benefits us to listen and follow
12 *Self-regulation*: The fight-flight and craving responses can be managed though the body
13 *Trigger*: Shadow (repressed aspects of ourselves) is revealed by triggering and infatuation
14 *Chaos*: The body is free and has no laws!

The embodied principles

This is what we are doing in embodied work. These came from observing my own work and that of other teachers and noticing that just a few principles were being applied. They are deep flexible core methods. Paul Linden invented one and called it an 'algorithm', and I have extended the idea. The principles can be thought of as keys to understanding embodied work or as templates for practise. While embodiment should never be practised 'by the numbers' without appreciation for individual differences, intuition, circumstances, etc., these principles aid clarity and can be used generatively. Note also that while these are presented in a simple and discrete linear fashion, application is often more complex than this.

The fundamental principle

1. The fundamental principle – *awareness and choice*

Awareness principles

2. Familiarity – *try and notice*
3. Exposure – *differ and see*
4. Contrast – *extend and compare*

5. Simulators – *metaphor and reveal*
6. Body listening – *reveal and dialogue*
7. Body reading – *see and ask*

Choice principles
8. Growth – *range and balance*
9. Centring – *notice and manage*
10. Emotions – *identify and shift*
11. Shadow – *identify and re-own*
12. Process – *follow and allow*

The principles in detail

These apply to one's own practice and also to facilitation. They are divided into awareness and choice principles but awareness often naturally brings choice, so don't hold this distinction too rigidly. The vast majority of embodied training works with these principles, and making them explicit speeds up students' path to excellence.

The fundamental principle

1. The fundamental principle (aka freedom principle)

    Distinctions – awareness – range – choice

    - Learn about a set of embodied distinctions
    - Create awareness of current patterns of posture, movement and attention through mindful self-observation, contrast or external assessment – create insight
    - Learn other options to create a wider range of possible choices and fewer habitual unconscious patterns – build range
    - Choose actions and responses to match circumstances, values and goals – increased responsiveness

This is at the very core of all embodied work. It underpins all other principles. Sometimes I simply refer to this as 'awareness and choice'.

Awareness principles

2. Familiarity principle

    Try – notice – clarify – reflect

    - Try a range of motions or postures (e.g. 4-elements movements)

- Notice which are familiar, which are uncomfortable and which are longed for
- Clarify what patterns might be present
- Reflect on how this shows up in life

I use this principle a lot with all kinds of models and it can be done with both individuals and groups. Be careful to distinguish between what is familiar (indicating a habit) and what is longed for (indicating a desire).

3. Deviation principle (aka exposure principle)

Try – deviate – notice – self-assess

- Try and do any physical form (e.g. a yoga posture or dance step)
- Notice deviation from the form (you may need help with this)
- Illuminate purely physical influences such as injuries
- See the pattern that is exposed
- Use models to make conclusions

You can use a dance step, martial arts weapon practice or any form with a client to reveal patterns. Here, 'mistakes' are not mistakes but interesting ways we reveal ourselves. For example, if a yoga student finds it hard to do warrior pose, perhaps they have an issue with fierceness or taking up space. In yoga this is sometimes called 'exposure', as patterns are exposed.

4. Contrast principle

Decide – embody – exaggerate – contrast – notice

- Decide on an area to work with, from challenges in life or from consistent feedback, for example
- Take the key issue and identify how it is embodied (through self-observation – if possible, do this first; and outside observation – often necessary when we have habituated)
- Exaggerate and contrast this pattern with its opposite, noting transitions, the middle ground and specific body markers of the pattern to make it obvious, and its movement comings and goings
- Notice the pattern via these body markers as it occurs habitually in life

This is useful for coaching around many things, for example, working with being pushy vs. being a pushover, or earth vs. air. This principle brings clarity to what is involved but also usually helps with range, as it shows that it is possible when we reach an extreme pattern to often 'swing back' into the other pole, so it could be used as process work as well.

A variation on this is seen in distinction coaching where one is not contrasting polarities but two confused things that need to be distinguished.

188   The Body in Coaching and Training

5. Simulator principle

    Identify – metaphor – observe – insight – apply – review

    - Identify an area to be examined
    - Create an embodied metaphor for the circumstances (e.g. being pulled in two directions)
    - Observe embodied reactions and possibilities
    - Gain insight into external circumstance (e.g. current patterns or new possibilities)
    - Apply insight back to external situation
    - Review and adjust

A useful one for bringing insight into a coaching challenge. The body has a way of feeling the symbolism of situations and reacting in a consisstent way to regular life revealing both habitual patterns and creating a place to study new possibilities.

6. Body listening principle

    Identify – welcome – expand – ask – design – review

    (a) Identify a theme / question through conversation, or

    (b) Start with a sensation already calling for attention within the body (e.g. pain with no obvious external cause)

    - If (a), ask body for a sensation which relates to this question / theme and identify it
    - Notice, accept and welcome sensation (a) or (b)
    - Ask sensation if any other parts of the body are involved and follow these until it settles
    - Ask sensation to grow (*note*: may have to set bearable limits)
    - Ask sensations what message they have. What is their job? What would they like? What would they like to say?
    - Design actions and practices based upon this if needed
    - Review and adjust

This is a way of accessing intuition and dialoguing with the unconscious. Note that self-care and rest are particularly important after body listening practice.

7. Body reading principle

    Permission – why – note – observe – identify – eliminate bias – feel – observation – state – ask – compare

Principles of excellence **189**

- Establish permission to body read
- State why an assessment is being made – 'for the sake of what?'
- Note immediate empathic emotional impact, both in own mirroring and in reactivity
- Consciously 'try on' what you see with micro or macro movements in own body for emotional tone and insight into the meaning
- Make concrete observations (assertions – like operational language), using as many of the eight embodied primary tools as possible (e.g. posture and movement style)
- Apply models of embodiment that you know to make an assessment
- Eliminate bias as much as possible – note cultural norms, obvious physical causes like injuries, own observer bias due to state (e.g. in a bad mood seeing negative things) and possible shadow
- State what is both observed and what assessment might be based on that, stressing it is just an educated guess and not 'the' truth
- Ask if this trait plays out in a general way in life / if others assess it in this light
- Compare the somatic tendency observed within their daily-life behaviour

The principle here is to resonate with someone and observe them clearly, by eliminating as much of our own bias as possible. See Chapter 5.

Choice principles

8. Growth principle

   Aim – identify – design practices – support – review

   - Name trait that in excess is causing problems that we'd like to move away from, or a value / virtue you'd like to embody more
   - Identify the embodied pattern of this trait, then the positive trait if you've started with an excess / negative. Use the contrast principle if needed to help find the pattern
   - Design a practice to grow the desired embodiment
   - Create support structures and engage with communities of support, feedback and immersion
   - Review and adjust

For example, someone says 'I have an issue with arrogance and I would like be less habitual and have more range'. You help them to discover how 'arrogance' lives in the body and find an alternative mode which they can practise. Often we are building range with this principle.

9. Centring principle

    Challenge – notice – learn – repeat – centre – increase – repeat

    - Introduce manageable challenging stimulus with permission. Start with a very gentle stimulus and calibrate upwards making it more intense and realistic until a noticeable but not overwhelming distress response is reached
    - Notice the distress response. Make / ask for specific body-based descriptions rather than evaluations. Repeat stimuli if not able to identify response
    - Apply an appropriate centring technique using culturally sensitive language and add metaphors, role-models and images if helpful
    - Repeat stimuli and employ the centring technique, targeting specifics of the individual distress response
    - Notice objective reduction in distress response, subjective feelings of distress and effect on the relationship (e.g. less hostile). *Note*: A coach should let a client discover this for themselves not tell them
    - Increase stimulus strength with permission. As long as the individual is not overwhelmed, you can keep increasing the strength of stimuli and centring
    - Repeat centring

This is what we do when we practise centring (see Chapter 4). Like all the other principles there are many ways of applying this one, for example, using many stimuli, and many centring techniques. *Note*: A well-designed yoga or martial arts class can be an expression of this principle.

10. Emotion principle

    Notice – name – cause – presence – shift

    - Notice sensations in body
    - Name and if appropriate express emotion
    - Identify message – underlying needs and story that have caused emotion
    - If another story would serve you better, shift to it
    - Stay present with sensations of emotion (this often helps it move)
    - Shift and centre body to change / moderate emotion as appropriate

This is a simple way to work with emotion through the body.

11. Shadow principle

    Identify – try – tolerate – play – re-own – mark – process

    - Find someone or an aspect of someone which you find annoying
    - Identify the specific embodied elements of what you find annoying
    - Try it on and learn to tolerate it. Go in and out as necessary
    - See the world from this perspective, increasing empathy
    - Play with it until you find the positive side
    - Speak from this embodiment as part of yourself
    - Find the body markers that will allow you to access this again
    - Verbally or creatively process this experience

Making the unconscious conscious. This is one of the deeper aspects of the work I do and should be approached with care, I have not included much in this book on the topic. Note that self-care and rest are particularly important after shadow practice.

The lite version – think of trigger, note tension, relax.

12. Process principle

    Frame – follow – allow – set aside – follow – meaning

    - Pose yourself a question you'd like insight into as a frame. This part is optional, and just 'letting the body do its thing' is also usually helpful
    - Follow sensation in the body
    - Allow movement to occur. This could be very briefly or over days. Music can facilitate this but remember, music is not neutral
    - Watch out for forms and set aside judgement and censorship – you can, for example, just say 'later' to yourself when this happens or focus on sensation again instead. In this way, it is a kind of moving meditation
    - Keep following sensation and movement, preferably until it comes to a natural rest point
    - You can make sense of the experience through discussion and creativity (e.g. drawing)
    - Self-care and rest

The idea here is to 'get out of our own way' and allow the body to follow its natural healthy process. There are other slightly different varieties where, for example, we are looking to complete a stuck movement (e.g. somatic experiencing). The seasons model is key to this principle.

Note: The above was developed for Embodied Yoga Principles and the Embodied Facilitator course, drawing on the work of Paul Linden, Richard Strozzi-Heckler, Wendy Palmer, Stuart Heller, Ginny Whitelaw and Dylan Newcomb.[7] I am somewhat proud of them as by making explicit the "meta-pattern" in much embodied work, they can vastly speed up student's journey to both excellence and creativity. This is one of the more advanced aspects of this book, however, so don't be alarmed if you're a beginner and they don't make sense right away.

> *Exercise*
> Review all the exercises in this book with these principles in mind to embed them. Then make up some new exercises. Only by seeing many examples through this lens, and working with them in your own way, will they become embedded.

In the real world

Life transfer and containers

I hope this book inspires you to practise an embodied art, but this time is wasted if that practice doesn't find its way into real life. This is the challenge of life transfer. Ironically, what makes a learning environment most effective is differences between the practice area and real life. For example, in a yoga studio one generally does not talk and social exchange is limited. This is helpful because by simplifying life, one can work on specific skills, and by making life lost less consequential, for example, it is hard to lose your job or your wife but in your class come on risks are reduced and learning enhanced as a result. The very things that make a yoga studio effective for learning embodiment also create barriers to transfer into life.

Gradients

A general principle that is very helpful is that of 'gradients'. This means that, for beginners, learning situations are made artificial and therefore safe and easy, but as one progresses, elements of realism and perhaps intensity are added back in. Traditional embodied practices often fail to do this, perhaps because in Asian traditions very long time-frames of practice were considered the norm and the long, slow way would get you there in the end. What it means, for example, is that a normal aikido or yoga class will never integrate such things as money, conversation or technology. It is necessary therefore both to simplify practice sufficient for beginners to learn it, and also add a scale of increasing realism so that they can apply it. This is another version of calibration, but applied to learning theory rather than ethics.

> **Final reflections**
> How are you already excellent as a facilitator? Where do you need to improve? Which of these two questions was easier to answer and what does this say about your self-assessment bias?

Notes

1. Taken from my first book, *Embodiment: Moving Beyond Mindfulness* (Unicorn Slayer Press, 2019).
2. This is the norm in many systems and leads to degradation like photocopying photocopies.
3. I generally make people work to find their own aims by asking them, 'So why am I doing this weird stuff with you, do you think?'
4. First published in EFC course notes 2012, in the Embodied Yoga Principles handouts.
5. Bodily changes that warn you that a pattern is engaged, e.g. your eyes narrow when you become angry.
6. These are the subtle application of larger forms, e.g. changing one to engage the entire pattern of an Embodied Yoga Principles pose.
7. These teachers are perhaps my six biggest influences and the work in this book would not be possible without each of their contributions. Some I have spent a lot of time with, some only a little.

9 Conclusion

Wow, what a journey! If you've engaged with the reflections and exercises in this book, no doubt you've got a lot from it. If you've just skim read it, that's OK, I understand that we're all busy, and why not block-out time in your diary to get the most from it at a later date?

Top tips for facilitators

As a review here's some top tips:[1]

- Know what you're trying to do. Clear aims matter
- Being is more important than tools. Embody what you're teaching
- Any training is a cycle. Flow matters (e.g. building trust and authority early, and helping people get clear take-aways at the end)
- Give clear instructions, involving a 'how' that a ten-year-old could grasp
- Speak the truth. I don't just mean, 'don't lie'
- Have a plan, but . . .
- Listen and adapt what you're doing in the present moment
- Take what you do seriously, but don't take yourself seriously
- Don't sleep with anyone you're teaching or take advantage of them financially
- Culture matters
- A little love goes a long way

Seven ways the body is vital to coaching

Here's a reframing of much of this book's content as applied to coaching as another review:[2]

1. *It tells you what you're screaming*
   Your bodily states and general disposition are always being transmitted to others. Our embodied way of being is one of the most dramatic influences on clients, regardless of the words we are speaking.

2. *It's your super-Google*
   While logical techniques and tools are helpful, it's only by accessing deep bodily wisdom and intuition that we can do our best work.
3. *It's your free legal high*
   Simple bodily techniques, such as centring, can be used to quickly self-regulate when faced with the challenges of facilitation.
4. *It's your X-ray specs*
   Your client's body is shouting a story of their history and dispositions. By learning about embodment, you can more accurately assess and adapt to clients.
5. *It turns you and your clients into transformers*
   If you develop a greater embodied range for yourself and then teach clients to do the same, new possibilities quickly open up.
6. *It's your psychic 'spy'*
   By tuning into your own body, you will become aware of how it mirrors others, giving you vital information about a client or group.
7. *It makes you human!*
   Being tuned into yourself makes you authentic, ethical and in touch with what you care about. If we aren't bringing that fully into our work, what's the point? Being embodied is being human.

Bonus: Can you link each of these to a chapter?

Exercise: Test yourself!

OK, kids, it's exam time!

- What is embodiment and how is it different from fitness, mindfulness and body language?
- What is the contexts model?
- What is embodied intelligence? Name all four areas
- Name three philosophers and three scientists associated with embodiment
- How do we become self-aware?
- How is state different from trait?
- How can we self-regulate? Name three techniques to do this
- What makes for effective practice?
- How can we learn social awareness skills?
- What is 'body reading' and how can we learn it?
- How can we build our embodied impact and influence?
- What is the 4-elements model?
- What is the cycles model?
- How does trauma impact embodiment?
- Name three cultural factors in relation to embodiment
- Name four deeper principles of embodiment
- Name three ethical considerations around embodiment

- What are some common mistakes embodiment teachers make?
- Why does all this matter?

Don't stress if some of these are tricky and you have to check back, this book takes a few readings to get the most from it. If reviewing this book with a facilitator colleague you may want to split this list up and dedicate and hour to 4-5 questions and look at then over several weeks.

Exercise: Can you teach it?

I find a good test of whether I've absorbed something is – can I pass it on to someone else? Try explaining some of the core things we've covered above to an interested friend or colleague. This often reveals what's not totally clear yet.

Exercise: What have I missed / extra chapter?

I like to encourage students to think critically . . . so what have I missed? What have I stressed too much? How have my personality and practice biased this book? What would you bring to the party if we collaborated?

What would be a great extra chapter? (You can get an e-book on selling embodiment in business at the following website: https://thebodyincoachingbook.com/ – that we did not include here due to length constraints – and a video of a facilitation workshop on the book's core content free that we normally charge £50 for.)

You could also try making a case against embodied learning to check you haven't become a 'convert' too.

Ongoing practise

At the risk of droning on, what matters most in embodiment is *practice*, so I hope that if you've found something within that your practise is ongoing. If you're going to teach embodiment to others, I would strongly recommend this – for the success of the work, for integrity and for safety reasons. Pick one regular twice- or three times-weekly devoted practice like yoga, dance or aikido, meditate as a foundation too, and set reminders to practise the smaller skills within like centring daily.

Review the book both for what inspires you and what you need. Note what skill-sets are lacking and find concerted ways to build them that you can practise regularly, and don't just leave it to chance!

Commit now and tell people, even if it's just for one minute of practice a week . . . or all this book did was bring you several hours closer to your death and increase your arrogance about what you think you know.

Resources

Book website and supportive videos

Embodiment is sometimes much easier to show than to tell. With that in mind I have uploaded many free videos over the years, and your understanding of the content here will be dramatically improved by spending an hour or two viewing these – practical demonstrations and coaching sessions especially. If you're reading a print version of this book and just want links to click on for ease (which will also be updated regularly) go to:

www.embodiedfacilitationbook.com

We have also uploaded the e-book extra chapter there I mentioned, and some extra pdfs for facilitators, as well as the first three chapters from my first book and a great workshop video to demo most of the content. This site is also a great portal to the various courses and communities I'm involved with, so if you've enjoyed this book, definitely check it out.

Video list

All of these can be found at www.embodiedfacilitationbook.com also.

Introductions

- What's being embodied: https://youtu.be/g3yuDEihmE0
- What 'embodiment' means: https://www.youtube.com/watch?v=MUkp3kK6IHo&t=1s
- What 'embodiment' doesn't mean: https://www.youtube.com/watch?v=UeN7ERj4MEA&t=1s
- How to be more embodied: https://youtu.be/CxNP5vKZ4qc
- Seven core models: https://youtu.be/FCNZkl2OEs8
- Embodied intelligence: https://youtu.be/Q4yJ7LCxrUo
- Layers of embodiment: https://youtu.be/KfXjC59t8Uc

Learning

- Learning embodiment: https://youtu.be/w3QHiMeEmi8
- Trolls of learning: https://youtu.be/lKGR_hxyomo
- Practice intro: https://youtu.be/iFDk-MonAVM
- Practice at home: https://youtu.be/KxaqSMbngJI
- How to choose a practice: https://youtu.be/ncB0BUNBJJ8
- How practice screw us up: https://youtu.be/va3NaPHV8CU
- Daily embodiment practice: https://youtu.be/3QWPWI_P44E

Meditation

- Meditation for embodiment: https://youtu.be/79UupboRkPU
- Choosing a meditation style: https://youtu.be/Mh9Wmc7xWmw
- Body-scan meditation: https://youtu.be/4mtwmxO4BkA
- Body awareness in daily life: https://youtu.be/qnRgpFmVOsk
- Mindfulness of breathing: https://youtu.be/r19qyGPYfhw
- optional videos
    - Body-scan systematic: https://youtu.be/ZqIKiW4K_H8
    - Metta meditation: https://youtu.be/8Lff46LtMrY

4-elements

- The four elements – overview: https://youtu.be/ZwWkprjdg9w
- Four elements – advanced: https://youtu.be/7bjSVOHjLNk
- Four elements workshop: https://www.youtube.com/watch?v=L4qbsKL-j14&t=1189s
- Demo (old): https://youtu.be/6UN5Fnwucso
- 4-elements in coaching: https://youtu.be/Kbd8AZCc5Gc
- 4-elements in meditation: https://youtu.be/Z3xAuRgtt_c
- Embodied form breakdown: https://youtu.be/P3lH-QMgbBo
- Embodied form: https://youtu.be/Ku3mux7VWV4
- 4-elements coaching demo: https://www.youtube.com/watch?v=2SHunOVrxes&t=854s

Cycles

- Cycles/ seasons – embodied change: https://youtu.be/wGqX5ATCVII
- Cycles applied: https://youtu.be/wWxUkjiF7x0
- Partner basic practice: https://youtu.be/VdjE3BsclAw
- Cycles in relationship: https://youtu.be/4wx4NoAdKcs
- Relational embodiment: https://youtu.be/5sFhgGsW0p8

Centring

- What is centring?: https://youtu.be/Y_CzQPzTcvQ
- ABC centring: https://youtu.be/wsXHcDBcuEI
- Centring application: https://youtu.be/ofm3HyoXnJM
- Centring for purpose: https://youtu.be/5L3Cwq4rwT8
- EROS centring: https://youtu.be/IibZ8gI4GT8
- Pleasure centring: https://youtu.be/0Mzs9XMhR-k
- Form and freedom: https://youtu.be/GpxW1nNFgT4

Conclusion

Techniques with clients

- Easy embodiment coaching: https://www.youtube.com/watch?v=Zs4Xe39q87A
- Trauma education for facilitators: https://www.youtube.com/watch?v=Oz2Xn3jDp-8
- Language use: https://www.youtube.com/watch?v=4fgvLcJjIY0
- EYP for coaching: https://www.youtube.com/watch?v=l6Op1OKnECA&feature=youtu.be
- EYP coaching demo with Ira: https://www.youtube.com/watch?v=NHOO9a6PNrc
- EYP coaching with Kate: https://www.youtube.com/watch?v=UcgOsG_mlvc
- 4-elements coaching session: https://www.youtube.com/watch?v=2SHunOVrxes
- 4-elements coaching part 1: https://www.youtube.com/watch?v=itt18059y8g
- 4-elements coaching part 2: https://www.youtube.com/watch?v=NjhUubNIpeM
- Embodiment coaching part 2 (Russian and English): https://www.youtube.com/watch?v=HOgTisCJKss
- Distinction coaching with Neilon: https://www.youtube.com/watch?v=3MecLe_Mgf0
- Distinction coaching (Russian and English): https://www.youtube.com/watch?v=If8F86TCRyQ
- Relaxation coaching with Chris B: https://www.youtube.com/watch?v=4YfCIajYtAI
- Purpose coaching (includes centring) with Sarah: https://www.youtube.com/watch?v=1V-jy2DqROw
- Body listening coaching: https://www.youtube.com/watch?v=eJBqO9oXPBE
- Embodied time management coaching: https://www.youtube.com/watch?v=aQgNPVnBSh0

You can find lots more coaching demos on the following page (mainly from Mark Walsh):
https://embodiedfacilitator.com/coaching-demos/

Paul Linden coaching demos:
https://www.youtube.com/watch?v=cDGqgiTKd0s
https://www.youtube.com/watch?v=u606bM0ucVE

Other resources

Many of the ideas presented here are fleshed out on my *podcast*, The Embodiment Podcast (freely available at www.embodiedfacilitator.com/the-embodiment-podcast, as well as on iTunes and the usual platforms). Podcast episodes feature me and a host of guests talking about various aspects of embodiment.

I also started The Embodiment Conference, a massive online event, which features many facilitators from a range of embodiment fields: https://

theembodimentconference.org/. By far the largest resource of online embodiment videos come out of this too, and can be found via the conference site.

If you're interested in accessible, online, peer-to-peer embodiment training, see if there are any 'Embodiment Circles' near you (www.embodimentcircle.com).

On social media I'm on Facebook by my name, and am @warkmalsh on Instagram and Twitter if you're into that. I travel a lot and often do dinners and coffees for enthusiasts so feel free to ask if I'm ever in your town. My travel dates are on https://embodiedfacilitator.com/

Courses

I run The Embodied Facilitator Course which runs in several countries and goes *much* deeper into this book's content. Go to: https://embodiedfacilitator.com/, and we also run the Foundation of Embodiment Certification annually for those who wish to study online: https://embodiedfacilitator.com/fec/

I also recommend the in-person training delivered by:

- Arawana Hayashi
- Bonnie Bainbridge-Cohen
- Charles Eisenstein
- Dylan Newcomb
- Gabor Maté
- Ginny Whitelaw
- Ilan Stephani
- Martha Eddy
- Max Strom
- Michalea Boem
- Paul Linden
- Philip Shepherd
- Stuart Heller
- The Strozzi Institute
- Tara Judelle
- Wendy Palmer and her European students (USA / Asia / Europe)

There are other great trainers too, but I know the above people's work.

Reading

Embodiment is primarily about experience so on completing this book I'd most like to encourage you to practise! However, theory and practice are 'two wings of a bird', to steal a Buddhist phrase, so some extra reading is useful and I know what we learning professionals are like! These will give you a wider perspective and aid your development. This is the EFC reading list adapted for this book:

Conclusion

Essential reading

These are my top picks for extending the knowledge in this book.

> Mark Walsh, **Embodiment Moving Beyond Mindfulness** (Unicorn Slayer Press, 2019)
> My other much more personal and poetic book, written in bite-sized chunks.
>
> Mark Walsh (e-book), **Centring: Why Mindfulness Alone isn't Enough**
> A centring masterclass in a short book! Available at: https://embodiedfacilitator.com/
>
> Steve Haines, **Trauma is Really Strange** (Singing Dragon, 2016)
> A short introduction to trauma with pictures.
>
> **Own It!** by Liz Peters (SRA Books, 2019)
> By an EFC graduate, this is a super-accessible intro to the work, and great for confidence teaching it!
>
> **Embodied Peacemaking** by Paul Linden (CCMS Publications, 2007 e-book)
> The best practical guide to embodiment exercises, generally. Don't be fooled by the name, it's an excellent book for coaches. Available at: https://embodiedfacilitator.com/wp-content/uploads/2018/11/Paul-Linden-3PeaceBook.pdf
>
> **Mindful Movement: The Evolution of the Somatic Arts and Conscious Action** by Martha Eddy (University of Chicago Press, 2016)
> History and theory of the field. Great for everyone, especially body geeks. An excellent book.

Core reading

These publications are highly recommended:

> **Leadership Embodiment** by Wendy Palmer (The Embodiment Foundation, 2013)
> Has a good section on neuroscience.
>
> **The Art of Somatic Coaching** by Richard Strozzi-Heckler (North Atlantic Books, 2014)
> Another angle on embodied coaching.
>
> **'The Art and Science of Somatics: Theory, History and Scientific Foundations' by Kelly Mullan (Master of Liberal Studies thesis)**
> An in-depth history essay. Available at:
> https://creativematter.skidmore.edu/cgi/viewcontent.cgi?article=1093&context=mals_stu_schol

The Awakening Body by Reginald Ray (Shambhala, 2016) or **The Science of Enlightenment** by Shinzen Young (Sounds True, 2016)
   Both these books are on meditation and can be seen as two ends of a spectrum. If a hippie, read Shinzen, if uptight, read Reggie!

Body Psychotherapy by Nick Totten (Open University Press, 2003)
   A small but deep book on an aspect of embodiment we look at only a little on EFC. It's hard to get a taste of it personally, so worth surveying.

Discovering the Body's Wisdom by Mirka Knaster (Bantam Books, 1996)
   Surveys a huge range of embodied disciplines. Very useful for people new to embodiment and good on the topic of practice.

Trauma Essentials by Babette Rothschild (W.W. Norton, 2011) or **Healing Trauma: A Pioneering Program for Restoring the Wisdom of Your Body** by Peter A. Levine (Sounds True, 2005)

Sensation: The New Science of Physical Intelligence by Thalma Lobel (Atria, 2014)
   An accessible book on embodied cognition.

Move to Greatness by Ginny Whitelaw and Betsy Wetzig (Nicholas Brealey, 2008)
   A clear embodied typology with a business focus. Their model has lots in common with 4-elements.

Retooling on the Run by Stuart Heller and David Surrenda (North Atlantic Books, 1994)
   Includes content on the 4-elements.

Extras

Read for pleasure and geekery, if you like reading.

Emotional Anatomy by Stanley Keleman (Center Press, 1985)
   Beautifully illustrated, if slightly inaccessible classic.

The Silent Pulse by George Leonard (Gibbs Smith, 2006)
   On practice and rhythm.

Integral Life Practice by Ken Wilber, Terry Patten, Adam Leonard and Marco Morelli (Integral Books, 2008)
   Provides a wider context and has an excellent chapter on practice.

Presence-Based Coaching: Cultivating Self-Generative Leaders Through Mind, Body, and Heart by Doug Silsbee (Jossey-Bass, 2008)
   An aligned approach to coaching.

Breakfast Essays: Brief Writings on Body Awareness and Life by Paul Linden (CCMS Publications, 2009 e-book)
   Digestible stories about embodiment. Available at: https://embodiedfacilitator.com/wp-content/uploads/2018/04/4BreakfastEssays.pdf

- ***My Tao Te Ching*** by Francis Briers (Warriors of Love Publishing, 2014)
  Where wisdom and humour combine, from former EFC co-lead trainer, Frankie. He has written several others I also recommend.
- ***Listen! Say Yes! Commit!*** by Harry Puckering and Julia E. Knight (Lulu.com, 2015)
  Improv principles, with applications to business.
- ***Intelligence in the Flesh: Why Your Mind Needs Your Body Much More Than it Thinks*** by Guy Claxton (Yale University Press, 2015) or ***Rip it Up*** by Richard Wiseman (Macmillan, 2012)
  Both accessible books on the science.
- ***Bone, Breath and Gesture*** edited by Don Hanlon Johnson (North Atlantic Books, 1995)
  A collection of writings from many seminal names in the field.
- ***The More Beautiful World Our Hearts Know is Possible (Sacred Activism)*** by Charles Eisenstein (North Atlantic Books, 2013)
  How the body is related to ethics and environment, with an emphasis on creative agency and self-ownership.
- ***Hakomi Mindfulness-Centered Somatic Psychotherapy: A Comprehensive Guide to Theory and Practice*** by Halko Weiss and Greg Johanson (W.W. Norton, 2015)
  Goes deeper into body therapy.
- ***Wisdom of the Body Moving*** by Linda Hartley (North Atlantic Books, 1995)
  A good intro to body-mind centring and dance movement therapy from a leading Brit.
- ***Everybody is a Body*** by Karen Studd and Laura Cox (Dog Ear Publishing, 2013)
  Another recommended dance movement therapy book.
- ***Sensing Feeling and Action*** by Bonnie Bainbridge Cohen (North Atlantic Books, 1993)
  An intro to body-mind centring.

More on meditation

- ***The Body*** by Paramananda (Windhorse Publications, 2007) or ***Meditation for Life*** by Martine Batchelor (Frances Lincoln, 2001)
  Both are good and light.

Also recommended: Anything by Thich Nhat Hanh (accessible), Ken McCleod (deep), Jon Kabat-Zinn (scientific/secular), Pema Chodron (heart-led) and Noah Levine (punk rock Buddhist alternative!). See also: Judith Blackstone's Realisation Process (various books).

Good meditation apps include Buddhify and Insight Timer, though there are many others.

Poetic endings

While this has been a technical and pragmatic book, I feel the need to finish with poetry, as in many ways what embodiment is all about is better evoked than explained.

Saltwater
She tells me saltwater can cure anything
As I cry and she bleeds.
She tells me the body is the sea of love
Not in so many words of course
But in how the moon tenderly holds the tides

No, don't misunderstand
Not love like a vapid pink card, bought as an apology for pleasantries
. . . She is on another shore now far from here . . .
But like what makes the waves return
To a beach that rejects them

She tells me saltwater can cure anything
As that this is what our body is made of.
But having seen men blown apart
I know what we are literally full of
is shit

And yet . . .
Having seen men dismembered by loss too
– near drowned in saltwater tears
I know
That the healing of brine is not so sweet, but healing none the less,

And what we all have in us
Is an ocean far greater
than our tiny floating minds can ken

– for Tess

The Mystery of the Body
A cloud floating over a pause
An invisible pregnancy
A sense of belonging, between the spaces in doubt
Ever fruitful yet elusive
You will never know the body fully

Married to a mystery
You turn your head quickly to see what always eludes
But she's already gone
to the edges in your smile, the commas in your dreams,
and the magic you stopped believing in as a child.

Gifts with the stamps of an African country that you didn't know exists
Arrive with rhymes but without reason
Sometimes when you need then most like fleshy angels
Other times inconveniently, like the erections of a teenager
You will never know the body fully

It's what happens just before a thought
On a day that the Romans wiped from history
You're trying to knit fog, or grasp an otter made of maybe
You will never know the body fully
But she will love you, like no other, until the day you die

Why embodiment?

I hope this book is successful as a practical guide for facilitators, and I also hope that the bigger picture of embodiment as a necessary reclaiming of our humanity is apparent. When we come home to the body, we come home to each other, and come home to the planet. Embodiment is not the only thing that is needed in the world today, but it is a central aspect of stopping disconnection and therefore stopping violence, on intrapersonal, interpersonal and planetary levels. That's why embodiment – this stuff – matters.

Notes

1 Taken from my first book, *Embodiment: Moving Beyond Mindfulness* (Unicorn Slayer Press, 2019).
2 Ibid.

Appendix 1

Top tips for Zoom (and other virtual meeting software) by Daniela W – The Embodiment Conference Manager

In times of Covid-19 and lockdown, thousands of facilitators moved into online teaching. The one thing which stuck out for me observing and helping many of them was that you simply can't copy and paste what you are doing off-line into the online world. Don't get me wrong, your facilitation skills are still valid and helpful working online, but applying your work to the online environment is a whole new skill-set. So here are my tips for moving your embodied work online.

1. *Adapt instead of copying*
   Don't try to copy and paste what you are doing face-to-face into an online environment. Instead, adapt your work to the tools and options you have available (breakout rooms and chat for interaction, interactive surveys, shared maps or digital whiteboards – be creative!)
2. *Try NOT to make it perfect*
   Perfectionism is your enemy. Techniques will fail at times and there is no way you can control everything (I learned that the hard way, but you don't need to). Better you get okay with that now. Be prepared (use backups where you can) but be okay with it when things go sideways.
3. *Self-regulate*
   This is likely the most important part for *any* facilitation work. If you don't plan to get an engineering degree before teaching online, self-regulation is likely the best alternative option to deal with the dodgy internet connection or glitchy software.
4. *Test and PRACTISE!!!*
   What you can do is to limit the chances things can go sideways. Try out the things you want to use in your session, test your internet connection, check video set – up and functionality, lighting, background and sound / microphone. You don't want to fiddle around with these when you are about to start a call.
5. *Less is more*
   In online facilitation there are tons of amazing tools and it is easy to get carried away by that. However, less is more. People might be not as tech savvy and can struggle with the abundance or get lost on the way. Whatever you use, you should know inside out.

6. *Interactivity*
   Get people to move and interact. Talking heads are what kills almost any online workshop, as people become passive consumers instead of active participants. Don't talk for more than 15–20 minutes. Use exercises, chat inquiries, breakout rooms or stretching breaks.

Appendix 2: Four-elements tables

Four elements: embodiment table

Element	Shape	Yin / Yang	I, We, It	8 tools strengths	Primary / relational direction	Dominant emotion + relation	Movement types (Laban system)	Breathing
Air	none	yang	all / none	responsiveness movement	up / away from	joy **excitement** disengage	**float** stillness light indirect disintegrated sudden free	upper chest in mouth, out nose fast 'light / inspirational'
Fire	triangle	yang	I	intention	forward towards / against	curiosity **anger** engage / challenge	**thrust** + movement light direct disintegrated sudden free	chest in nose, out mouth emphasise in-breath fast 'heating / growling'
Water	circle	yin	we	relaxation acceptance	backward receiving	awe **fear** receive / accept	**flow** + movement heavy indirect integrated sustained bound	lower back in mouth, out nose emphasise out-breath slow 'flowing / sighing'
Earth	square	yin	it	structure	down standing ground	sadness **despair** resist	**hold ground / sink** stillness heavy direct integrated sustained bound	belly in nose, out mouth slow 'steady / grounding'

Four elements: extended

Element	Fears	Desires	Primary virtues	Ways to engage	When you may need more of	Communication styles	Music
Air	being controlled boredom imperfection	freedom creativity perfection	curiosity transcendence innovation humour	inspire, be original explore, adventure study, learn with joke go fast	when needing clarity, fresh ideas or lightness	creative humorous	jazz new-age funny experiential
Fire	not being enough not doing enough losing	recognition achievement / progress / results winning	courage vitality fierceness get things done	motivate action be competent challenge compete give goals go fast	when you have goals to achieve, need energy or bravery	direct challenging	hip-hop heavy metal Wagner
Water	rejection conflict loss	relationships harmony loyalty	humanity creativity responsiveness empathy	listen to, care, be sincere enter into relationship with/socialise share feelings go slow	when in relationship or conflict	empathic relational	romantic Chopin singer-songwriter
Earth	change lack of control rushing	stability control correctness	justice reliability groundedness temperance	show them the facts / numbers be reliable regularity structure and analysis go slow	when things get chaotic, unfair or ungrounded	factual practical	classical country traditional African

Four elements: further correlates

Element	Thinking: questions	Emotions	Work activities	Relationships and conversations	Lifestyle	Places and environment	Season (Kinda)
Air	What is possible?	create with your emotions / rise above them	vision and strategy leadership invent brainstorm reflect	co-create be flexible joke inspire	be spontaneous, make time for creativity and deep thought	bright light open space colours and chaos hills and mountains	spring
Fire	What needs to be done?	express your emotions – get energised and assertive	take action get results hire and fire prioritise	tell challenge be sincere make headway	do more, faster, stronger	cities and deserts bright light hard surfaces functionality	summer
Water	What needs to be accepted?	accept your emotions and flow with them in relationship	have meetings get feedback staff-care and HR network celebrate	listen accommodate care support	allow more time for flow and relationships	rivers and sea soft light and soft surfaces comfort	autumn
Earth	What is true?	balance your emotions – calm down	planning management budgeting make lists keep traditions	support be reliable hold your ground / maintain standards	slow down, consider, be careful	gardens, forests and parks contained spaces (e.g. houses) order	winter

Four elements: developmental practices

Element	Breathing practice	Sitting practice	Standing practice	Walking practice	Movement practice (in any activity)	Long-term practices (see yoga box for note on how you do any art)	Eye practice	Environmental practice
Air	upper chest in mouth, out nose fast 'light / inspirational'	upright, tall light spine	legs together arms and palms up	'floating', extending, changing directions, from hands and head, unpredictable	stillness light indirect disintegrated sudden free	improv, art, comedy acro-yoga, badminton, scuba diving, jazz dance, play, reading poetry brainstorming experimental cooking	looking up slightly, looking at big picture	go wild / make fun inspirational pictures
Fire	chest in nose, out mouth emphasise in-breath fast 'heating / growling'	leaning forwards, at front of chair	one leg forward with front leg bent, arms in front palms forwards	fast with purpose and direction, from chest	+ movement light direct disintegrated sudden free	karate, kendo, MMA, boxing, running, squash, aerobics, weight-lifting hot yoga tango, flamenco speed cooking	narrow 'hard' focus	minimise and make functional

(continued)

Four elements: developmental practices (continued)

Element	Breathing practice	Sitting practice	Standing practice	Walking practice	Movement practice (in any activity)	Long-term practices (see yoga box for note on how you do any art)	Eye practice	Environmental practice
Water	lower back in mouth, out nose emphasise out-breath slow 'flowing / sighing'	sitting back, relaxed	one leg forward with back leg bent, arms to side, palms front	'flowing' – flexible, keeping in relationship to ground, people and place	+ movement heavy indirect integrated sustained bound	salsa, many forms of partner dance swimming, water sports yin / Scaravelli yoga team sports, jiu-jistu, aikido	wide 'soft' focus, letting in	add family pictures and plants
Earth	belly in nose, out mouth slow 'steady grounding'	steady, grounding down	legs wide apart. arms apart, palms down	slow, 'planting', stop-start, feet, steady from belly centre	stillness heavy direct integrated sustained bound	gardening walking, rugby and American football (though depends on position) spell checking! judo, sumo, Iyengar yoga, African dance, ballroom	looking down slightly, detail orientated	organise clean up

213

Four elements for facilitators

Element	Primary virtues	When it's needed in facilitation	Communication style	Facilitation activities	Risk when in excess
Air	curiosity transcendence innovation humour	when needing ideas, fresh insight or lightness	creative humorous	creative brainstorming and intuition humour visioning	vague / ungrounded chaotic / silly
Fire	courage vitality fierceness get things done	when you have goals to achieve, need energy or bravery	direct challenging	encourage action, priorities and goals challenge direct feedback and powerful questions	brutal (pushy) rushed
Water	humanity creativity responsiveness empathy	when in relationship or conflict	empathic relational	listening, empathy and care trust, intimacy and relationship-building connection and support	weak (push-over) colluding
Earth	justice reliability groundedness temperance	when things are getting chaotic, unfair or ungrounded	factual practical	establishing facts – straight teaching assisting with planning managing accountability	stuck uninspiring

Index

Page numbers in italics are figures; with 't' are tables; with 'n' are notes.

3-minute listens 137
360 feedback 84, *84*, 90

AAI (awareness, acceptance and intention) 114
ABC centring 109
Abramović, Marina 36, 37
acceptance 20, 22, 25–6, 79t, 114
accountability xviii
addiction coaching 171
aesthetics 14
agency 22
aikido 122–3
'am I right?', body reading technique 148
anger management training/coaching 171
applications 171–4
arm-raising technique 73
art therapy 37
assertiveness training 172
autonomic nervous system (ANS) 58
awareness 24–5
  see also self-awareness; social awareness

balance 20, 23
  see also centring
Barrett, Lisa Feldman 47
Berceli, David 109
Blackaby, Pete 69
Blackstone, Judith 70
Blake, Amanda 14
bodily capital concept 38
body language 37, 44
body listening 67, 68, 134–9, 186, 188, 199
body practices 41–2
body psychotherapy 35, 36, 40
body reading 145–51, *147*, 186, 188–9
body scanning, and self-awareness 65
body-subject 37
bodywork 40, *42–3*
Bourdieu, Pierre 38
box, sitting outside the 13
brain, and meditation 47–8

breath/breathing 19, 22, 79t, 138
Briers, Francis 2, 183

cafe empathy 138
calibration xvii, 108, 117
'calm Karen down!' technique 161–2
capacity xvii, 120, 154
Carter, Gary 69
centring coaching practice 159
centring principle 21, 100–8, 190
  categories 110
  expressive practices 111
  practicing 112
  and stress management 174
  techniques 109–10, 111–12, 114–20, 161
challenge 29, 57, 59, 120
change management training/coaching 171
chaos 185
charisma 154
check-ins, for awareness 64, 73
chemistry 154
choice principles 186, 189–92
Christianity 30n2, 35
circling and authentic movement practice 140
clients
  and self-awareness 72–5, 87–94
  and self-leadership 113–21, 129–31
  and social awareness 140–3, 149–50
  and social leadership 159–64, 166–8
clowning 156
coaches see facilitators
cognition 14
  embodied 45–6
  and enactive view 38
Cohen, Bonnie Bainbridge 69
comfort 76, 127, 185
  see also familiarity
communication skills training/coaching 171
communities 29, 184
competitive moods games 156, 162

confidence/assertiveness training 172
conflict resolution skills training/conflict resolution facilitation/embodied peacemaking 171–2
Conrad, Emilie 2
conscious movement methods 69
  and self-awareness 68
conscious/unconscious embodiment 4
consent xv–xvi, xvii, 108
containers 94, 120, 126, 127, 192
  bodies as 35–6
contexts 11, *12*, 50, 184
contrast principle 88, 90, 127, 185, 186, 187, 189
coordination, group 119
copying
  and pattern awareness 77, 85
  and social awareness 137–8
corporeality 33, 38, 39, 44, 52
creativity training/coaching 172
cross-cultural training/coaching 172
Csordas, Thomas 39
Cuddy, Amy 45, 48
cultural trauma 56
culture and cultural embodiment 50–5
  and body reading 150
  and embodied practices 131
  and emotion 47
  and groups 75, 94
  and regulation 121
  and self-awareness 75, 94
  and self-leadership 121, 131
  and social awareness 143, 150
  and social leadership 164, 168
cycles model 13, 175, 176t, 177–8

dance 36–7, 41, *42–3*
  conscious 68, 69, 111
dance movement therapy 36, 40
dance reading 148
dating/attraction/intimacy coaching 172
death-matches/meditations 156–7
Descartes, René 35
designing embodied workshops/coaching sessions 175–9
developmental trauma 56, 57
deviation principle 76, 80, 90, 127, 155, 185, 187
disembodiment xvi, 35, 64
distinction coaching 88–9
dual relations xviii

eating, and self-awareness 67
embodied cognition 45–6
Embodied Facilitator Course 183, 183–4
Embodied Yoga Principles (EYP) 80, *81–6*, 85, 90, 173
embodiment 2–6, *6*, 33–4, *42–3*
  contexts 11, *12*
  cultural 50–5
  influences of 39–41
  science and 44–50
  scope and history 34–9
  and training and coaching 6–9
Embodiment Conference 29
emotion principle 14, 46, 47, 190
emotional intelligence 43–4, 172
empathy 136
  walks 138
empowerment xvii
enactive view 38
Erichsen, J.E. 55
ethics xv–xvi, xix, 15, 182
Eulenburg, Albert 55
exaggeration technique 88
exposure principle *see* deviation
expression 18, 35, 37, 41, 50, 100, 121, 155
expressive practices 42, *42–3*, 111

facilitators xiii, 10, 182–3, 194–6
  four elements for 214t
familiarity principle 76, 80, 90, 185, 186–7
feedback
  and leadership 154
  and pattern awareness 76, 80, 84, *84*, 87–8, 90
feet
  and centring 110
  and self-awareness 65–6
  shoe exercise 96n.16
Feldenkrais, Moshe 41, 63, 68
'fight-or-flight' reaction 101, 104, 105
filtering students xviii
financial skills coaching 173
form (top-down processing) 23, 70–1
four elements model 12, 71, 77–8, 79t, 91–3, 120, 149–50, 155–6, 209–14t
four seasons cycles model 13, 175, 176t, 177–8
freedom (bottom-up processing) 22, 23, 42, *42–3*, 70–1
freedom/fundamental principle 185–6
functions, body 14–15

gateways *see* intelligence
gender 54–5
Gendlin, Eugene 68
gesture 119
'get me across the room' technique 161
Golec de Zavala, Agnieszka 49
Goleman, Daniel 16, 43–4
gradients 192
groups
    centring techniques 118–21
    self-awareness techniques 73–4, 90–4
    self-leadership techniques 130–1
    social leadership techniques 161–3
growth principle 186, 189
guidance 185

habits, embodied 76
habitus concept 38
hand on chest listening 139
Harris, Adrian 12–13
hatred, body 25
health, and movement 23
Heller, Stuart 23, 75, 76, 80, 100
hello frame, and self-awareness 66
holography 185
humour 161

I, we and it of centring 79t, 103
identity 14
imagery/imagination 27
improv 41, *42–3*, 53, 111, 156
individual adaptation 118
insight 14–15
inspiration 15, 166
integration 127, 185
intelligence
    embodied 4, 7–8, 10, 11–13, *12*, 16–28, *17*
    emotional 43–4, 172
    intention 20, 22–3, 52, 79t

Jackson, Benita 49
Johnson, Mark 9, 46
journaling 64–5
joy 185, 209t

Laban, Rudolf 41, 79t
Lakoff, George 9, 45
language 15
    body 37, 44
leader-follower practices

and social awareness 138–9
and social leadership 155, 160
leadership, social *see* social leadership
leadership training/coaching 173
learning 14, 28
learning communities 184
Levine, Peter 56–7
life purpose coaching 173
life transfer 192
limits, know your xviii
Linden, Paul 15, 103, 108
linguistic creation/language 15
listening *see* body listening
Lobel, Thalma 46

Marcher, Lisbeth 36
marry me!/give me a pay rise practice 159
martial arts 40–1, *42–3*, 53
massage, group 73
meditation 24, 40, *42–3*, 47–8
    and self-awareness 65
Menakem, Resmaa 56
Merleau-Ponty, Maurice 37
messengers, bodies as 36–7
mimicry *see* copying
mindfulness 42, *42–3*, 43, 45, 47, 63
    and self-awareness 65, 76
mirroring techniques 87
mistakes 180–1
    in teaching centring 118
modifications, body 37
motivation 14
movement 14, 23–4, 79t
music 119
'Mystery of the body, The' (poem) 205

naming, practices for social awareness 137
nature connection *42*
neuroscience 46–8
Newcomb, Dylan 96n21, 120, 200
Newfield Network 15, 162
noise, making 73
numbing, and self-awareness 66–7

object, body as an 34–5
objectification 3, 35
    see also disembodiment
observation, and social awareness 136
one-to-one
    awareness techniques 72–3

centring techniques 115–18
pattern awareness 87–9
social awareness techniques 140–1
social leadership techniques 159–61
Oppenheim, Herman 55
owl eyes/ears technique 111

paired movement practices 140
Palmer, Wendy 70, 88, 98
parasympathetic reactions 56, 57, 58
parenting coaching 173
pattern awareness 75–7
  helping clients to develop 87–95
  and self-leadership 124–8
  techniques for developing 77–86, 79t, *81–4*
Pause technique 73
Peper, Erik 49
perception 14, 39, 45, 52, 77
performative arts 41, 53
philosophy 35, 37–9
places 12–13
podcasts 138
poems 204–5
polyvagal theory of trauma 57
Porges, Stephen 57, 104
post-traumatic stress disorder (PTSD) 55–6
postmodernism 37–9
posture 14, 20–1, 44
  and body language 44
  research on 45, 58–9
  and responsiveness 26
  and self-awareness 65
power dynamics xvii–xviii
practices 28, 29, 185, 197
  committing to 168–9
  culture of 53
  recommending 166–7
  self-awareness 64–94, 79t, *81–4*
  self-leadership 100–21, 124–8
  social awareness 137–43
  social leadership 154–64, 166–8
principles 183, 184–92
process principle 181–2, 185
professional culture 53–4
PRRIMAARI 19–27
public speaking coaching 173

'quick-win' centring techniques 115

radical embodied cognitive neuroscience 46
regulation *see* self-regulation
relating 14
relationship 2, 4, 11, *12*, 33, 185, 198, 210–11t, 214t
relaxation 19, 21–2, 26, 79t
resilience training 173–4
resources 197–204
respiration *see* breath/breathing
responsiveness xv, 20, 26, 79t, 186, 210t, 214t
reviewing the embodied foundation, and social leadership 154–5
role modelling 166
roots and wings technique 112
Roth, Gabrielle 13, 175

safety xv, xvi–xix, 5
'Saltwater' (poem) 204
science 44–50
self-assessment, pattern awareness 80
self-awareness *17*, 18, 24–5, 95, 161, 185–6
  state 62–75
  trait 75–94, 79t, *81–4*
self-esteem, and yoga 49
self-leadership *17*, 18, 64, 77
  state 98–121
  trait 121–31
self-regulation *17*, 18, 19, 99, 100, 110, 185
Selye, Hans 57
sensations, awareness of 24–5, 63
service xvii
sex, and self-awareness 67
shadow principle 54, 93–4, 191
shake and settle centring 109–10
shoes, and the familiarity principle 96n.16
sideways state shifting 120
Siegel, Dan 58
simulator principle 155, 160, 186, 188
skills, learning 28–9
social awareness *17*, 18
  state 134–43
  trait 145–51, *147*
social engagement 57
social leadership *17*, 18
  state 152–64
  trait 164–8
social regulation *17*
social skills training 172
somatic experiencing 57

somatic psychotherapies 40, *42–3*
somatics, western 4, 41, *42–3*
space *see* places
standards of excellence 183
stereotypes 52
Stirk, John 69
stress management 173–4
stress traffic lights 104–5
stressor progression technique 116–17
Strozzi-Heckler, Richard 110, 175
structure 21, 45, 79t
subtle influencers 156
support 120
survival mode 57
sympathetic reactions 56, 57, 58

tango 86
team-building 174
techniques 183
　video recording 87
technology 29
　using Zoom 206–7
　virtual considerations 74, 94, 121, 143, 150, 163, 167
tenets 184–5
tense-relax centring 109
tension 21, 23, 36
theatre 41, *42–3*, 111
thumbs up technique 73
time management training/coaching 174
tone 119, 156
top-down
　letting go technique 111–12
　processing 23, 70–1
touch xx–xxi, 108
　self-awareness practices 72
train spotting technique 148
trainers *see* facilitators
transcendence 5
trauma xviii, 54, 55–9, 74, 105–6

and awareness 94
and body reading 150
resources 106–7
and social awareness 143
and social leadership 163–4, 167–8
therapy 174
treatment methods 107
and windows of tolerance 58–9
triggers xv, 52, 54, 105, 106, 185
　see also stressor progression technique

up-down centring 109

values 15, 112
Varela, Francisco 38
video recording 87
virtual considerations 74, 94, 121, 143, 150, 163, 167
visualisation 19, 65, 110, 112, 117
VUCA (volatile/uncertain/complex/ambiguous) 8

'Wake Bob Up' technique 162
wars, and trauma 55–6
welcome frame, and self-awareness 66
wellness training/coaching 174
western somatics 4, 41, *42–3*
what's true technique 112
Whitelaw, Ginny 80, 96n21, 200
'who's X' practice 139–40
windows of tolerance 58–9

Yehuda, Rachel 56
yes frame, and self-awareness 66
yin and yang *see* four elements model
yoga 2–3, 40, *42–3*, 49, 53, 70–1, 111
YouTube 138

Zoom 206–7